The Talking Point: Creating an Environment for Exploring Complex Meaning

Thomas R. Flanagan and Alexander N. Christakis
A Collaborative Project of the Institute for 21st Century Agoras

INFORMATION AGE PUBLISHING, INC.
Charlotte, NC • www.infoagepub.com

The Talking Point: Creating an Environment for Exploring Complex Meaning

DEDICATION

We dedicate this book to the living memory of our friend and colleague, Dr. Hasan Özbekhan, a Turkish American systems scientist, cyberneticist, and philosopher whose pioneering work on *Toward a General Theory of Planning*, published in 1968, provided a transformational stimulus to the way that people approach complex plans. We further dedicate this book to all those who take up the human burden of helping groups find their way toward a common constructive purpose in this world.

Library of Congress Cataloging-in-Publication Data

Flanagan, Thomas R.
 The talking point creating an environment for exploring complex : meaning a
collaborative project of the institute for 21st century agoras / Thomas R.
Flanagan and Alexander N. Christakis.
    p. cm.
 Includes bibliographical references.
 ISBN 978-1-60752-361-1 (pbk.) — ISBN 978-1-60752-362-8 (hardcover) —
ISBN 978-1-60752-363-5 (e-book)
 1. Dialogue analysis. 2. Group problem solving. 3. Communication. I. Christakis,
Alexander N. II. Title.
 P95.455.F55 2009
 302.3'46–dc22

                                                           2009043804

Printed in the United States of America

CONTENTS

SECTION ONE
THE ARENA

SECTION TWO

THE PRACTICE

PROLOGUE

"It is misleading to study the history of ideas without constant remembrance of the struggle of novel thought with the obtuseness of language."

Alfred North Whitehead
Mathematician and philosopher

The Talking Point is an experiential book.

True to its premise that you cannot form a collaborative language unless you discover it in dialogue, half of the text positions you as witness to, and participant in, just such a discovery.

The other half prepares you for the journey.

It is a preparation worthy of the time of all who value discourse as essential to the moderation of conflict, the formation of social capital, and the improvement of the human condition.

The first five chapters are a fascinating exploration of the subtleties of language, the nature of shared meaning, the implications of power and leadership, the creation of priorities and erroneous priorities, and the practice of collaborative learning.

For those whose interests lie in exploring the complexity of situations in search of the root causes of existing conditions and the deep drivers for changing conditions, *The Talking Point*'s chapters on the dynamics and the management of dialogue in real time are engaging and will remain forever valuable.

The Talking Point is the work of Thomas Flanagan, a neuroscientist, and Alexander Christakis, a theoretical physicist, who have brought all the rigor of their scientific discipline to understanding and facilitating the structure and practice of authentic dialogue. The authors have applied their approach, called "structured dialogic design" (SDD), for complexity resolution from local communities to very complex international partnerships.

What makes their work unique is their respect for the communicative subtleties that emerge during truly complex design. Their hope is to take us on a voyage to the talking point and beyond, because authentic communication requires understanding our limited powers of conception and supporting the natural ways we talk and relate to each other.

That their book is accessible to readers not immersed in the language of group process is a gift. That the work that made their book possible is a monumental human achievement becomes apparent as you participate in and become increasingly aware of the process.

There are larger issues of governance and scientific exploration that are part of the ethos in which *The Talking Point* is written but that are beyond *The Talking Point*'s essential purpose. Nevertheless, they are not lost on the authors, and for those familiar with these issues they will resonate in the text.

Among these is the future of democracy—whether, as Prime Minister Tony Blair observed, the challenge before democracy in the twenty-first century will be to decide where individual rights end and common rights begin, and whether American Democracy's eighteenth-century contentment with "muddling through" can engage the breathtaking speed and complexity of the twenty-first century without surrendering its principles to less egalitarian forms of governance. Such issues are worthy of immediate consideration.

If we are going to answer these questions, we are going to have to return to, and allow ourselves to be changed by, the practice of democracy itself. *The Talking Point* is an invitation to this practice, and the Structured Dialogic Design process was invented for just such an engagement.

At the beginning of the scientific era, Francis Bacon cautioned, "Whosoever shall entertain high and vaporous imaginations, instead of a laborious and sober inquiry of truth, shall beget hopes and beliefs of strange and impossible shapes." It is one of the revelations of *The Talking Point* that what seems to make sense may not be accurate and, I can testify from my own experience, may be completely erroneous.

All too often these "hopes and beliefs" comprise erroneous priorities that are generated by people and organizations because plans seem to make sense in the context in which they were created, but in the complexity of the larger social system they can have vast, unforeseen, and unpredictable consequences.

The authors speak directly to this, because it is for the engagement of complexity in the service of democracy that the structured dialogic design process was created. In *The Talking Point* the authors echo Bacon's caution: "The point we are making is not simply that we are likely to underconceptualize the priority of items in a complex system without applying a systems design approach (which certainly is the case), but also that we are certain to select erroneous priorities without constructing a systems view based on our shared understanding of our complex situation."

With observations like this, *The Talking Point* enters the arena of historical significance. The evidence is clear that in modern democracies, "deliberative" and "participatory democracy" are increasingly incompatible. The consequences of isolation and the decline of civic engagement and its potential are among the compelling reasons for exploring the talking point.

Its methodology and insight reveal a process that has the capacity to find answers to Robert Putnam's question about "how to reconcile the tension between active citizenship and diversity." In fact, SDD may be among the first methodologies that has the capacity to systematically, objectively, and without malice or prejudice expose in dialogue Karl Mannheim's observation that "ruling groups can in their thinking become so intensely interest bound to a situation that they are simply no longer able to see certain facts that would undermine their sense of domination."

The authors acknowledge that they speak on behalf of "a global quest for democratic renewal." Through the Institute for 21st Century Agoras, they and other experts in large group design and decision making practices share their experiences and insights from a diverse and rapidly evolving world.

The Talking Point is a primer in a sophisticated methodology. The methodology—a technology for the practice of democracy—needs a scholarly center where the research can be continued, its discipline can be taught and its practice integrated with the full spectrum of dialogue technologies.

Finally, and admittedly more speculatively, the scientific method has enabled us to successfully penetrate the complexities of the physical realms and given us some capacity to understand and articulate their dynamic interrelationships. However, the complexities of the social realms remain very much obscured.

It may well be that *The Talking Point* and the methodology on which it is based are early contributions to a new discipline in the history of science. Not to take the work of Tom Flanagan and Alexander Christakis seriously is to run the risk of participating in the classic oversight that Mannheim and Whitehead suggest all too often accompanies compelling emerging insights.

Have the courage to read this book.

Craig H. Lindell, Chair
South Coast Community Collaborative Design Studio (SoCoDesign Studio)
New Bedford, Massachusetts

PREFACE: A NEW PARADIGM FOR COLLABORATIVE LANGUAGE

Our goal in this book is to reflect on forty years of work with highly diversified groups in many different social and business sectors across the globe. We will share our understanding of how groups actually do engage in collaborative learning as they deal with complex problems.

Have you ever been in a really complex problem-solving discussion with a lot of folks whom you really didn't fully know as individuals yet? Have you taken your turn speaking, asked for questions, sat back down, and then felt that others in the group just didn't quite "get it"? Have you left that well-intended and well-mannered meeting with an empty feeling inside and suspecting that nothing significant had been resolved? If you have, then you have experienced what we call "cross talk." Cross talk happens when groups carefully manage sharing their meeting time so that everyone can speak, yet fail to manage the communication process to ensure that meaning is effectively exchanged. Important information that is voiced is not examined, captured, or used.

We are seeing a progressive need for collaborative design events for solving complex problems. These events avoid cross talk by weaving together a design during a group's dialogue. At the same time that we are hoping for greater participation in solving problems, we also are seeing increased time pressures acting on individual participants. The idea of committing a day to a collaborative problem-solving discussion is far from universally appealing. Why? Time is money, of course, but individuals also may have had bad experiences with this sort of thing. Some discussions have left participants feeling manipulated or coopted. In the most pervasively damaging cases, individual participants in collaborative problem-solving discussions may emerge with the conviction that such collaborative planning cannot possibly lead to solutions for complex problems. Cross talk does more than wastes time—it kills opportunities.

To prevent cross talk, and to help groups that are dealing with complex, boundary-spanning challenges, we need to get the group to the talking point—the point at which they are effectively engaged in exchanging meaning through open and focused dialogue. For group participants, this is a personal experience as well as a shared voyage. Comparatively little has been written about this personal perspective. This book fills this gap with personal accounts and reflections from participants and from individuals providing support for participants.

Some participants jump into a talking mode very easily—and often too easily. High-performance individuals in high-performance environments are primed to contribute actively and visibly. Other individuals—through introspection or skepticism—take a reflective approach. Reflective individuals often have a variety of modes for expressing their thoughts and may seek to discover the melody of the group before they are quite ready to join in the song. In parallel with speaking styles, we also have a range of listening styles. Impatient listeners tend to react to words. Profound listeners tend to mine for meanings. The challenge for individuals who would help groups collectively devise powerful solutions for their complex problems is the need to orchestrate this symphony of styles. But whereas psychological studies typically focus on individual types and categories of types, this study will focus on the interactions among individuals in the circumscribed context of a collaborative learning environment.

This book is written as a view from the streets and the trenches. It is a perspective that seeks to capture the attitudes, styles, and transitions of individuals who experience authentic collaborative design for the first time. It is also a voyage in itself. It is a trip to the talking point. The voyage will include signposts for participants, sponsors, and support personnel. The story will begin with a view of a sponsor discussion, move toward an inside look at preparatory work within the support team, and then walk through a series of experiences encountered by first time participants. All accounts will be based upon real-life events drawn from over forty years of experience with group problem solving. Footnotes to scientific principles and decision support approaches will be included for those wishing to dig deeper into the methodology. By sharing in this voyage, you will understand what it means to reach the talking point, and you will have some practical guideposts to help you revisit your experience in the real world.

The Talking Point is not without a precedent effort. Malcolm Gladwell's *The Tipping Point* discusses how self-sustaining, fully participatory momentum takes over in social systems. The parallel in *The Talking Point* exists with the momentum that is fueled by the social hunger for authentically shared deep learning. As a sufficient portion (we estimate 20%) of the group begins to interact in a fashion consistent with authentic learning, the group accelerates its march toward the talking point. Stated another way, the group needs to discover that it can create and share valuable learning opportunities. Once a group reaches this point collectively, its ears are open and its language is synchronized. The group has adopted a learning norm that is effective for that specific group. When this point has been reached, the dialogue managers move from the highly visible dialogue control role into a group support role that guides the group's transitions by introducing a sequence of integrated decision tools.

An alternative subtitle for *The Talking Point* might have been "a new form of group languaging." Although we were tempted, we didn't use this subtitle. But we do address the critically important subject of group languaging in this prologue, and in Chapter 1. An inspiring example of how structured analysis serves to open new possibilities is offered by Michael Goodman in his essay "Systems Thinking as a Language":

> We say someone is fluent when they begin to think in a particular language and no longer have to translate. But fluency means more than just an ability to communicate in a language; it means understanding the surrounding culture of the language—the worldview. As with any foreign language, mastering systems thinking will allow us to fully engage in and absorb the worldview that pervades it. By learning the language of systems thinking, we will hopefully change not only the way we discuss complex issues, but the way we think about them as well.

We agree with Goodman's perspective. As an example of how new languages (which include new ways of thinking about and working with quantitative and qualitative information) lead to breakthroughs, the Doppler effect was predicted by Einstein on the foundations of the general theory of relativity, which itself was based on the less-used geometry of Riemann. In hindsight, without the language of the Riemannian geometry, the general theory of relativity would not exist today. Although the Doppler effect would be as real as ever, our understanding of it would be different. Within the field of structured dialogic design (SDD; see Appendix I: The Structured Dialogic Design Process)—a new systems thinking language allowed Kevin Dye to discover the basis for a long-anticipated and profound limitation to the accuracy of traditional group-based design. This limitation is called the erroneous priority effect (EPE), and it could not have been discovered without the language of SDD. SDD itself would not be around without the existence of a digitized/discretized languaging geometry invented by Alexander Christakis, called Archanesian geometry. A formal understanding of the principles that have shaped the evolution of SDD is beyond the scope of this particular book. Our goal is to convey an impression of when, where, and how SDD works. The story of why SDD works is presented in the recent book *How People Harness Their Collective Wisdom and Power to Construct the Future* (Christakis & Bausch, Information Age Publishing, 2006). Our goal in this book is to provide readers with an exciting voyage. Participants and support staff who have been part of an SDD program over the history of its practice retain a lifelong impression of the experience. We add this comment both as a note of celebration and also a note of caution—participating in effective collaborative problem-solving discussions can be seriously addictive.

SECTION I

THE ARENA

"Organizations are made of conversations."

Ernesto Gore
Author, *Conocimiento Colectivo (Collective Knowledge)*

Note: The reflections offered in this section are intended to evoke consideration of aspects of working in the arena of collaborative large group design without providing the detailed academic documentation of the foundation of the practice. Highly scholarly works related to the practice of structured dialogic design and its precedent methodology are represented by landmark publications of John Warfield and Roxana Cardenas (*The Handbook of Interactive Management*, 1994) and Alexander N. Christakis and Kenneth Bausch (*How People Harness Their Collective Wisdom and Power to Construct the Future in Co-Laboratories of Democracy*, 2006).

CHAPTER 1

ABOUT THE TECHNOLOGY OF DIALOGUE: MANAGING MANY-TO-MANY NETWORKS

In the beginning was the Word, and the Word was with God, and the Word was God.

John 1:1 (King James Version)

The discovery of shared meaning—and the invention of dialogue—begins with the use of words and involves a process of "languaging" that results in an expression that is understood by a community. To explain what we mean by "languaging," consider the example that Richard Ogle provides in his book Smart World. The Roman numeral system—which presented a language for thinking about and working with numbers—was displaced by the Arabic numeral system. Why? Compare the ease with which we can think through the design process of subtraction—or division—with these two "languages." Taking 333 from 666 with the Arabic numeral is a fluid mental process, while subtracting CCCXXXIII from DCLXVI is, well, painfully disengaging. Our words and our language enable or encumber us. Through "languaging," we invest intelligence into communication artifacts that represent our cultural mind. We build up to "languaging" by constructing a shared linguistic domain that is founded on meaning that we put

The Talking Point: Creating an Environment for Exploring Complex Meaning, pages 3–12
Copyright © 2010 by Information Age Publishing

behind our words. As a result, we think and design not only with what is in our head but also with what is in our culture at the time.

More than a mechanism for solving momentary problems alone, languaging is critically important to dialogue and to the creation and survival of cultures. Dialogue is the original vehicle for sharing all meaning. Because of its importance, it is used ubiquitously. It is as essential and as common as oxygen, and for this reason, we rarely reflect upon dialogue. It simply exists. It is here. It will always be here. Unlike oxygen, however, there was a time is some ancient past when humankind had to invent dialogue. The gift of the capacity to manipulate and string words together has enabled humankind to reach beyond its biological legacy. In this context, dialogue is the most profound evolutionary technology in the history of humanity.

MEANING

If women are from Venus and men are from Mars, we probably should marvel at those occasions when meaning is effectively shared across genders. Ramp up the complexity . . . take individuals with different trainings and traditions from a dozen or so different organizations—maybe even from different corporate, government, nonprofit, and civic sectors—and challenge them to take on the task of resolving a really big or "wicked" problem in a situation in which success requires that they work collaboratively.

> Wicked problems have incomplete, contradictory, and changing requirements; and solutions to them are often difficult to recognize as such because of complex interdependencies. Stakeholders have radically different world views and correspondingly different frames for understanding the problem. (http://en.wikipedia.org/wiki/Wicked_problem)

If the problem isn't "wicked" enough already, constrain the group's time so that the group can only come together for several hours, two days a month—six days, over the course of a year. And then let's agree that they have nearly no money to spend to support extended deliberation, and that as individuals they all have a dozen equally pressing crises that demand their immediate attention. Does this sound contrived to you? Does this sound like a Hollywood doomsday screenplay? Or does this actually sound a bit too familiar for comfort? If you haven't been in this situation yet, you will be facing it as we march into the Information Age of the twenty-first century. Complexity is increasing exponentially, and we are going to be continuously running in our efforts to catch the meaning.

So what do we do? Unless we believe that artificially intelligent manmade machines will come to our rescue, we are ultimately left to our innate capacities to think through our problems. On the upside, the human brain is a marvel. Individuals have some awesome capacities. If we can assemble all that brainpower, there can be little that will be beyond our collective reach. But here, of course, is the rub. On the downside, we have only recently made genuine progress in efforts to link individual brainpower effectively and efficiently.

We are floating in a sea of data and information. Individually, there is more complexity surrounding complex problems than any single human mind can fathom. We cannot independently construct accurate new understandings of our highly complex social systems themselves. Social structures are embedded within and also carry other social structures in a multilevel complex that systems scientist Ervin Laszlo calls "holarchies." Holarchies assemble as individuals concede legitimacy to small groups and concurrently become bound by them, and as the small groups legitimize and adhere to constraints of larger groups, and so on. Our knowledge of even a single complex social system is both incomplete and continually evolving.

No one really knows just how rapidly we are accumulating and storing information. We know that the rate is accelerating. Scholarly published research is comparatively easy to monitor, but the accumulation of local knowledge—in the form of individually authored text and images—is difficult to track. The capacity to produce stored knowledge is driven by information technology and access to that technology, both of which are continually expanding. We simply cannot track all of the pertinent knowledge that we may already have recorded in print or electronic records. Even if we could index and access all that we already know, we have no hope of being able to read our way into the deeper understandings. Our modern necessities drive us back to reliance on our use of dialogue—a powerful yet still imperfect tool. In the end, as in the beginning, we must master our use of dialogue to exchange meaning so that we can capture complex understandings and forge new adaptive and sustainable solutions. This gives us reason to reflect on our first uniquely human technology—our ability to exchange conceptual meaning through dialogue.

Meaning unfolds, if we will allow it to do so.

WORDS

Words are inventions created to transfer meaning, but conversation is an imperfect process. Diction is the stuff of puns and poetry. And although pictures are worth a thousand words, only with the power of a single word or phrase can we transfer a precise, distinct meaning. In order to transfer meaning, we have to first step into a process that allows us to harmonize our meanings. As we do this, our innate skills allow us to invent ways of telegraphing our shared meanings. Some shared meanings will be nonverbal, and some verbal; some will be pictorial, or graphic. Our capacity to find ways to share meaning is hardwired into the neurological structures of our minds and the cultures of our social institutions. When we bring different ways of thinking and different traditions of learning together, we need to step back into the fundamentals of a process that we call "languaging." Languaging is the essential skill of capturing meaning in words, symbols, and structures. Without languaging, we cannot effectively express and faithfully transmit meanings across boundaries.

This is of central importance in understanding the talking point. Words play an essential role in the process of languaging. Universally, languaging is an underlying process of cultural groups. Over time, individual communities will develop their own ways of using words to express meanings. On one hand, this human feature shapes local identities. On the other hand, it can confound expansive, cross-community collaboration. Groups must take the time needed to be certain that they share a "linguistic domain" for exchanging complex meaning.

All around us, words are the common stuff of questions and proclamations, and yet, as a construction material, they are also remarkably slippery. Michael Hancher (Humpty Dumpty and Verbal Meaning, *The Journal of Aesthetics and Art Criticism, 40*(1) (Autumn, 1981), 49–58) makes this point using a passage of Lewis Carroll's *Through the Looking Glass* in which Alice objects to Humpty Dumpty's use of language:

> "I don't know what you mean by 'glory.'" Alice said.
>
> Humpty Dumpty smiled contemptuously. "Of course you don't—till I tell you. I meant 'there's a nice knock-down argument for you!'"
>
> "But 'glory" doesn't mean 'a nice knock-down argument,'" Alice objected.
>
> "When I use a word," Humpty Dumpty said, in rather scornful tone, "it means just what I choose it to mean—neither more nor less."

The passage shown above is relevant because experience with diversified groups throughout the world has shown us that participants generally want to initially agree upon the lexicon of their dialogue. That is, people want to seek clarity by first freezing meaning on words rather than by discovering the meaning that specific speakers attach to words. The risk is that individuals who seek to dominate the definition of the meaning of key words can exclude the authenticity of original meaning that others are trying to express. **Open dialogue must create an environment where meaning and language can coevolve.**

Poets and philosophers—and all of us, at some time or other—know that words fail us. When they do, we respond by inventing new words—or perhaps by modifying and reusing words. We see the precision of words in the jargon of technical communities—"bits," "bytes," and "baud" and the revisionist power of common use—"gigabyte" takes on the imprecise meaning of "a great amount." Even when words have codified formal meanings, they still retain the capacity to "capture" additional—and sometimes—contrary meanings. What used to be "hot" then became "cool" or "sweet," and what was once praised as "good" became—for a while—equally praised as "bad." The flexible use of words and syntax is a local, national, and global phenomenon. Playwright George Bernard Shaw captured the spirit of this situation when he proclaimed that "England and America are two countries divided by a common language."

Word choice matters. During the engagement of stakeholders in collaborative design, word choice impacts responses to questions posed to dialogue. Within dialogue, words need to emerge and connect equitably with all participants so that groups can draw fully on the skills, perspectives, and traditions of diverse participants. The result will be a superior design. Organizational leaders should be sensitive to this when they engage stakeholders in framing mission statements and when setting goals. Words that have been used to the point of exhaustion are ineffective: "stakeholder," "collaborate," "empower," "creative," "sustainable," and so forth. Imprecise or incorrect words will make specific audiences bristle: "facilitator" is a fine term but doesn't capture the essence of a "collaborative design manager," and "negotiation" doesn't substitute for "design." Those who manage dialogue-based design have a particular responsibility to be sensitive to the impact of the choice of words within design sessions.

Beginnings are fragile times. We cannot begin a design project without words (or images that carry meaning like words). Therefore it is important to "test" word choice when a triggering question is framed for collective consideration. This is a two-direction challenge for design managers. On one hand, the meaning—or the design intention—must be clear and explicitly understood. On the other hand, word choice must refrain from distracting members of the group by strongly connecting with other, unrelated meanings.

An example from the arena of practice will illustrate this point. About twenty years ago, the leader of the Winnebago tribe of Wisconsin, Chief Reuben Snake, wanted to engage tribal members in designing and implementing a self-sufficiency plan for the tribe for the year 2000. He collaborated with one of the authors in framing the triggering question for the stakeholder engagement. The question presented to the tribal members was: "What are inhibitors to our implementation of *the* self-sufficiency plan of our tribe?" When the question was posed to the group of participants by Reuben Snake, to his surprise, they all refused to respond. As it turned out, they were objecting to the use of the word "the" in the triggering question, feeling that by accepting the word "the" they would be constrained to discuss the self-sufficiency plan produced by Reuben, a plan they did not own. When the triggering question was modified to read "*a* self-sufficiency plan," all agreed to participate in designing and implementing their plan. Simply changing "the" to "a" allowed us to motivate the Winnebago tribe members to engage in their plan of action for future years.

How far one carries concerns about word choice when introducing a design project depends upon the nature of a specific collaborative design project. When community sponsors seek to transform a community, considerable sensitivity is warranted. For example, opening a discussion to plan approaches to assimilate immigrant families into the community can raise formidable word choice issues. The siting of renewable energy infrastructure in urban settings may require considerable sensitivity. Generally, wherever special-interest groups have used language to define their protected interests, use of that language by the design managers is risky, because a deeply valued meaning may be misrepresented unintentionally. Design managers work closely with community sponsors on issues of meaning and language. This is practical as well as reasonable because dialogic design managers "own" neither the meaning nor the language of the designers. A glaring error common to many "facilitation" approaches is the practice of "suggesting" or "correcting" word choices of participants in group deliberations. The proper approach for dealing with word choice issues is to encourage the community of stakeholders to understand the differing meanings that lie beneath specific words, and then to allow the author of a statement to clarify his or her meaning to the group. Often the author will shift his or her use of words to accommodate the distinct meaning that emerges in the group dialogue. Dialogue managers and sponsors work together when they are framing a question to focus the design so that collisions of words can be minimized.

The whole business of inventing, modifying, and applying words to convey meaning is part of the process of languaging. The words we use—the language we use—is not the essence of the meaning that we wish to share. Rather, it is an instructive shadow of this meaning. The essential point in what we are seeking to say in these few pages is that we must listen carefully; whether in play or in desperation, people will use or invent words to capture elusive meanings. There is considerable imprecision in the use of words, and we must take care to appreciate meanings and not words alone.

In written expression, we have little choice to hold ourselves and all other authors strictly accountable to the lexicon of accepted meanings of the words that they use. But written works lack the nuance and subtlety of the vocal inflections and the body language that are so much a part of dialogue. There are things that we can do in dialogue that we can never achieve in writing. Rather than trying to constrain the way individuals use words within a dialogue—thereby limiting the universe of evolving meanings that need to find expression—we should encourage an active exploration of the meanings that lie behind spoken words. When given the environment within which to explore meaning, groups will come to understand that words need to be clarified before meaning is understood.

We must resist the tyranny of words if we are to liberate the universe of meaning.

DIALOGUE

Epochal boundaries get a bit fuzzy as you get very close to them. Before we had spoken words, we shared dialogue with our eyes. The primordial language of eyes and of eyebrows is not uniquely human—nor has it been left behind in the dialogue of modern man. Dogs have eyebrows, and as any dog owner can attest, canines know how to use eyebrows, ears, the tilt of the head, and body posture to speak. Cats are disdainfully envious of eyebrows, but this is another story: cats are distinctly more verbal. From the human perspective, spoken dialogue is a social technology uniquely suited for communicating complex concepts.

With the leap taken in the paragraph above, we have just summarized several million years of human history. But history marches forward. Dialogue technology is still evolving. It moves slower than glaciers most of the time, but every now and then it takes a quantum leap. With new technology, a new version of languaging can emerge, and the power of dialogue then jumps into a higher level of effectiveness. Just such a giant jump forward is in progress today. It is a long slow leap, because it takes a while for a global species to leap into a new generation of languaging, but the change is under way. **The convergence of the analytical rigor of matrix algebra with the reduced costs of microprocessors and projection and recording equipment has ushered in a fusion of engineering and sociology that is being manifested as a new languaging capacity.**

Challenges that we face today in the practical application of dialogue as a means of defining and resolving complex problems include too many unexplored meanings, too many unclear words, too many different approaches to languaging, and too many conflicting demands. Complex meanings need to be "unpacked" into elemental or "digital" concept units, voiced and clarified for others, assembled into ways that illuminate relations among "digitized" ideas, and presented in "language forms" that are flexible. This whole process needs to be "scalable" so that it can support concurrent discovery and sharing of complex meaning across the range of perspectives that collectively "own" the situation that is linked to the meaning.

As we hope to convince you, dialogue can be the defining aspect of community life. Anthropologists recognize a concept of "communitas" wherein communities are organized around inclusive rituals that have taken on high social significance. Community dialogue must always happen within some space, and that space can be "controlled" by whoever manages the dialogue process within that space. For this reason, it is appropriate to ask who actually owns the dialogue space that exists between two or more people, two or more organizations or cultures, or two or more related thoughts. Who has both the responsibility and the right to claim such ownership? We believe that the space where community dialogue happens is owned by those who share their understandings in that space. Ownership in this sense includes the broader right to act on the community's interests based upon that shared understanding. Ownership can be narrowly held or broadly held. Convening a broadly diversified community is an awesome responsibility and a tremendous privilege. Developing and preserving the spirit of community once stakeholders have gathered to take on a complex problem is the essential work of community building. Groups may gather with openness, uncertainty, and expectancy—or with strong preconceptions, commitments, and expectations. Opening the space for a community to construct a consensual linguistic domain and share complex understandings is serious work. Ensuring authentic participation for stakeholders who convene in a community dialogue is difficult. Opening doors is essential, but not sufficient.

Authentic participation in dialogue requires equity in time to think, listen, reflect, speak, understand, draw distinctions, and make decisions. In any group, there will be a flow—or a network—whereby information is exchanged and individuals are linked. Options for these linkages can be put into three categories: one-to-many networks, many-to-one networks, and many-to-many networks. It is at the level of this third class of networks that the greatest breakthroughs are now emerging, but let's consider all three forms briefly.

One-to-Many Networks

Speakers, lectures, seminars, and many training presentations involve a one-to-many format in which a speaker or a lecturer "presents" information to groups. To the extent that time and inclinations allow, the audience may participate by applause (or derision) or by questions (written or spoken). Audience participation may be equitable *during the presentation* but is typically absent in the preparation of the presentation. There is a distinct "power" imbalance between the expert at the podium and the audience in their seats. This didactic "classroom" approach is an ancient practice designed to help questioners understand the wisdom of the speaker.

Many-to-One Networks

An extension of the one-to-many network exists when audience feedback is an essential goal of the dialogue. Once again, a presentation of some form is used to focus group discussion, and following this extended introduction audience question and commentary (note) is invited and (ostensibly) captured. The model has been embraced in dialogues defined to be "stakeholder processes," such as "design charrettes." The potential for the input of many individuals to be heard, understood, retained, and incorporated

in the work product of "the one" genuinely does exist, and equity of participation may be cultivated by specifically soliciting input from all members
of the audience. The limitation, however, is that ideas that are offered by
the many may be in conflict with each other, or with those of the original
concept author. In these cases, reconciling conflicting ideas and underlying
meaning becomes a "back office" task for the sponsors of the dialogue. The
audience is left behind, and the legitimacy of the final product is thrown
into question. Audiences who participate in these events may feel coopted,
and stakeholders who do not participant may rightly feel disenfranchised.
This is the twentieth-century model for a "public hearing." The intent of
the questions is to understand the reaction of the public.

An extreme form of this practice is found in the "public comment"
approach to participation that has been promulgated by agencies of
government. In these cases, a policy document is posted or distributed, and
citizens are expected to find, read, interpret, and understand the meaning
and intentions of the document's authors, and then to contribute a meaningful input to shape a policy that is asserted to be actively evolving. Participation rates are low, and understanding rates may be considerably lower.

Many-to-Many Networks

There are two fundamentally distinct forms of many-to-many networks.
One form involves the familiar social networks in which individuals move
through concurrent, distinct discussions in sets of small group dialogue. In
this way, they carry bits of topical interests from group to group. The alternative form involves a single focused discussion to which all participants
contribute in turn. The small group approach can build a sense of shared
understanding within individuals. The large group process is needed to
confirm that a consensus does, in fact, exist within the larger community.
The challenges that frequently exists when one tries to consolidate impressions of consensus based on small group dialogue into larger group consensus relates to different languaging practices experienced in discussions
among small groups. Meanings that are collected individually as stakeholders work in small groups produce uncertainty when those meanings are
directly aggregated across individuals in the form of a report to a larger
group. But if a consensual linguistic domain is first constructed within the
large group, and if this language is then used within smaller groups, aggre-
gating small group understandings becomes more reliable.

Collaborative design in small groups is an ancient practice. Most groups
of five to ten individuals can (if they genuinely wish) assure equitable participation of stakeholders in their design activities. Scaling up the small
group process to enable more participants has been a formidable challenge
for democratic practice. The reason that the many-to-many network breaks

down is because the number of moving parts exceeds the unassisted cognitive capacity of individuals in the group. Ideas need to be clarified and tracked, and a record of the connections that have been made needs to be recorded. In essence, the group's consensual decisions need to be captured in a systemic way. The scaling problem can be formidable.

Consider the number of one-to-one reciprocal communication links that exist among groups of different sizes. The equation for calculating this communication load is given by Robert Metcalf's network power function: $N(N-1)$. Bidirectional communication in a network of two individuals has a power function of 2; with three individuals, the power function is 6; with four individuals, 12; with 5 individuals, 20. Traditional facilitators often work with groups of up to eight individuals, who, if they have genuinely distinct perspectives and are engaged in a truly complex problem, will communicate with a network power function of 56. As the group doubles to include sixteen individuals, the power function rises to 240. The method described in this book is typically used for complex problem solving with diversified groups of twenty to forty individuals, representing power functions of 380 to 1560, and has been used with groups of over seventy individuals from different organizations and backgrounds, representing a power function of 4830. Our point is that as group size increases, methods that have been effective in supporting small groups will eventually fail. For large groups to construct collaborative systemic designs to respond to complex problems, they must use specialized dialogue management approaches to reach what we are calling the *talking point*.

THE FINAL WORD

Too much information is formally equivalent to too little information—in both cases, the situation leads to underconceptualization of problems and poor choices.

The central challenge of our time is to master working in the many-to-many dialogue space. To navigate this complex and typically unstructured terrain, principles that have been implemented in what John Warfield and Alexander Christakis have called "the science of generic design" can serve as our compass. Prior technological enhancements for dialogue have been based largely on approaches for managing speech. Generic design emerged as a means for concurrently managing speech and meaning—specifically, for use with many-to-many learning networks. To really understand what this means, you will have to follow us deeper down our rabbit hole.

CHAPTER 2

ABOUT THE ESSENCE OF MEANING: HOW WE THINK AS GROUPS AND INDIVIDUALS

"Borders? I have never seen one. But I have heard they exist in the minds of most people."

Thor Heyerdahl
Norwegian explorer

We think just like babies. There: the sad truth is out. We have learned to be faster and better, but we are essentially doing the same things. We make an observation and put it into a framework, and then behave in a fashion consistent with the fit of the observation within our framework. It works something like this—for a baby: if I have it, it is mine; if I see it, it is mine; if it is in your hand, it is mine; if you own it, it is mine. The relationship of "it" being "mine" is a bit primordial, and durable, too. It is a simple framework. It links to a framework that says, "if I own it and it feels nice, it goes into my mouth; if I own it and it doesn't feel nice, it goes onto the floor (but I still own it)." The point is that from an early age, we begin making observations and putting them into some frameworks. It is like building a house. We have a few simple rules for stacking bricks, and so we build until things

The Talking Point: Creating an Environment for Exploring Complex Meaning, pages 13–24

collapse—and then rebuild. For babies (of all ages), the first few times that frameworks collapse are particularly painful. A primordial emotion cries out, "It is not supposed to be that way!" With a certain passage of time, we come to cope with the deflation and collapse of some of our frameworks. Understanding the role that cognitive frameworks play in our everyday lives reveals a lot about what we might expect from an effort to come together and make a collective decision.

LIVING WITH FRAMEWORKS

The essence of all learning—the augmentation of prior knowledge or understanding with new information—has been approached through assimilation theory (Ausubel, 1968). From an early age, individuals continuously construct a framework for understanding their world. New observations are fit into that framework, and frameworks can evolve to have many elaborate associated frameworks. It's a bit like "the house that Jack built," where things are connected in some marginal sense, and generally more tightly held together in some particular instances, but are largely constructed in the ad hoc way that we experience life as individuals. We interact by activating closely related frameworks in each other: a shout of alarm can activate a common fight-or-flight framework and its attendant physiological and emotional preparatory responses. A cooing song or the purr of a cat can sometimes sooth us. Words are triggers for activating frameworks of meanings, too. As the baby learns the word "mine" and finds a need to construct new frameworks when "mine" does not fit, he or she becomes progressively more receptive to words like "yours" or "Mommy's" or "Daddy's"—and, according to the literature, "sister's" and "brother's," in rare, well-behaved cases. So, then, frameworks (or "cognitive frameworks") are the essence of meaning. And words and other communicative symbols activate the frameworks and, by rattling that framework, also signal when a framework needs to be repaired, extended, or replaced. By the time we are emerging as adults, we carry a huge library of frameworks. Some are unique to us, but many are largely—if imperfectly—shared with and by others.

Things that are everywhere often go unnoticed. Many of us are fully unaware of the air that we draw into our lungs and then expel a few long seconds later. We agree that it exists, but pondering it can seem quite pointless. Frameworks are a bit like the air around us. We rarely think specifically about a framework within which we insert or reject observations. If we don't have a bin for an observation built into a framework for assessing a situation, we are likely to ignore an observation that is right in front of our eyes. What was the color of her coat? What type of shoes was he wearing? What was the make of her father's car? Who played tight end for the New

England Patriots this season? On what side of the plate does the salad fork belong? So are these trivial observations? That wholly depends upon the context. If we have an existing framework for handling these observations, we have already decided that they are not trivial.

Societies are complex places cluttered with norms and conventions, all of which can potentially signal things that can trip us up. We may fail to hold a door open for someone in one context and get a demerit, but in another situation we may get a demerit for holding that same door open. We sail through life prisoners of our frameworks and the frameworks of others. But it is amazing how given the proper incentives, we can hastily rebuild a framework: an attractive new friend might even get us to rethink our framework for judging the merits of broccoli—or sushi.

Not all frameworks are amenable to change. Some frameworks are seared into near permanence by strong emotional experiences. Emotions, or feelings, are indeed linked to the cement that we use to build and rebuild deep frameworks. For some of us, the elegance of a complex framework is like a work of art unto itself. We might marvel at the genius that was poured into the framework that explains how cells use DNA to copy instructions for rebuilding themselves and assembling themselves into complex organisms. We might reflect in awe at the beauty of a mathematical proof or the balance and energy in a poetic verse. Chances are that we will also fall victim of the intentional tickle on a framework that results from a joke— the thing that is not supposed to fit and that surprises us with the way that it doesn't.

So we walk around as a bundle of frameworks, tapping on the frameworks of others to see whether anyone is home. Sometimes our verbal taps will be rejected abruptly, because they clearly break established rules. Sometimes our verbal taps will resonate, because we sense a shared desire to rebuild some defective social rules. In many cases, our frameworks will rap against each other when we stare through the same window out onto the world and yet see different vistas.

As individuals, we are likely to disagree on interpretations of new information based upon differences in our frameworks. When we come together as groups, we will reach agreement intuitively or explicitly, either by aligning our individual framework with some "leader's" framework, or by jointly constructing a new and shared framework. When we are dealing with deep frameworks, there is an inertia that locks us into a struggle for preserving the "truth" that we feel we have uniquely captured in our framework. With the explicit goal of constructing a framework for understanding new information in complex situations, individuals must collectively confront the inadequacies of their individual frameworks. This psychological process cannot be rushed; individuals may need to take a period of time to "grieve" for the death of their personal worldview. It can be a time for both individual and collective sorrow (and group members can be less accommodating than they might have envisioned themselves being). In moments like this, a kind environment will set the tone for the emotions that will be used as mortar for constructing the new framework. This is a moment that is too fragile for haste.

When sufficiently diversified groups of individuals are engaging a complex learning situation, new knowledge generally includes both assimilating new information into existing frameworks and constructing or modifying frameworks for assimilating that new information. Different bits of observations will trigger a framework crisis for different individuals, and it is because of this that all salient observations must be explicitly presented at a pace that ensures reflective understanding. Processes that move too quickly will ensure that those inconvenient learning opportunities will be lost. The cartoon of the dog listening to its owner only to hear, "*blah blah blah* cookie *blah blah blah blah* lie down" speaks to the notion of getting only part of a message. And we should add that in addition to thinking like babies, we also are apt to listen the way our pets do. Woof!

MIND MAPPING, DIALOGUE MAPPING, AND DECISION MAPPING

In the 1970s, Joseph Novak and his colleagues at Cornell University extended Ausubel's assimilation theory through descriptive studies of early learning using a dialogue process they called concept mapping. In essence, a learner's recalled ideas (in circles) are connected by lines to represent how information was organized by individual children. The practice has persisted in the form of "nonlinear" outlining and has been offered as a means of tracking group conversations through a variety of rather simple graphic programs. Cognitive mapping is descriptive—and revealing. Its variants include semantic mapping and, when coupled with an analyst's expert understanding of materials and flows, systems dynamics maps. Cognitive mapping of dialogue—mind mapping—has become a core feature of some group consulting practices.

Cognitive mapping isn't always only descriptive. When a map is used to guide the design of a course of action, the map is prescriptive. Maps that have evolved specifically to chart the flow of dialogue are historic. They record what has "happened." Maps that specifically record and chart many small decisions that have been made are both historic (because they record decisions) and prescriptive, because the pattern of decisions can define a preferred course of action. In this sense, the decisions that we are talking about emerge as a sequence of yes-or-no votes related to well-defined relationships between pairs of items under consideration by the group. When a dialogue is structured so that many incremental—or "micro"— decisions are accumulated by a group, the resulting map isn't tracking the dialogue, but the decisions. And by mapping only those pairwise relationship decisions for which a supermajority (greater than 75%) of a group sees a "significant" relationship, we tap into the collective cognition of the group. We are building a cognitive map once again, but this time we are constructing a map based on collective cognition.

So here is the basic taxonomy of cognitive maps:

1. A mind map (or semantic map, or systems dynamic map) results in a framework of an individual's "mental model."
2. A dialogue map results in a historic record of the way that a dialogue unfolds and the way that topics link to each other.
3. A decision map results in a historic record of many incremental decisions made through supermajority consensus within a group and results in a framework of a collective "mental model."

These cognitive mapping approaches all provide frameworks for assimilating new observations, yet they serve distinct purposes and are produced in different ways. Mind maps are produced through iterative insertion and reposition of objects and connections by their author. Dialogue maps are produced during a dialogue by a facilitator and record the path of the discussion. And decision maps are generated as a record of decisions that have been made by a group and are captured by a dialogue manager. Distinct types of maps play different roles in recording and guiding thinking and discussions among their authors. Mind maps record the intimate interactions of their authors and some subject matter and result in an individual cognitive structure. Dialogue maps are a record of the sequence of ideas raised and discussed by groups in the form of a historic structure. Decision maps are a record of a group's decision making activity and result in a collective cognitive structure.

These different types of maps also have different susceptibility to the influence of individual mapmakers. Mapmakers who have preconceived notions of how a resulting framework is "supposed" to look can influence the flow of dialogue in a group, thereby shaping the resulting dialogue map. Mapmakers can also prompt subject matter for consideration, thereby influencing individual mind maps (which may be a desired approach in a classroom setting). Mappers have limited capacity to influence the structure of group decision maps, because individuals within the group name the items for consideration—and because even the sequence in which decisions are made by a group (in a thorough pairwise decision process) alters each pairwise decision itself.

So, which map is "best" for a group? If it is your purpose to discover the way that a group of individuals with diverse perspectives understand a complex situation, you will want to systematically ask them to make relational judgments as a group as you record consensus decisions so that you can record where strong agreement exists within the group. This means that you want to use a decision map to understand the collective cognitive mind—the mental model—of the group.

Mind maps are the easiest to use, and dialogue mapping is a close second. Why are these approaches potentially able to mislead us? So far, we have not considered why mind maps and dialogue maps might fail us. The problem with these framework-building tools is that they capture strong individual views but lend themselves poorly to building consensus. They capture an expressed consensus rapidly but frequently fail to capture a shared understanding deeply—but both these comments require further clarification.

Mind maps are created by individuals and small groups for individuals and small groups and typically require expert interpretation to unpack. Moreover, frameworks created from individual perspectives tend to lack point-to-point relationships to "comparable" maps created by other individuals. The maps are profoundly helpful at surfacing items for collective discussion and can be modified by input from others to iteratively converge on a mutually acceptable view. In sufficiently complex situations that require input from diverse perspectives, the objects and the language used to discuss the objects may need to be reconstructed to accommodate the group. Consider a systems dynamics model for explaining how a school system works: teachers, instructional material, students, and tax dollars are flows that interact in buildings, classrooms, and administrative office overtime. The systems dynamics map will feature materials and flows based on historic information and may even accommodate some assumptions about some alternative futures. It is a powerful and broadly used method, but it is weak at capturing the hopes, expectations, and intentions of a diverse population of stakeholders in a complex system. Nevertheless, it is very good at reporting a history of matter and energy flow for that particular school system.

Dialogue maps can depict discussions of matter, energy, hopes, fears, strengths and any manner of subject matter that emerges in a group's discussion. With an attentive facilitator, these maps can capture these concepts in the form of labels that are expressed in the language used by the group. This is indeed a powerful tool for helping a group recall what it has discussed and for suggesting relatively unexplored subject matter that a group may wish to subsequently consider. As the dialogue map is constructed, information is recorded in the "chunks" with which it surfaces. There may be moments when clarification is clearly required and dutifully provided, but there also is a tendency to move at a naturally rapid pace. Dialogue maps capture ideas well if—and only if—the pace of the dialogue is managed to assure clarification of meanings and full inclusion of participants. Free-ranging dialogue—and many facilitated dialogues, too—float information through a stream of consciousness in chunks that are too large for some participants to assimilate. When this happens, participants can become disconnected and cease to effectively participate. The quality of decision making can erode. While hidden meanings can be addressed, the mapping process does not assure that they will be addressed, because structuring decision making within the group is secondary to the goal of mapping the flow of the discussion.

Decision mapping is arduous and requires that a dialogue be designed so that decision making opportunities are maximized. This process is discussed and illustrated elsewhere in this book, but for the purposes of comparing the challenges of working with these three framework tools, decision mapping requires explicit attention to preserving the authenticity of individual ideas and explicitly capturing supermajority decisions. The supermajority decisions require defining a pairwise relationship for voting, collecting votes, discussing variances in perspectives, revoting, and then recording the decision. In all dialogue-based frameworks, the elements in the map (the ideas) need to be explicitly clarified, and the clarification has to be protected by assigning ownership of each idea to its original author, exclusively. The challenge is that when new ideas emerge, each original idea needs to remain intact and authentic. This is important, because during decision making the group will vote on a specific meaning and will become confused if multiple individuals claim authority for describing an idea in different ways. In decision mapping, meaning will unfold around an idea as the group discusses an idea, but the exclusive arbitrator for a specific idea must be preserved as the author of that idea. In this sense, every participant is an expert in the idea that he or she puts onto the table for the group to consider, and every participant reserves the right to introduce a new idea when he or she is able to explain to the group that an important new distinction has been discovered through dialogue.

When large groups discuss complex situations, it is important to distinguish between the goal of exploring ideas and the goal of decision making. Identifying and exploring ideas is a diverging process. Decision making requires convergence. We use our individual frameworks to make decisions, and for this reason, when coming to consensus with a group, we collectively use a framework that is latent within the group's collective consciousness. The quality of decisions that we make as groups is critically dependent upon our capacity to "discuss and understand" the issues *and* the relationships between the issues. Quality in this decision making is preserved by avoiding information overload—or, stated another way, ensuring "parsimony" through logical selection of the issues and the relationships that need to be assessed. Overload is not a consequence of the complexity of an idea alone but also includes ambiguity around and nuance associated with an idea, and its relationships with other ideas. Failing to protect participants from information overload during deliberations of complex situations results in leaving one or more of them behind.

CONSOLIDATING OR REVISING COGNITIVE MAPS

An interesting point relates to whether we best remember what we happen to have "said," what we have explicitly "decided." Cognitive dialogue maps and structured dialogic design (SDD; see Appendix I: The Structured Dialogic Design Process) decision maps differ in this respect. The differing approaches vary in their ability to convert short-term memory into long-term memory.

Cognitive psychologists and cognitive neuroscientists tell us that consolidating a memory requires a form of rehearsal whereby we repetitively activate the same sets of nerve cells that were involved in forming an initial understanding. The hypothetical cellular assembly underlying cognition has historically been called an "engram." Somewhat paradoxically, small bits of information are harder to retain and recall than larger interconnected concepts. It is as if an idea needs to engage a sufficiently rich set of frameworks to become "fixed" in the brain; reflecting on this idea consolidates it in the brain. For example, in the business of remembering things, cognitive psychologist tell us that having a "rich context" (e.g., multisensory or multifactor memory) helps etch, freeze, and recall the footprint of the idea.

Individuals actively or passively forget unused or less frequently used frameworks. Can you write out the equation for the Pythagorean theorem just now? If we happen to "like" a certain framework, we may replay it over and over to etch it into place. Certainly there is some emotion—some pleasure—attached to our efforts to actively remember a specific way of thinking about observations (or maybe there is a relief from the discomfort of the coercion that might have been compelling us to have once memorized that theorem).

In the human brain, emotions are linked to learning and memory. Cognitive neuroscientists have tracked this reinforcing function to a portion of the brain called the amygdala. If groups have a collective mind, is there also a "collective brain?" And if there is a collective brain, is there a collective amygdala that plays the parallel role of reinforcing institutional memory? One way of thinking about this is to consider the role that the arts play in retaining and reciting institutional experiences in our communities. Through story, song, art, drama, and sculpture, we reenact experiences and decisions as a record of collective activity. Through artifacts, and stories told with and through artifacts, we hold the memory of our important advances. Active forgetting is the deliberate dismantling of culture and cultural artifacts by revolution or conquest. In the context of our work with groups, it is very important to appreciate the role that artifacts generated through collective decision making contribute to the capacity of a group to retain the memory of what they have decided upon. Without such memory, groups are continually at risk of stalling their intended action. Without effective—rather than voluminous—artifacts, groups are fated to stumble into a premature dementia and lose their capacity to collectively respond.

Here is the echo of the challenge that is presented by the need for groups to remember: groups also must retain the capacity to unlearn so that they can work with current information and knowledge. If we use artifacts to bond us to what we have learned in groups, how do we "tweak" our artifacts to update our memory? We can, of course, add or delete text or add or delete images in a collage. We also can redraw our maps. Dialogue maps (mind maps) could result in gaps or disconnected additions. Decision maps use a methodology that easily accommodates deletions and that weaves amendments and augmentations into previously determined structures. The method that we use with groups applies a software tool (an inference engine) so that maps can be updated by prompting for the smallest set of relational judgments needed to position a new idea within a map. With tools such as these, groups can arm themselves with a continuously current script from which refreshed narratives of their shared understanding can be generated. The narrative remains linked to the most current picture of the essence of the group understanding.

REVELATION OF THE FRAMEWORK OF A GROUP'S COGNITIVE MAP

Mind maps and dialogue maps hold few real surprises for their authors. This is because the authors' thoughts or expressions are experienced as they are recorded. Conversely, decision maps emerge in the background of the dialogue and are presented in an "Aha" moment for the group after the group has completed pairwise decision making. This "grand finale" presentation intensifies the evocative feelings that rise in the group as they see their newborn shared framework. Reflecting on this explicit statement of "the way that the group thinks" is a powerful experience. The point of considering how the collective cognitive map stirs the neural juices of its creators is found in the necessity of using emotion to drive commitment to action. Is the SDD decision map art? If one defines the core requirement of art as being something that evokes strong emotion, then, yes, the artifact represented by the SDD decision map is art—at least for those who have created it. For this art to have emotive power on others, it is translated into other art forms, including inspiring narratives that use the decision map as their script.

AN EXAMPLE FROM THE ARENA

In 1987, Reuben Snake, the chairman of the Winnebago Native American tribe of Wisconsin, was reluctant to join a group of fifteen other tribal leaders from different tribes to engage in a structured dialogue for the purpose of collectively defining the problem situation confronting tribal America. When he finally agreed to participate in the SDD session, which was managed by a Greek national, he was antagonistic and sarcastic about the process—ridiculing it as another cultural invasion by the "White Man." He objected that the Greek philosophers caused great damage to the philosophy of his Native American ancestors.

When the group completed one day of disciplined dialogue and their map was presented on the wall of the collaborative facility at George Mason University, they were in a state of emotional awe. They suddenly saw clearly, and for the first time, that their collective brain was able to map the deep predicament of their people. The map depicted a vicious cycle of issues that were strongly coupled. All their issues were all emanating from the fact that Native Americans had fallen into the trap of perceiving themselves the way others—namely the immigrants to their land—were perceiving them. In an emotional statement, Reuben said that the only way they could escape their predicament was to drastically change their perception of themselves. He went so far as to joke that perhaps each Native American should adopt 500 white Americans to help jointly change each group's perception of the other.

That night, the group of leaders had dinner together in a hotel in Washington, D.C. My memory is that they consumed a lot of alcoholic beverages to numb their pain. The following day they got together and were able to design a pragmatic action plan for escaping their perceptional trap. The results of this breakthrough discovery emerged and bore fruit after ten years of sustained commitment to the vision that tribes would be able to develop effective plans for economic development ensuring their emancipation.

Reuben and the Greek dialogue manager became very good friends after the 1987 experience at George Mason. Reuben invited him to visit the Winnebago tribe for a planning session focusing on the strategy for the self-sufficiency of the Winnebago tribe by the year 2000. He introduced the process to his tribal relatives by saying that the method was the closest analogue to the traditional way of building consensus used by their ancestors as they passed around the peace pipe. He brought this process to the tribe to experience it as a contemporary way to reignite their spirit and unite them with their ancestors.

THE FINAL WORD

We understand complexity by connecting an idea into a system. Our species is hardwired to perform this task, and we perform it both as individuals and as groups. We need to construct frameworks to reveal our individual and collective cognitive or mental models so that they are both durable and also flexible. In natural, or freeflow, dialogue, the sequence with which information emerges from within a group follows a general logical pattern that results in a history of how a shared understanding has emerged. In the structured sequence of tasks in a SDD session, ideas emerge and are clarified without mapping the history of their emergence. But in SDD sessions, decision making is mapped in the background and the resulting map is presented to the group to show the group how their many small decisions have accumulated into a "structure" that reports their aggregate understanding. Dialogue mapping results in an artifact that can help groups recall what they have discussed. Decision mapping, as rendered through SDD, presents the group with a framework of what they have collectively decided, thereby serving as a communal platform for developing a joint action plan.

CHAPTER 3

ABOUT THE NATURE OF LEADERSHIP: POWER POLITICS EXPRESSED IN DIALOGUE

"The manager administers; the leader innovates. The manager has a short-range view; the leader has a long-range perspective. The manager asks how and when; the leader asks what and why. The manager has his eye on the bottom line; the leader has his eye on the horizon. The manager accepts the status quo; the leader challenges it."

Warren Bennis
Professor, University of Southern California

"If the people lead, the leaders will follow."

William (Bill) Ellis
Nonviolence activist

The most familiar model for leadership is the hierarchical leader–follower structure, in which highly visible individuals voice decisions on behalf of the group. Leaderless communities are less familiar, and they also require

The Talking Point: Creating an Environment for Exploring Complex Meaning, pages 25–46

identifiable individuals who will be willing to play coordinator roles to extract decisions from groups. Individuals who play either of these very different leadership or coordinator roles exercise power on behalf of the group. The power associated with traditional leadership roles has been extensively discussed by many authors. The power of coordinators—or sponsors—relates to decisions about when, where, how, and why groups will be engaged for the purposes of establishing a group perspective. In many cases, an end result of engaging a group is the creation of a collective perspective that will result in a change (a new direction or a transformation). Change and active resistance to change are both expressions of power. Some forms of power act on the choice of a target question for a group to deliberate. Other forms of power act on the processes groups use to make collective decisions.

LEADERLESS COMMUNITIES

Leaderless communities deserve special attention. Some communities are stable because they are defined around geography and traditions of paying taxes and jointly electing municipal officials. Leaders of these communities may hold office specifically to direct (or prevent) change. In contrast, leaderless communities may elevate a citizen to a leadership (or coordinator) role only on an "as needed" basis. Weak or ad hoc leadership may be shaped by initiatives from sponsors who have some stake in the actions of the leaderless community. This all is very central to the theme of this book, because we each belong to countless leaderless (or "latent") communities that are just waiting for some stimulus to trigger us to collectively spend the time, energy, and money needed to organize around a leader. The tenure of that leader or coordinator is a separate matter, but the style of that leader is a primary concern in shaping the capacity of the group to respond collaboratively.

The key consideration of leadership in leaderless communities is that as sponsors and internal coordinators seek solutions to community problems, they have an extremely powerful role in specifying the frequency and the direction for communities to focus their attention. If they solicit community decision making events too frequently or too frivolously, they can saturate the bandwidth available to the community for collective deliberations and make it more difficult to convene the community in the future. In effect, an "evil" leader can be installed by a sponsor or a special interest group in a leaderless community for the specific purpose of consuming all of the community's available planning time in unproductive—though perhaps even kindhearted—"dialogue." Before you judge us too harshly for our attitudes about idle dialogue, let us say in our own defense that we do fully appreciate dialogues and deliberations as capacity-building practices that enable struggling communities to learn how to speak to each other and how to reason together. The shortfall of stopping with dialogue and deliberation is that these forms of group activity do not lead to effective design for collaborative action. Yes, you can throw in a vote at the close of a dialogue and claim that the group has selected an action option—and some members of a diversified community are likely to do their part in following up, too. Our point is that much more work is involved in planning for *collaborative* action. **Collaboration begins with a shared strategy, while cooperative action is tactical and is based on shared logistics.** Cooperative action can lead to fragmentation of a community because the community is not cohesive in its decision to act. Sometimes this doesn't matter much; sometimes, it matters a great deal. For example, in an effort to envision and create a harmonic future for health care and for wellness—involving advocates, practitioners, patients, insurers, and administrators—sending folks off on fragmented missions has a slim prospect of resulting in a strongly cohesive collaborative culture.

The difference between cooperation and collaboration is a matter of involvement versus commitment. As the adage goes, the difference between involvement and commitment is like ham and eggs: the chicken is involved; the pig is committed.

WAKING THE COMMUNITY

Boundary-spanning missions typically involve engaging a community that is defined by a specific shared interest and that frequently does not yet have an identified champion, leadership team, or coordinator for orchestrating collective action. How does the community come together? Who is the convener? Who sounds the convocation? Who remains accountable for the investments of trust that will follow? Frequently citizen activists (who have not already polarized themselves too much within the community) will gather a "steering committee" of some sort. In this small group, an initial trajectory is plotted to address a shared problem within the community. Sometimes the process begins with an executive in a company that either employs or works with a great number of members of the community. This can be viewed as a top-down launch. A third option is through leaders of nonprofit education, religious, or community development organizations. The nonprofit—or independent—sector either originates or accepts the proposed target from grassroots activists or corporate sponsors and manages the organization of a diversified steering body. At the very start, an individual champion aggressively seeks to distribute the leadership role to include others. The first circle can be imperfectly selected, but it must be transparently committed to being inclusive if the event is to result in authentic boundary-spanning collaboration.

All beginnings are fragile times, and this beginning is no different. A steering committee is subject to the criticism that it brings biases from individual life experiences to the planning table with its members. But how can it be otherwise? Members may manage their biases well, but, as we will see in Chapter 5, we all will make some decisions beneath the level of our own cognitive review. The legitimate role of the steering committee should be to assess the extent to which the community recognizes a significant, widely shared problem that can only be addressed through their collaborative action. The question that they should be asking their neighbors is, "Who else do you know who might have a stake in solving this problem—in one way or another—who might contribute a different way of looking at the problem?" If the problem is broadly distributed but not strongly felt, the steering committee has a new problem. In this situation, it will need to launch an education/communication campaign presenting what it feels is an unbiased account of the community need, reassessing the extent to which the community cares.

Community activists can inflate passions for action, but the inflated passions may not contribute to the reflective environment that will be needed for collaborative design and sustained collaborative action.

Corporate sponsors must be expected to encounter suspicions of extracting wealth from communities with whom they interact. Corporate philanthropy is good business, and good business is good for a community, but not all community members have strong confidence in this chain of virtue.

Academic centers that seek to serve communities run the risk of being believed to hold the community as an object of experimentation, or as a classroom for teaching students. Certainly learning from the wisdom of the community can serve many audiences, but academic priorities do not always place community benefits above academic benefits.

By default, but also by first principle, community foundations and community development organizations (and related municipal economic and community development offices) are chartered to serve the community first. Organizations that seek to promote their neutrality are ultimately judged by the company that clings most closely to them. A case—regardless of how weak or prejudice—can always be made that a neutral party has knowingly or naively fallen under the thrall of some dark force. We can agree that this may occasionally happen, but we have had no first-hand experience of this in over thirty-five years of working with diverse communities. Once we experienced a team of sponsors who dissolved after having achieved a breakthrough with structured dialogic design and—content with what they had achieved through democracy—reverted to command-and-control management. Usually, however, by the time that an organization reaches out to apply structured dialogic design, they have already deeply made the commitment to listen to the voice of the community.

ADVOCACY AS A CATALYST AND AS A DECISION CLOSER

Advocacy is a means of waking up a community. It is an exercise of power through the use of personal persuasion to build up collective "political will" to investigate a problem or to endorse a specific solution. In boundary-spanning situations, we will use advocacy as a means of recruiting stake-holders to participate in collaborative design. People must be willing to solve a problem together if they are to actually solve a problem together. Unfortunately, we recognize that advocacy can also be used to preempt, derail, or negate democratic deliberations. For this reason, we can probably all benefit from an evolution of language able to describe different uses of advocacy.

In a political system, the use of advocacy as a means of "buying" support for a vote from individuals constitutes a "fungible" economy. This means that if one person agrees to support someone in one initiative, he or she can expect to receive support in return from that person in a totally unrelated initiative. This isn't a problem when the support is limited to "please help us understand and solve a shared problem," but it can be damaging when it is directed at a request for an affirmative (or negative) vote on specific proposal that may or may not have been authored by "special interests." Buying political support through a marketplace for political favors corrupts the democratic process. For this reason, we feel that advocacy is good as a catalyst but very dangerous as a decision closer.

The devil is always in the details, however—even as well-intentioned community mobilizers seek to recruit individuals to come and discuss a problem, some (possibly many) members of the community will look at the invitation as a means of gathering advocates for their preconceived notions of appropriate solutions. It often can be difficult to avoid the resulting "collision of good intentions." In the approach that we have used when working with groups, we make a point of focusing the community expectation on the goal of coming together first to frame a collective understanding of the situation that the community faces. In our experience, it is critically important that advocacy be used *only* to engage individuals in a commitment to collectively understand and address a problem. Advocacy is needed because focusing a community's attention toward any one urgent and important problem removes the community's focus from alternative, competing problems. At this "metalevel" of problem solving—the level at which the community senses which problems it needs to engage at which time—we acknowledge that an economy of reciprocity may be both unavoidable and also healthy.

Within a structured dialogic design session, advocacy is restricted. All collaborative design participants are engaged in design and decision making tasks as autonomous individuals. Their individual autonomy is protected through preservation of the individual authorship of their ideas and through individually cast votes on the nature of influence among ideas. Individually they are free to express strong conviction about relationships among ideas, and, through persuasive dialogue, they are expected to influence each others' thinking—but not in the form of reciprocal transactions.

EMERGING AND INTERMEDIATE LEADERS

Steering teams may or may not reach directly into and across the expanse of the community to engage a sufficiently diversified community of stakeholders to truly "represent" the community perspective. In such cases, members of a steering team (including *de facto* leaders, sponsors, and grassroots champions) may work through "brokers." Brokers exercise power based on traditions of trust that they hold with individuals in the community. These brokers may become recognized as new leaders as a community initiative gets under way, and, indeed, many brokers have come into the practice of structured dialogic design. At this level, brokers are beginning to ask individuals in the community to follow them—literally. Brokers lead stakeholders into a forum for collaborative design (we call this forum a "colaboratory").

THE BASIS OF LEADERSHIP POWER

Brokers must use a power that is effective for their followers, and the situation of their followers will define the source of power that is needed. Mary Parker Follett crusaded for research on the "followership" 80 years ago. Today we recognize five bases of social power[1] that bind followers to leaders:

- The leader's position or legitimacy
- The leader's knowledge as an expert
- The leader's ability to reward followers
- The leader's ability to coerce followers
- The leader's referent power (the extent to which followers identify with, respect, or admire a charismatic leader)

Some leaders can apply multiple bases of social power, but some of the power bases are eroding. The expert role, for example, has been lessened by

---

[1]French, J., & Raven, B. H. (1959). The bases of social power. In D. Cartwright (Ed.), *Studies of Social Power* (pp. 150–167). Ann Arbor, MI: Institute for Social Research.

the sheer volume of information that is available to average citizens through the Internet or related electronic systems. The authority of experts, including experts who leaders might choose to recruit for their cause, doesn't wield the power it once did. Positional power, or respect for rank, title or office, has also been eroded a bit. The authority of positional leaders depends upon the perceived rational standing of the organization or administration that they lead. With the many well publicized small and large flaws in our complex institutions and organizations, no organization assures bulletproof credibility. Personal respect or admiration or charisma can be fleeting, even though they are constant targets of popular media. The powers to reward and punish are dangerous, because inequity or perceived inequity in their use can create a powerful backlash. The reduction—or redistribution—of social power has a real impact on the way that leaders need to approach ways of managing their followers. In such a case, leaders will have a looser hold on followers, followers will follow a leader for different reasons and be held to the leader by different convictions, and leaders will have to know when to be strong and when to be gentle.

CONFIDENCE (THE CRITICAL FACTOR IN EMPOWERED COMMUNITIES)

It is not enough that a stakeholder might be willing to follow the leadership of a broker. Stakeholders need to understand that their fellow stakeholders are also prepared to follow leadership that is committed to addressing the community challenge. Based on the different mechanisms through which power holds onto followers, a leader's social powers often may not reach beyond his or her own organization. Sometimes there may be a language barrier—sometimes a difficulty in expressing a concept. Sometimes the followers are coming together from different parts of an organization or types of organizations that don't share a reporting hierarchy. Sometimes the social power base of the otherwise preferred leader isn't a good fit with the different motivations of the essential followers. A business executive, for example, might not have the expert social power to effectively motivate a cadre of engineers and scientists; an engineering manager might be equally ineffective in motivating a cadre of sales professionals.

When the diversity of the perspectives (i.e., skills or competencies) in a community is great, and when the experience of having worked together on complex problems in the past is low, confidence in self-governance becomes a concern. Communities that do not believe that they can govern themselves probably cannot govern themselves. Community collaborations can falter when stakeholders are not confident in emerging leaders, when they question the governance approach that will be used, and when they doubt the commitment their fellow stakeholders are prepared to make in order to solve the problem. Even an exceptionally skilled leaderless community will fail if it lacks confidence in its capacity to collaborate effectively.

WHY WOULD ESTABLISHED LEADERS YIELD ANY OF THEIR POWER?

Often, it is difficult to delegate a leadership role to an individual who will be leading a group that has a big problem and that has not worked effectively together in the past. This is beginning to sound sadly like business as usual. Ingrid Bens is a world-class trainer who works with groups to improve their performance. She specifically trains managers to improve the quality of their team facilitation skills. One of the points that Ingrid makes is that managers have to be able to use multiple management styles, because the tasks that managers need to manage do not lend themselves to only one stylistic archetype.

First (and most traditionally), there *is* a time for managers to tell their teams what is going on. This is a direct command-and-control role, and it can be as polite or as dogmatic as suits the individual manager and his or her essential followers. Followers will have a common motivation of reward through employment and may have additional individual motivations. The ideal situation for this approach is one in which followers (e.g., employees/staff) lack some specific skills but are willing to learn.

Second, managers are almost certain to find some times when they want to "ask" for input from their teams. Requests for input have to be taken seriously to ensure that responses will be full, complete, and accurate, and leaders need to project a tone of respect for the wisdom of followers. Leaders retain all of the decision making functions. This is particularly important when the followers have some skills but need to help leaders understand where gaps exist and how they might best be filled.

Third, managers are likely to have times when they want their teams to "participate" in a collaborative action at a tactical level. Here leaders don't want to participate in routine, day-to-day decisions, but they do want to maintain control over strategic directions and overall performance. Accountability is still to the leader, but cooperation and best efforts are needed to get the job done.

The fourth role is a "delegating" role. Overall control of the initiative is put into the hands of the followers—and typically into the hands of a specifically selected follower. This follower will decide when and how the leader will be involved. This situation is characterized by the presumption of high competence and high commitment among the followers, as well as a presumed comfort in their own ability to manage the effort.

Leaders do not always intend to yield power. Sometimes communities take the lead. Here is a case in point. The dean of a school of engineering convened his faculty to design a partnership project with industrial companies that wished to be linked with the university. During the construction of the consensus view for how this should be done, the dean, who was a very domineering individual, was continuously and consistently on the minority vote. When the final consensus map was displayed on the wall of the facility, the dean stood up and very strongly advocated for the systems view presented in the map—without actually realizing that his individual contributions were not reflected in the results. When relaxing together later, we told him that his votes were consistently minority votes. He was totally amazed. He continued to fully embrace the group view and, we are told, has become less dominant in his behavior toward his faculty. Discovering the confidence that a manager can have in a group allows a manager to delegate more power to the group, enriching—and perhaps transforming—the manager's individual style. We see this as an example of an accelerated transformation from command and control management toward what Chris Argyris calls a "commitment model" of management. Important value and behavioral differences can be transcended when leaders recognize the combination of competence and confidence that exists within their groups.

TRUSTING THE NET (THE POWER OF METHODOLOGY)

Individuals gain confidence in their group when they have a reason to trust its leadership, its communication/decision making capacity, and the conviction of others in the group to follow through on their expressed intentions. Of course, organizational development experts and human resource managers recognize that even when small teams come together, individuals pass through phases as their team gels and performance increases. Facilitators offer a range of exercises and skill-building drills to accelerate this small group socialization process. Ultimately the team and the team leader learn to work together, and with a history of productive work, they have confidence in their team. This has a great deal to do with personality styles and behavioral strategies. It may be that we have reached near perfection with what can be achieved through small group collaborations. A fundamental problem exists, however, when group size increases much beyond ten individuals. At this level, the group leader cannot rely on the "Ping-Pong" tactic of testing and bouncing ideas back to individuals in the group, because progress is too strongly dependent upon the individual team leader's skills in understanding and reacting to an overwhelming diversity of expert information. In these situations, the dialogue shifts from hub-and-spoke coordination with the leader at the center and instead operates by linking every node (individual) directly to a corresponding expert at the moment that that expert input is needed. The leader directs traffic among ideas but does not touch or take ownership of the ideas. As a result, the team leader becomes a nonjudgmental coordinator of high-speed information flow. The team leader is, in effect, pulled out of the "content" space of the team process so that the team can access, share, and store information connections more effectively. Human behavioral issues are certainly still involved, but information management practices now dominate over psychological issues, and confusion and dispute are preempted rather than managed.

A high-speed exchange of unfolding information is very much like a square dance. Everyone is involved. Everyone is positioned to learn something new. Everyone is tapped to contribute. At some point, everyone does engage each other directly. In principle, a large group operates as effectively as a small group—swapping only the deeper wisdom of the large groups for the agility of the smaller group.

Folks who have not been part of a square dance can find it bewildering, with its swings and turns and foot-stomping promenades. It takes a bit of practice, but then it can become powerfully attractive. Some individuals would be reluctant to admit that they actually enjoy the dance itself more than dancing with any specific partner. People can come back again and again for the social process of a square dance—firmly committed to it.

Now you might have to suspend some disbelief, but it is at least theoretically possible that some individuals will also become just as strongly attached to a genuinely effective collaborative planning practice—not simply because of the relief that is offered over alternative approaches, but because of the powerful pleasure of learning and solving problems as a well-orchestrated group. We see this as a measure of the strength of the leader–follower bond that stakeholders have with the structured dialogic design process. It reflects their trust in the net.

YOU CANNOT TRUST A NET THAT YOU DO NOT USE AS A NET

Neither of us has ever been an aerial acrobat, nor is this likely to be waiting for us in the future. Still, we know that high on a trapeze, an acrobat appreciates the net suspended below. Climbing and bouncing on the net offers proof that ropes and knots are in place. It is still only in the launch from great height that the virtues of the net are fully known. Structured dialogic design is a net to protect collaborative designers as they share in the discovery of complex problems and in the creation and implementation of strategic solutions. The net is strong, and the confidence that stakeholders learn to place in the strength of the net provides the group with the power that it needs to take on challenging collaborative design problems. Without the net, the trapeze would be quite dangerous. Without structured dialogic design, engaging a boundary-spanning group of individuals who have not worked together in the past to form and implement an action plan to resolve a wicked complex problem would be hazardous.

To extend this metaphor: We have been asked to provide a sample "demonstration" of structured dialogic design. This has been like providing protection for a trapeze artist whose feet are only six inches off the ground. The net is not needed. When the net is not needed, it is a nuisance to set up and to test. It is not appreciated. If groups do not have a serious, boundary-spanning challenge to engage with structured dialogic design, then they could only experience it as a trivial toy or an over-engineered gimmick. On the other hand, with the experience of having served over 300 groups taking on serious challenges, each having more than thirty participants, we have exposed 9,000 individuals to the dance of structured dialogic design and its power as a safety net. Our colleagues have collectively shared the experience with many more individuals. Everyone who experiences SDD finds something familiar, something unfamiliar, and nothing comparable to it. Not everyone wants a net when they perform, but responsible communities do.

RECOGNIZING POWER DIFFERENCES AMONG STAKEHOLDERS

All group practice managers have special challenges serving confrontational or adversarial temperaments that slow or stall group learning. In some groups, a participant may assert that an aspect of the group learning was either unnecessary (because it essentially confirmed much of his or her original individual preconception) or irrelevant (because it did not sufficiently confirm his or her original individual preconception). While these personal assessments are at odds with the collective assessment, SDD managers seek to assure these individuals that their contributions have shaped the group view, and that the group view is a reflection of what was learned by others. Individuals who reject an outcome that does not fit their expectations are inconsolable and may seek opportunities to undermine the group's efforts to implement its collective plan.

Individual Power of Eloquence

To make decisions democratically, all stakeholders need to be operating as distinct and equal individuals. Distinction among stakeholders is reflected in the preservation of the authorship of individuals as they express their personal views on complex ideas. Equality among stakeholders is reflected in the respect that is shown for inclusive individual participation. Equality is more challenging to ensure than distinction. To maintain distinctions, we track authorship and prevent group authoring. Equality requires that balancing opportunities be heard by the group. Individuals enter a structured dialogic design session with different inclinations toward oratory and pontification. The format of SDD does provide opportunities to constrain excessive verbiage by asking speakers to provide a concise statement of their main point for the group records. Unequal eloquence in conversation, however, is beyond the control of the methodology and does allow some individuals to sometimes sound more persuasive than others.

We see the power of individual eloquence first during clarifications. Poetic, precise, or humorous statements may cause some participants to favor an idea a bit beyond its naked cognitive content. We do not have any specific evidence that this is the case, but we must remain open to the possibility. Elegantly expressed ideas may draw less scrutiny through questioning. Inelegantly expressed ideas certainly do draw questions for clarification, and in this sense fuzzy statements may be explored more frequently, if not any more deeply, than other statements. Individual eloquence is also expressed during explanations for votes taken during pairwise connections of idea. Here an eloquent explanation can seem more coherent—both linguistically and logically. The influence of eloquence is somewhat buffered in this instance, because only a supermajority (>75%) of the group's collective votes will result in a decision to record the relationship as being significantly influential. We have seen the explanations offered by individuals who lack eloquence fully reverse group thinking frequently enough to convince us that eloquence is not a dominant factor in decisions made with structured dialogic design, but the role that the power that eloquence may play in distorting democratic decision making remains incompletely explored. Structured dialogic design is no more adversely influenced by individual eloquence than other dialogic approaches, and because of the large number of pairwise group decisions evoked by this approach through the course of the group deliberations, structured dialogic design may be considerably shielded from the power of individual eloquence.

Individual Power of Appreciation and Reflection

Appreciation and reflection together constitute a power that is encountered in all exchanges between speakers and listeners. The appreciative power of individuals is manifest in the depth to which individuals probe ideas for understanding. While structured dialogic design does not permit any "value judgments" to be expressed by other participants during the clarification of meanings of authors' ideas, insightful questions for clarification can strengthen or weaken the appeal of an idea. The power to ask profound questions can enrich the learning of all participants, provided that incisive comments are not cloaked in tone and body language that might signal a desire to undermine the author of the idea.

A case in point might help in clarifying the issue of the dark intent that can be cloaked in a question. When an aspiring director of a center in a federal agency that we were working with was passed over from being assigned the directorship of the center by a younger female candidate for the position, he was clearly upset and angry. During an SDD session with fifty members of the center as participants organized by the new female director, the objective of which was to redesign a core process for the agency, he attempted to challenge the knowledge and authority of the newly assigned director by pursuing questions of clarification of the meaning of her ideas in a "darker intent" mode. He pretended that he could not understand her ideas and wanted "exhaustive clarification." When the dialogue manager recognized the dubious motive of this individual, the dialogue manager had to declare that the statements offered by the new center director were "as clear to this individual as they can ever be." Without inserting himself as an expert in the interpretation of the content (which would be a violation of the design team's content neutrality), the dialogue manager declared an end to a specific line of inquiry. This is a move that can only be achieved when it is clear to the dialogue manager that the group itself is in support of moving on. The timing for the intervention must be appropriate, and the dialogue manager must be able to "read the group" accurately.

During review of the group's collective influence map describing their situation, reflection aids in the construction of narrative accounts of the group's shared view. Individuals can draw additional depth into elements in the map by recalling aspects of clarifications that were shared earlier in the design process. Power in this reflection always acts to the group's advantage, because the summary statement is limited to the content upon which the group reached strong agreement.

Individual Power of Judgment

Structured dialogic design segregates idea exploration and idea analysis (judgment) to distinct phases of the design process. Professionals who manage groups recognize that group participants judge more than ideas alone. Individuals also may hold judgments (or prejudices) toward fellow participants based on distinct business professions, affiliations, or hierarchical professional or social positions. Powerful egos can become engaged in performing on stage for the prize of top dog, or push against all others to be king of the hill. Disparaging remarks must be addressed directly by restating the rules of engagement that are set out in the agenda for the community event, but disparaging postures, eye rolling, or focused disinterest in a specific individual's contributions are more difficult to manage. It is reasonable for individuals in a community to initially with-hold full support for the ideas of others. It is reasonable for individuals to enter a collaborative dialogue with the belief that they have some pretty powerful thoughts to contribute. As a dialogue unfolds, participants who may never have interacted directly before come to discover that they are all sources of experience and wisdom; this dissolves some preconceptions. As even power-focused individuals discover, real power exists in the capacity to be understood, believed, and accepted by others. An authoritative, judg-mental demeanor can be an impediment to succeeding in the free market for the exchange of ideas, and intelligent individuals learn this rapidly.

Structured dialogic design does allow participants to add to an author's idea by linking a comment to the idea (again, without judgment). This practice achieves two goals: (1) it allows a group to "park" a comment that might emerge for collective exploration at a later date, and (2) it allows a group to offload a potentially colliding idea without forcing a judgment of the merits of the two ideas in ways which could defeat the expression of the author's original idea. For example, a comment might be, "A similar idea was raised last year." The comment may point to an idea that was unpopular at a prior time, yet recognize that the same idea is being revisited in the present discussion. The dialogue manager would declare, "We will take this statement as a 'comment' within our record of the author's idea."

Individual Power of Cultural Vocabulary

What was once "cool" became "hot" (or was it the other way around?), and what was "gnarly" or "rad" (radical) today is "sweet" or "sick" (but will probably have changed again by the time that this page is read). Using and sharing "cultural passwords" builds group cohesion and concurrently sets up a means of identifying individuals as being within (or outside) a group.

Individuals who introduce new words (jargon) into a community express their power for building a new cohesion or a new boundary.

The words that we choose to express our ideas also have a genuine impact on the way that we are understood as individuals. We can hint at our inner feelings or reveal our cultural gaps. "Individuals' choice of words can hint at their social statues, age, sex, and motives. We sense if the speaker or writer is emotionally close or distant, thoughtful or shallow, and pos-sibly extraverted, neurotic, or open to new experience."[2] These hints can

---

[2] Pennebaker, J. W., Mehl, M. R., & Niederhoffer, K. G. (2003). Psychological aspects of natural language use: Our words, our selves. *Annu Rev Psychol, 54,* 547–577.

accelerate or impede the emergence of trust within a group, and trust is needed to collectively explore deep hopes and concerns related to uncertain futures. Individuals who are confident in revealing their inner self through an engaging cultural language can play leadership roles in cultivating trust within a group. The power of this leadership role, of course, will depend upon the strength of the followers.

MANAGING POWER DIFFERENCES DURING DIALOGUE

Like its kindred discipline—facilitation—dialogic design management relies upon norms that convey respect while also allowing participants to dig for knowledge and understanding. Inquiry that thrusts too deeply and too quickly into a subject is likely to be perceived as aggressive—as is commentary that ridicules or dismisses points offered in clarification of an understanding. Rules of engagement are presented when the agenda for the event is introduced, and norms emerge as the group begins to apply the principles of SDD. It is an orderly, or structured, dance. But it was not always this way.

The history of formal approaches to protecting speakers in dialogue is rather recent. Parliamentary process might be considered a poor example by those who have viewed parliamentary exchanges. Efforts to apply rules of discourse to more rough-and-tumble audiences led a young naval officer named Henry Martyn Robert to compile a set of rules that became known as Robert's Rules of Order (originally titled *Pocket Manual of Rules of Order for Deliberative Assemblies*). The precipitating moment for the emergence of the code arrived when the officer was assigned to oversee a community dialogue at a church meeting in the then-thriving global whaling port city of New Bedford, Massachusetts. The rules were actually modeled after practices that had emerged in the U.S. House of Representatives—by individuals of Benjamin Franklin's vintage who were influenced by Quaker traditions. For all of the huge leap forward that Robert's Rules of Order contributed in public assemblies, deliberation still easily could be dominated by individuals with high position or with forceful personalities. A crowd mentality within a meeting could make it clear than those holding the minority view were unlikely to prevail through the power of rational argument alone. Robert's Rules of Order offers no mechanism for fostering a reflective deliberation. Rather, the early objective was to manage the traffic jam in the race to the podium.

Dialogue that emerged along the traditions of the courts, not surprisingly, engaged competing positions in the fashion of a debate. Deliberative dialogue frequently begins before hard positions have been established.

The goal of dialogic deliberation, or in Greek *dialogic syzitisis* (searching together), is to define and design a consensual solution. In this sense, dialogic deliberations differ from contests, in which individuals vie to promote the survival of their individually-framed preferred solutions. Examples of the later form of dialogue emerged from "round table discussions" and have been traced back to tribal cultures among indigenous peoples—such as the Native American councils of the Iroquois Nation—and to some religious sects, such as the Quakers (the Religious Society of Friends). Here, more than regulating the sequence with which speakers would raise questions and make statements, the broader goal was to ensure that all participants would speak and would be heard. The approach can be rightly called a democratic dialogue. Beyond the simple act of counting votes (which in many "democratic processes" today typically substitutes for participating directly in the dialogue that frames the question on the ballot), democratic dialogue ensures that all participants are engaged in shaping the motion for action.

Structured dialogic design fashions itself upon principles of democratic dialogue. A specific topic is presented to the group for dialogic deliberation, and the group is asked to understand and accept that topic before the group begins. Individuals reflect individually and then contribute in a "round robin" fashion to gather all individual perspectives sequentially as parts of a coherent story and to record them to ensure transparency of inclusion in the process. Sequencing is not based upon seniority, rank, or personal urgency, but rather upon the sequence with which individuals are seated at the table. Each individual makes a statement, and then the entire group has an opportunity to ask for clarification of the speaker's meaning. This allows meaning to unfold to meet the needs of the assembled participants. As one can imagine, this takes some amount of time. To honor the investment of time, the design management team creates a continually updated record of the group's ideas and the construction of the ideas into a shared framework.

Structured dialogic design is not as spontaneous as other forms of dialogue, but the tradeoff for the rapid expansion of ideas that occur with less structured processes is found in the powerful and reliable convergence of group perspectives that results from structured dialogic design. Managing power during dialogue is no different than within a well-facilitated deliberation using alternative methods. Facilitators and dialogic design managers will both intercede to prevent a forceful participant from marginalizing other participants. They will both use body language, redirection, humor, and process management authority to protect the group. Facilitators and structured dialogic design managers (as a specific practice of dialogic design) will present participants with tasks that will be managed individually, in small groups, and as a whole group for specific aspects of the dialogue.

SIGNIFICANT DIFFERENCES IN DIALOGUE MANAGEMENT METHODOLOGIES

A significant difference in approaches to power management between traditional facilitators and structured dialogic design managers relates to the relationship of the process leader and the group. Many traditional facilitators play a role in moderating the content that a group provides, frequently suggesting revisions to language—and sometime simply applying their own words to thoughts voiced by the participants. In traditional facilitation practices, the group is constantly aware of the facilitator's active presence, and may feel lost without constant guidance. Participants find themselves bouncing ideas off the facilitator, and the facilitator prompts specific members of a group to pick up on specific comments made by other participants. The goal of this approach is to get some level of participation from all members of the group. In structured dialogic design, the dialogue manager works to speak as little as possible—striving to direct the dialogue with hand gestures, and to steer the questions and answers directly among the participants who are seated facing each other in an open circle arrangement. Structured dialogic design managers do not alter the expression of any of the ideas from the group, nor do they allow any group member to alter the language of another participant (although all participants are free to reword their own comments to improve clarification of their meaning at any time in the dialogue).

Structured dialogic design engages all participants to the same extend as both speaker and listener. All voiced ideas are honored equally, and in instances in which a duplicate idea is discovered through dialogue, the group defaults to retaining the first expression as the authoritative statement (and will always go to the first author for a clarification of the meaning of the statement when a situation calls for more clarification).

Both traditional facilitation and structured dialogic design use voting as a means of getting a view of collective preferences. In structured dialogic design, voting is a means of stimulating dialogue, while in many traditional facilitation processes, voting is taken as a signal that dialogue is now over. The way that structured dialogic design treats the results of voting is to seek to learn from those who hold a minority view of the situation. This honors the "underdog," avoiding the sociological stigma of presenting a minority view. In seeking to learn first from the minority view, we seek to preempt any "tyranny of the majority." We model the inquiry so that the majority camp is the first to ask "what can you teach us." After the minority perspective is expressed, individuals from the majority perspective then present their view. Typically, there are multiple perspectives associated with both majority and minority preferences. Only by engaging in dialogue after voting does the group come to really understand the different perspectives. At this point, we take a second vote to see whether the group feels that there is strong consensus on the specific issue, and subsequently, we record those instances in which the group strongly concurs.

Through many, many small decisions, a group builds up a common structure of strong consensus, which the dialogue manager presents back to the group graphically on the screen and the wall of the facility. This differs with a convergence process under traditional facilitation approaches, whereby a group is confronted with a range of perspectives and then cornered into making one last great guess at what is most important. From the perspective of power management, there is no "final battle" to be fought with structured dialogic design, because many small decisions have paved the way to a reflection on where agreements have brought the group. The global system of connections among ideas emerges from a sequence of local decisions by supermajority voting. Traditional facilitation leads groups into a final showdown when preference votes are the final determinant of outcomes and where strong personalities can see how a strong post hoc argument might turn the tide. With structured dialogic design, groups ponder the conclusion that they have reached—and how they came to reach that conclusion—in a reflective fashion, whereas traditional facilitation raises the final decision above collective reflection. By immersing the participants in a cascade of localized decisions, structured dialogic design enables the community to synthesize their "pluralities of realities" and collaboratively construct a global pattern that is a reasonable approximation of the collective reality. Their agreements reveal the wisdom of the group. In essence, making their own collective wisdom explicit transforms people from all walks of life into experienced practitioners of the scientific approach for building consensus.

AN EXAMPLE FROM THE ARENA

In one design session, one of the participants was presenting a response to the triggering question "What must we do today to ensure our community that we will have the health quality that we will need in five years?" The participant named one idea—"tell the truth"—and during clarification stated that they all needed to be sure that the way those issues were covered in the newspaper were accurate.

The editor of the local newspaper, who was sitting in the room, was clearly turning dangerously red. So the dialogue manager placed himself between the speaker and the newspaper editor and, while looking toward the editor, began to explain: "All right, we have heard a clarification of the meaning behind this statement. We do not have to agree with it. I don't know what to think, because I have no idea what this means. You may or may not already know what it means. You do not need to believe it, anyway—all you need to do is understand what this idea means. At a later state in our process, we get to vote on things that we feel are important, and some ideas will surface as highly important to the group. You do not need to worry about this as being an important idea or not just now. For the moment, you need only be sure that you understand the meaning behind the idea. Now, do we have any questions for the author of this idea?"

The dialogue manager nodded to the editor of the local newspaper, who was clearly ready to speak, and who now recognized that he was not alone in sensing the implications of the statement. The editor asked with a steady voice, "Do you mean that you feel the reporter or the newspaper has lied?"

The speaker said, "No, that isn't my point. I mean that there is more to the story than what comes up at first, and we need to work more closely together so that the press gets the full story before it puts out any story." The dialogue manager then stepped between the editor and the author once again and asked the editor, "Do you understand the author's meaning?" The editor said, "Yes, but I don't like the way that it was stated." The dialogue manager said, "Okay, we will add a comment to the record saying, 'The way that the meaning was expressed can cause some tensions.'"

Turning back to the author, the dialogue manager asked, "Now, you do not have to change anything that you have said; however, you do have the opportunity to change the way that you have expressed any idea if you choose to do so." The dialogue manager stopped short of asking the author if he wanted to change his words, and instead looked out to the rest of the group and asked, "Are there any more questions for clarification on this idea?"

In the example above, the author did choose to change the wording to "report more fully," but this is not the point that this example seeks to make. The point is that a strong, influential participant in the dialogue was obliged to rely upon the goodwill of another participant to fix a situation that caused him some discomfort. A powerful individual can, of course, storm out of a room if he or she does not get his or her way, and it is the dialogue manager's job to see that this does not happen. The dialogue manager can "take the hit" for the pain that may be caused. But in a democratic design of a social system, the presumption is that the participants have a mutual goal of fixing a situation or capturing an opportunity together. Individuals are not convened for the purposes of inflaming conflicts. Individuals who are actively in conflict with each other are not ready to collaboratively design solutions together, but in some instances they can be drawn into a larger community in which they might find a way to begin to work together.

If the editor had become intensely upset, the dialogue manager may have suggested that reflection on the author's expressed idea might lead to the discovery of a new idea for the editor to introduce to the group. This new idea might provide a balance even if it were antithetical to the original idea. Because neither of these two opposing ideas would be subjected to value "judgments" as they are introduced, both could be clarified and carried forward into the planning process.

THE FINAL WORD

Power is a fact of the human condition. It is either the reward or the reason for individual leadership. Even when power is reduced by restricting the use of titles of authority and by the transparently equal treatment of ideas, individual human beings cast a personal aura that announces the power of their presence. This power cannot be eliminated, so it must be managed. As a group is building up a norm for equality in dialogue, we need to move deliberately, yet cautiously. A well-known story relates to ways that gradual change can bring about a transformation without triggering alarm. We've all heard how frogs are unable to recognize rising temperature in a heated pot until it is too late. And we do need a better example for situations when decision making processes allow a group to construct a shared understanding without triggering a showdown among strong personalities. This is a "soft landing." The ship begins moving so smoothly that we fail to notice the moment when we left port. Structured dialogues allow a group to anticipate and navigate a smooth transition into a new way of interacting as the group makes its way into the deep waters of complex and difficult design challenges. In a sense, the group immerses itself in the overwhelming complexity of the situation and is ultimately humbled by the diagnosis of this wicked complexity. Even the powerful and arrogant discover humility. Everybody recognizes that nobody can embrace the complexity alone, and that everybody must help in making progress toward the design of the solution. When that moment comes, the atmosphere within the group is transformed into one of humility, empathy, and equity.

Structured dialogic design splits leadership roles into control of the process management (under the structured dialogic design management team leader) and control of the content (under a leaderless democratic group of participants). The dialogue management team leader has highly visible power at the launch of the dialogue, but the group soon senses that like King Lear, the dialogue management team has very circumscribed limits to its power. The dialogue management team is at the same moment both a king and a servant of the rules of engagement. The overarching power exists within the rules of engagement.

From the participant perspective, every individual retains his or her individual power to speak or not speak (and to listen or not listen), but no individual participant makes an individual decision that binds the group. Individuals use the power of persuasion that exists in their life experiences, their understandings, and their expressions. All individuals are equitably positioned to contribute to the emergence of a powerful, newly constructed group language for understanding their situation and designing collaborative action. The strength of consensus is not measured by votes on a single view, but rather by a deep reservoir of local but important decisions that connect through an explicit logic to reveal a global systems view of the group's understanding.

Group leadership requires a social commitment to collaborative action. The commitment is vested first in collectively developing a definition (or an understanding) of their shared situation. Then it is reinvested in collectively creating the future by designing options for action. And ultimately the options are collectively configured into an action plan that can be coordinated through a project manager. Social commitment is not delivered—it is discovered and forged. Social commitment does not emerge simply because a group follows a single super majority vote, but rather because a group has collaboratively constructed a bridge through a continuous cascade of strongly shared decisions.

Benjamin Franklin commented that although the finished Constitution of the United States of America was not as perfect as he had personally hoped it might be, it was probably as perfect as it could possible be. As a collaboratively constructed bridge, it has sustained a nation's 220-year march in a direction that no nation had gone before. We are faced with challenges to construct similarly durable bridges today, and we must do this with far greater social diversity gathered at the planning table than was present in Franklin's day. The founding fathers of the United States of America were never fully at ease with the prospects of putting the power to shape the fate of a nation directly into the hands of "average citizens." They lacked the sociotechnical tools to reliably manage the process. Historic scholars today offer high praise for the personal virtues of the thirty-nine highly accomplished delegates from twelve colonies who labored in secrecy through four months in the heat of the Philadelphian summer of 1787. As a result, the final product of their efforts offers a model for nations of the world, yet the process that they used to reach this result does not provide a precedent for contemporary society. The feared consequence of putting power into the hands of stakeholders who do not know how to effectively exercise design and decision making power causes many individual leaders to delegate leadership to groups only as a last resort. Delegation of leadership power is done out of necessity. Structured dialogic design provides the safety net.

CHAPTER 4

ABOUT THE ART OF SENSING IMPORTANCE: SETTING PRIORITIES

"Not everything that counts can be counted, and not everything that can be counted counts."

Albert Einstein
Theoretical physicist and philosopher

What matters? It depends, of course. Without understanding a situation, we can guess wrongly. Here is where we can get stuck in "the chicken? or the egg?" dilemma. We need to know what is important so that we can construct an understanding of our situation, and we need an understanding of our situation so that we can recognize what is important. We need to understand the importance of barriers or tasks so that we can build an understanding or a plan, and we need to have a systems understanding or an integrated plan to fully appreciate the importance of individual barriers or tasks. This can make planning a bit complicated. We can have gaps in our understanding of barriers or tasks, gaps in our understanding of how things fit together, and gaps in our understanding of how things are likely to change. Change, of course, is certain. Our situation can change due to circumstances fully beyond our control—and once we put a plan into action, the plan itself is supposed to have an impact on the situation—hopefully, in positive ways.

The Talking Point: Creating an Environment for Exploring Complex Meaning, pages 47–58
Copyright © 2010 by Information Age Publishing

47

If you ask a group of folks to choose what matters, you need to provide a context for making choices. The quality of the choice can only be as good as the quality of the current understanding of our situation.

"What matters" continually changes. The task that we once agreed was a central concern ceased to be important to us after we had completed it. Like a slalom racer speeding down a snow-covered mountainside, the very next "gate" is the critically important gate—until the instant we pass it. Looking down at all the gates in the slalom run and asking the same question before we have started our run gives us different situational information to guide our choice. We are asking a larger question when we take in the larger view; we should expect to choose differently. Our understanding of importance is very much a matter of perspective. Even in extremely complex situations, if we deeply share a perspective on our situation, we can agree upon items of importance. If we fail to share that perspective, we can collectively fail to identify important items.

BUILDING LISTS AND EXPRESSING PREFERENCES

Constructing lists is not a mechanically difficult task. And choosing an important or preferred item from a list of options is something that we do every day. Individually, we order from a menu. Collectively, we might also order from that same menu—though now with added discussions of preferences. If the items of the menu are unfamiliar, it takes us longer to reach agreement. As simple as this commonplace task might sound, it is not something that we always perform to complete satisfaction. We are not suggesting that you bring a flip chart to the restaurant on your next trip. Trying to accommodate different perspectives through voting can lead us to outcomes that may fail to please any of us. Philosophers, for example, recognize the voting dilemma as Arrow's Paradox.

Kenneth Arrow received the Nobel Prize in Economics in 1972 for work he had done in the early 1950s. This work mathematically established that no voting system can convert ranked individual preferences into ranked collective preferences when there are more than two discrete options to choose from. Perhaps Professor Arrow had struggled through many dinner menus. It took the Nobel committee twenty years to recognize the powerful implications of Arrow's work. In a nutshell, if groups vote on a list containing more than two items, Arrow tells us that there isn't any way to aggregate their differing preferences that will result in a ranking of the list that will accurately reflect the group's thinking—without the influence of a dictator. If we knew nothing of Arrow's work, we could still think of times when folks cannot come to agreement because of other more mundane causes.

We suspect that most of us have been in a facilitated group session in which we are instructed to vote on options that are put into a list. As individuals, we vote. As a group, we tally the votes and identify the "winner."

The democratic voting seems fair, so we tend to place a lot of implicit trust in the quality of the results. Fair, however, need not be accurate.

"Multivoting" is an attempt to improve the accuracy of capturing a group's assessment of ranked importance of items in a list. The approach allows individuals to cast a specified number of votes (typically five, depending upon group size and list length). This pools highly preferred options. As with one-vote processes, the formal goal is not to use the votes to select the "winner," but rather to use the voting to focus discussion on a small set of highly preferred options. Repetitive cycles of voting with an increasingly narrow list of options may convince a group that it has used a rigorous approach to converge on a consensus of the most preferred option. (A derivative of voting and multivoting that allows participants to put multiple votes on a single option has been called "power voting," and because it can distort the process of convergence by consensus, it is not a process that we recommend you apply.)

Voting is fun. It is interactive and highly visible. This can create a good feeling, and good feelings can help groups believe that they are choosing wisely and fairly. Decision scientists will advise groups to heed Arrow's paradox and apply formal decision matrix methodologies—if the decision "really matters." And of course we cannot argue with such advice, provided the decision making process can be tuned to the capacities of the decision makers in the group. We all have our cognitive limitations, and since we are not really machines, we need to have decision making technologies meet us at least halfway. The good news is that powerful decision support technologies exist and can indeed go much further than meeting us halfway. Using such technology requires exacting discipline on the part of dialogue managers, and, indeed, most of the profession is not inclined to tool up to meet requirements that exceed the "normal" needs of a group. Our pragmatic instincts will encourage us to keep things as simple as possible, but no more so. The point that we are making here is that while voting is easy and can often be pleasurable for participants, voting based on intuitive individual understandings of the structure of a complex situation is only a preliminary technology for responding to complexity.

SENSING IMPORTANCE

Importance is an emotional assessment. It is our opinion that as a species we all blend contextual understandings on multiple dimensions into a feeling of "importance" that we then attach to an idea. We recognize and remember ideas precisely because we attach emotional significance to them.

Properties of ideas such as *large*, *fast*, *expensive*, and *rare* are objectively measurable attributes. Importance however is subjective. The fact that something is expensive may not be a basis for being important to us—in some comparisons. While we may not be consciously aware of it, we continuously rank and rerank the importance of things in our lives as our individual situations continuously change. Our favorite ice cream at 2:00 in the afternoon may not be our favorite ice cream by 2:00 in the morning. Our favorite shoes or tie from last year is bumped from the list by something else.

If we are asked to name our favorite song *at this instant*, we may catch ourselves "feeling" as much as we are "thinking." The powerful machinery that we have for "feeling" the importance among ideas can complicate our efforts to avoid making subjective preference decisions as groups. Try as we might, as human beings we cannot fully leave our feelings behind.

We have thought a great deal about the emotional aspects of thinking, learning, and problem solving (puzzle solving), because such reflection is central to our work helping groups address highly complex—"wicked"—problems. Our reflection on where groups' initial preferences appear in the subsequent systems structure that emerges from structured dialogic design work suggests that as a species, we may have innate capacities for attaching emotional significance to a small set of features that are common to all ideas.

First, it seems to us that we may be hardwired to feel the importance of some things based upon their "immediacy." By this we mean that we can feel the urgency of something that is close to us or that feels like it needs to happen soon. At the same time, however, we may have different feelings for what amount of time represents "soon," and correspondingly distinct thresholds for triggering a sensation of urgency. This emotion may be linked to "fight-or-flight" anxieties, and comparable relief when the threat has been harnessed or deferred.

Second, it seems to us that we may be hardwired to sense bottlenecks and dividing pathways—perhaps a vestige of our hunter past, when we might have herded large game into a narrow passage in our efforts to catch our dinner, or when other tribes might have been seeking to herd us into their traps. Again, there may be an anxiety related to anticipating a trap, and a corresponding elation in seeing a path through that trap.

Third, we believe that individuals in groups are able to sense when something is likely to be large, costly, or otherwise immovable. Perhaps we recognize that moving it out of our way is going to depend upon a lot of other things fitting together just right. Perhaps at an early stage in our biological evolution, our ancestors needed to know whether the band of hunting animals coming over the hill significantly outnumbered us.

Fourth, we have pattern recognition capacities. Pattern recognition underlies higher-order decision making skills. We sense connections. This allows us to make inferences that reach into unknown dimensions of experience. Pattern recognition also underlies the composition of musical progressions. Musical progressions play on emotions that are related to the temporal and harmonic "fit" of individual sounds in a larger system of sounds. As we listen to music, we come to recognize, and then anticipate, patterns, and we can react to the way that sounds confront and reward our expectations. Looking at an unstructured list of preferred ideas, we may or may not easily see a pattern that links them.

In a complex situation, chances are that a group of individuals will see multiple patterns, and for this reason, the group needs to reconcile these perspectives to truly understand how their preferred ideas fit together. Individuals who are asked to view a list as a system may experience a mildly haunting sensation of a missing element or misplaced connection, and—once that element or connection is named—a corresponding sense of reassurance. The point that we are making here is that without focused attention to the influence of relationships among ideas in a system, the leverage among ideas is unlikely to be conceptualized, and attention is likely to be biased toward immediacy, bottleneck, or size.

Our notion of the four emotions that drive individual preferences during group exploration of complex meaning is not without generic support from the field of cognitive neurology. A region of the brain that is strongly associated with emotions—the amygdala—is also strongly linked to learning. We are not seeking to claim originality in linking emotion to learning, but in light of the intense level of learning that occurs during structured dialogic design sessions, we are sensitive to the fact that we are working in an emotionally intensified environment. The implication is that not only will participants find themselves buffeted by the tension and release of discovery and resolution of ideas, but they additionally will find themselves exhausted at levels that are deeper than they may have anticipated. Our sensitivity to this fatigue is reflected in the attention that is given to the physical features of the design facility that the group will use.

RESULTS OF VOTING ON PREFERENCES

We have explained some of our perceptions of the emotional complexity that confronts individuals as they engage complex problems together in groups. Structured dialogic design session participants who are faced with the task of placing votes onto lists of items collected through group efforts will all vote individually and subjectively. That is to say, each individual makes his or her choice to follow his or her strong feelings, to look around and follow the choices made by others, or, perhaps, to even refrain from voting at all. The individual votes suggest the general area where the group agrees that important ideas exist. We always expect a spread of votes as a result of the complex function of emotions that individuals attach to proximity (urgency), bottlenecks (dividing paths), size (immovability), and connectivity (systems). Statisticians would speak of this as a problem of "precision." The arrows are hitting the target in a cluster, and the cluster has a spread. Of perhaps more central concern, however, is how closely that cluster of votes lands with respect to the true center of the target. Structured dialogic design provides us with a unique method for making this assessment.

Structured dialogic design provides a means for measuring the precision of a group's understanding by looking at the spread of individual voting results across the set of ideas contributed by the group. Convergence is seen when many individuals vote for the same idea. Tight convergence on a small set of ideas reflects precision in a shared view. This precision can also represent evidence of "groupthink," a condition in which a group forces itself into tight agreement and may fail to appreciate the value of fringe or marginal ideas. Primarily because voting is so easy, groups frequently seize upon voting results to chart their course.

Structured dialogic design also provides a means for measuring the accuracy (or error) in a group's initial understanding. Accuracy is assessed when a group looks at its preferences in multiple ways and then measures the extent to which the preferences have remained constant or have shifted. To measure accuracy, structured dialogic design guides a group in a process that maps out the highly preferred ideas based upon their interrelations. An example of this approach is illustrated by root cause analysis. Root cause analysis regards a list of ideas as distinct causes of a single complex process and asks a group to assess which ideas exist at the root of the problem. When a group understands a complex situation in terms of problems that are at the root of the situation, its members reassess their priorities. Structured dialogic design supports groups as they develop their understanding of the propagation of influence across ideas that they sense as being highly important. Highly influential ideas are like ideas that sit at the root of complex problems. We have found that in complex problem situations, some of the most influential ideas always fail to appear among the most preferred ideas, and some of the most preferred ideas always fail to have significant influence on the structured situation. Results from preference voting alone are always less accurate than they could be.

Researchers using structured dialogic design have tracked how individuals vote when they vote in groups and have observed two empirical phenomena called "the law of uncorrelated extremes" and "the erroneous priorities effect." These phenomena illustrate and explain how systems thinking can cause groups to completely flip priorities.

The Law of Uncorrelated Extremes

John Warfield is a systems scientist who has been the driving force behind what is called the science of generic design. According to Warfield, during a systems design process, the initial view of the observers of the situation about what matters and the final view about what matters will be uncorrelated. Individuals learn to see the situation differently; thus, the initial observations and the final observations are extremely different. This, of course, does not sound particularly profound at face value. The law is founded on empirical studies in which individuals who felt they understood a complex problem prior to a group investigation of that problem subsequently discovered that their preformed understanding was significantly underconceptualized. Individuals and groups can challenge themselves to test their understanding of a complex system by applying a formal design methodology and can convince themselves that appropriately diversified groups of stakeholders are needed to effectively understand complex situation. Stated another way, if a group of diversified stakeholders who share a situation all share the same preformed understanding of the essential features of the situation, then they are are not dealing with complexity and are unlikely to learn from each other. They cannot expect to improve their individual or collective understanding of their situation. When working with groups that are facing problems that they feel are truly complex, we frequently conduct a survey of stakeholders to establish the diversity of perspectives on the problem and to illustrate the opportunity that stakeholders have to learn from each other.

The Erroneous Priorities Effect

Working independently of Dr. Warfield, Kevin Dye and colleagues took a close look at decisions that were made by groups when they began, and then when they concluded, specific stages of structured dialogic design. First, Dye noted that as a group begins to converge on a shared understanding of a complex problem situation, a large number of ideas that individuals had contributed to the group were subsequently judged by individuals, and by the group, to be comparatively more important than other ideas. The group was learning. When the group votes its preference for important ideas after listening to others in the group, voting tends to focus on about one-third of the set of ideas. The remaining two-thirds of the idea set is still important and remains available for inclusion in a future action plan, but the subset of ideas emerges and reflects what the group comes to agree to as being of greater importance. This happens only because some of the authors of original ideas have changed their minds and have adopted the ideas proposed by others in the group. These authors have discovered that new ideas were more important than the ideas that they initially proposed and felt were highly important.

Second, even though the group is learning, the resulting list of aggregated priorities after individual and subjective voting proves to represent "erroneous priorities." Dye's further analysis reveals that after the group structures its aggregate list of preferred choices, the rank order of ideas based on voting does not match the rank order of ideas based upon their influence upon the problem situation. Early preference votes of relative importance fail to identify "high-leverage" ideas. The high-leverage ideas were recognizable only through the use of systems design tools. This phenomenon turns out to be broadly encountered in complex situations. Groups are unable to use their intuition to recognize and agree upon leverage that is propagated across a set of ideas. Dye's study of the "erroneous priorities effect" contributes a specific understanding of individual and group cognitive mechanisms that underlie Warfield's law of uncorrelated extremes. The point that we are making is not that we simply are likely to underconceptualize the priority of items in a complex system without applying a systems design approach (which is certainly the case), but also that we are certain to select erroneous priorities without constructing a systems view based on our shared understanding of our complex situation.

DISCOVERING LEVERAGE AMONG DESIGN ELEMENTS

Leverage refers to cases in which relatively small things can exert comparatively large effects on a larger system. The concept of leverage is traceable to the ancient Greeks' using it to construct their temples by lifting very heavy stones. Similarly, the key to a car can be used to start the car, and can therefore be used to put the car into motion. Having that key is a high-leverage circumstance in a system that involves getting the car to move. In effect, "getting the key" significantly influences our ability to "get the car to move." The key is itself a tiny thing, but it has tremendous leverage.

When we are dealing with complex problems, we might overlook the leverage that small items will have on the overall success of our efforts. In a community-building program, the item "identify a community liaison" may stand out as a highly leveraged part of the plan. If the group comes to understand the influence of this item in terms of the overall success of their effort, then the group's collective priority for this specific item might be increased. Formal systems thinking approaches help groups to see influences that otherwise are not apparent. Erroneous priorities always include omission of some of the high leverage items in a group's collective list of important items.

Structured dialogic design results in a graphic tree showing the "influence" that the group has decided exists among all of the highly preferred items identified by the group. The tree maps highly influential items as "deep drivers" at the base of the tree and also allows the group to see items that influence many others yet that may sit in the middle of the tree. By reflecting on the magnitude of the strong influence of items, groups change the way that they think about their priorities. The group combines its sense of urgency (proximity/visibility) and complexity (size/cost) with its newfound sense of influence (leverage/dependency). Triangulating among these three dimensions of importance, individuals come to "feel" differently about their original preferences. A simple example of such a tree structure is shown below.

In **Figure 1,** preliminary preference voting identified "get a plan and a leader" as most highly preferred, with 14% of the total votes cast. The

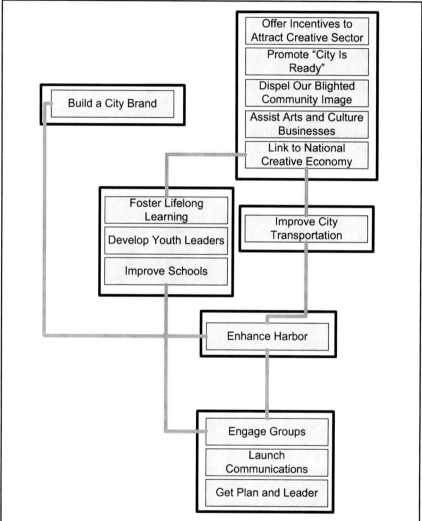

Figure 1. The design challenge was to create a visual image of consensus that was established through a focused dialogue among forty-five design sector stakeholders. The structure enabled the group to focus recommendations for immediate action on a set of three deep drivers that are shown at the bottom of the structure. Influence is propagated from bottom to top of the structure.

Modified after Flanagan, 2008.

second most preferred item was "build a city brand," with 13% of the votes, and the third most preferred item was "offer incentives to attract members of the creative sector," with 12% of the votes. After "structuring" the ideas, the group agreed to focus on the most influential ideas at the bottom of the tree. The most influential ideas adopted for immediate action planning included the highly preferred idea of "get a plan and a leader" but also included the sixth- and seventh-ranked ideas: "launch communications" and "engage other groups in the community." If the group had acted on their three most preferred ideas first, they would have secured a "plan and a leader" and then begun building a brand campaign and developing incentive packages before they got around to communicating and engaging others in the community. The nature of the ideas themselves are not rocket science, but the fact that the group reached a consensus for action that differed from the choices they were initially considering tells us that structuring lists leads to insights that can guide groups to effective priorities.

TIME—THE FINAL FRONTIER

Rational worlds do not exist in isolation from political worlds. Politics is very real, of course. The dark side of politics involves social interactions intended to capture gains in the form of authority or power. Demands are placed on groups to perform certain tasks or deliver certain products according to timelines that are beyond the group's knowledge or control. External pressures for performance timelines cannot be ignored. Due dates can complicate a work plan based upon a well-rationalized systems view of a problem situation and may necessitate the insertion of interim "deliverables." The important thing is for groups to recognize at what stage of the planning process they should take on the dimension of time. If responding to the political reality of a timeline is a group's overarching priority, then the group may not be able to implement a best-case response based on its systems view. We attempt to take this into account on the very front end of the planning process by imposing a planning horizon on the triggering questions. For example, we may guide the sponsor to ask "What must we consider so that we can deliver the necessary result in two years?" This will constrain ideas to only those ideas that individuals feel can be achieved within two years. Even with this caution, when chains of ideas are assembled, highly influential ideas may involve more time than can be invested to have their influence propagated in a way that will enhance the plan and still fit within the timeframe.

Time and money are sometimes interchangeable, and in some instances external political realities can take the form of too little funding and too much expectation. A political "sale" can be made before the product and production path have been designed or assembled. In complex regional economic development plans, for example, some items will have specific "political value" (for example, "launching a regional branding campaign") requiring high-priority response. This can happen when sustained support for a program in a community needs to generate visible evidence of "progress" to secure continued support. To be responsive, a group may have to move a specific task forward within an action plan. For example, the idea of "designing a regional branding campaign" would logically precede "launching a regional branding campaign," yet the political necessity may be to launch the campaign now. A group may find itself forced to agree to introduce a new item into its systems view at the time sequencing stage in the planning process—"launching a [prototype] regional branding campaign" might need to be considered in terms of the overall feasibility of adding this item into the systems view. Marketing people will cringe at the risk of launching an "inappropriate" marketing campaign because of the elevated costs of going back later and doing it right. This challenge may, then, put a very high priority on adding another item—"designing a low-risk prototype regional branding campaign." The decision to add a new item into an action plan may involve a tradeoff analysis, in which the gains of addition are balanced with costs of an alternative action. Project managers are well aware of the measures that may be required to make a plan work under evolving real-world constraints. The decision map generated with structured dialogic design provides a tool for project managers to explain what is happening to the plan as it moves through its implementation path.

The point of raising a discussion of timing and political realities in the context of "priorities" within a plan is that new priorities can emerge. To support groups that are dealing with complex plans that involve both many (rapid) external changes and many (delayed) discoveries, the group's understanding needs to be updated in a fashion that does not overwhelm the group. Structured dialogic design provides a means of dealing with changing or emerging priorities through a graphic representation of the group's influence pattern. When new information surfaces, members of a group can add the new information into the structure and preserve the familiar image of what has already been designed. Working with the interim deliverable presented in the example we have just discussed, "launching a [prototype] regional branding campaign" might strongly influence another item in the decision map (such as "recruit strategic industry sector partners into an industrial park development discussion").

Project managers understand that whenever planning and design groups come to "feel" that changing information is eroding their understanding of, and confidence in, their own plan, then the group loses its capacity to self-govern its collective venture. If this happens, the social commitment to collectively seeing the implementation of the plan fractures; the individuals in the group resume the role of individual agents instead of sharing priorities based on the wisdom of the group. By working with and preserving the essence of an easily communicated graphic representation of a complex understanding, project managers have a superior means for retaining coordination among sets of diverse partners, sponsors, and contractors.

Converging on an action plan under conditions of constrained resources (i.e., time and money and people) may involve tradeoffs among alternative approaches. Once again, when a group starts by building a consensual linguistic domain for exploring and understanding its situation and options, it has a strong foundation for shaping plans that can be readily compared. Structured dialogic design guides groups in a process of constructing sets of alternative action plans within subgroups. This process is supported in each individual subgroup by the use of a shared "menu" of options that itself is constructed from clearly shared understandings of options and relationships among options. Once the scenarios have been designed, alternative action scenarios are compared to identify a core structure common to all scenarios. The group is then guided in making tradeoff decisions for incorporating the nonidentical action options into a final consensus action plan. The groundwork that paves the way for assembling and sequencing this action plan is securely based on a systems view of the problem and a strong understanding of the leverage that can exist among options for action. As conditions change, rebuilding the plan can be supported by the design products used to craft the original plan.

THE FINAL WORD

In the increasingly complex world in which we must make collective decisions, we cannot rely on impressions of what "feels" right when we set our priorities. Our capacity to sense "importance" provides us with a shorthand for the more lengthy process of thinking a situation through all of its logical alternatives. Innate skills for rapidly assessing matters of immediacy, bottlenecks, and barriers can certainly have survival value, but responding without a shared systems view of our situation can put us onto social trajectories that we would otherwise avoid.

Frameworks for setting priorities based upon a systems view are not difficult to construct. Moreover, the frameworks can provide contextual relevance for setting priorities, which can provide decision making continuity through cycles of change. Shifting our attention from our list of priorities based on the aggregation of individual preferences to the framework with which we can be guided to identify highly leveraged options will reduce our risk of selecting erroneous priorities. Structured dialogic design is a thoroughly validated collaborative planning methodology that fully embraces a framework-based approach to group decision making and effective priority setting.

CHAPTER 5

ABOUT COLLABORATIVE LEARNING: INFORMATION OVERLOAD IN REAL TIME

"Power without wisdom is often dangerous, yet wisdom without power is always tragic."

Thomas Flanagan
Social entrepreneur

Learning results in a change that enables a different way of seeing things. Collaborative learning results in a change that enables new paths for approaching challenges together. Collaborative learning is the essence of all successful group design and all effective community-based planning.

INDIVIDUALS CONSTANTLY PROCESS INFORMATION

Without seeking to manipulate any specific outcome of authentic collaborative learning, it is worth recognizing how individual decision making can be influenced by shortcuts that we naturally take. Cognitive shortcuts, which are applied beneath the level of conscious awareness, set trajectories that can limit our decisions. In complex situations, as individuals listen to the observations of others, they tend to rapidly judge ideas in terms of

The Talking Point: Creating an Environment for Exploring Complex Meaning, pages 59–80
Copyright © 2010 by Information Age Publishing
59

how "familiar" or how "unimportant" they might be. These are mechanisms for dismissing the newness of some ideas. Structured dialogic design fosters clarification and comparison of ideas as the means of exploring familiarity and promoting distinctions. When overburdened, individuals lose the passion and capacity for exploring strange, new ideas. The point to appreciate for group work is that individuals dealing with complex situations are at risk for taking shortcuts that result in cognitive traps. Even when sitting together, individuals can take shortcuts that create significant problems for group decision making. Structured dialogic design exists to liberate individuals from the many individual cognitive traps that result in poor individual and collective decisions.

Biases in Individual Decision Making in Complex Situations

In their recent book, *Nudge: Improving Decisions about Health, Wealth, and Happiness* (Yale University Press, 2009), Richard Thaler and Cass Sunstein review some of the principles of what they call "choice architecture." Their goal is to help leaders understand how their efforts will shape the direction that choices are likely to follow—and they illustrate a subconscious decision making intervention brilliantly with reference to efforts to control highway speed along Lake Shore Drive in Chicago. Drivers consistently failed to slow to twenty-five miles per hour around a pair of very tricky S-curves, with frequent collisions as a result. The city of Chicago painted a series of horizontal lines across the highway and adjusted the distance between the lines so that they would be progressively closer as the driver approached the S-curves. Passing through a series of white lines that grew increasingly closer created the impression of acceleration, causing drivers to "automatically" apply their brakes and slow their vehicles. Tricky? Yes. Effective? Yes. Predictable? Also yes.

   The point to appreciate for group work is that the context for individual decision making is continually being shaped through "subliminal" observations. As individuals listen to the observations of others, ideas that seem "familiar" or "trivial" risk being automatically processed using cognitive shortcuts. Juggling too many choices at a given moment causes individuals to apply mental boundaries for what matters and what does not matter. The cognitive psychologist Amos Tversky (who was on track for a Nobel Prize before his death) called this "elimination by aspects." In essence, complex choices are represented by options that have different aspects or attributes—size, proximity, cost, comfort, familiarity, excitement, and so forth. The elimination by aspects shortcut ranks the attributes, then rejects options first that don't score well on the most valued attribute—for example, "familiarity." This is fine if and when criteria can be reliably ranked, and in situations in which criteria do not strongly interact with each other, but otherwise the shortcut results in both logical underconceptualization and choice inconsistencies: we choose poorly and inconsistently. In this instance, biasing ourselves to place a high value on new ideas only if they are "familiar" ensures that we will not come up with a profoundly new way of seeing our situation. Shortcuts are used not because they are appropriate, but because the decision maker often is overwhelmed with the complexity of the decision making task. When we are overwhelmed, we will still make choices, but we will make them poorly.

Another category of shortcut involves imprecise generalization. In effect, we seek first to fit new ideas into categories that we have individually constructed based on our own experiences. Sometimes the fit is inelegant. If we are in a hurry, the socks go into the shirts drawer. Understanding new information is not a matter of putting ideas into preformed bins. Active learning requires individuals to make distinctions and construct new bins. Structured dialogic design fosters clarification and comparison of idea as the means of promoting learning. In doing this, structured dialogic design raises what might initially seem to be a trivial observation to the status of "strange." Strange ideas require us to look at them in new ways. Group dialogue has the power of doing this better than individual reflections, because in group dialogue there are more options for applying a perception to a new idea in a way that will expose an aspect of that new idea's strangeness. The challenge, of course, is to manage the pace of information flow so that participants are confronted with strangeness and allowed to learn together without becoming overwhelmed and resorting to decision making shortcuts. If overloaded or excessively distracted, individuals will resort to using cognitive shortcuts.

Cognitive shortcuts are not inherently bad things. We all use them. They primarily exist to allow us to accomplish "tactical doing" activities and "strategic thinking" activities in parallel. For example, as a soccer player is running downfield, the soccer player is not thinking about the mechanics of running, but rather about the strategy that is unfolding around him or her. As the player runs, he or she may be responding to shadows or hints of motion in peripheral vision even before processing the full implications of the observation. Some will call these responses autonomic, referring to ancient reflex behaviors that may have ensured our primate ancestors' survival by causing them to leap when their foot felt something wiggle beneath it or grasp when their hand gripped something solid. Some behavioral reflexes are triggered well below the brain stem: consider the knee reflex when the patellar tendon is rapidly stretched with a slight tap—this is the canonical "knee-jerk response." Other behavioral reflexes are actually acquired skills based upon repeated experience. Skilled musicians create "muscle memory" so that when they "think" of certain chords or riffs, their fingers automatically find their way to the correct positions on the instrument. Muscle memory is similar to the spatial memory that lets us move briskly through narrow spaces within our own homes without bumping into immovable objects. We are not thinking *turn left at the table and take a sharp right at the sink*, but we navigate with this whole-body mental map in ways that parallel the way musicians find their way to the correct notes. Subconsciously, we fit observations into our existing mental maps to minimize the need to rearrange our furniture.

Using cognitive maps provides the basis of habits, and cognitive maps are not uniquely human. Cat owners will recognize with some amusement that cats develop expectations based upon chains of events, and this "chaining" can cause a cat to expect to be tapped on the head with a spoon before food will "magically" appear in its dinner bowl. Konrad Lorenz, the Nobel Prize–winning Austrian zoologist, introduced this notion in his study of the routines of behavior of his domestic goose. As the story goes, as Lorenz's goose was coming down the stairway, it always glanced outside the window before proceeding to the door. One day the goose forgot to glance at the window, and it was in a full panic by the time that it reached the door. It fled back to the stairwell and repeated its descent—this time including the glance out the window—and thus calmed itself, allowing itself to complete its passage outside. The instinct to protect our maps is strong. It runs deep in the essence of who we are as biological organisms.

Without being slaves to our habits, we do still risk becoming victims of our habits. Consider how a person driving a car may multitask—listening to radio broadcasts, holding animated conversations with other passengers (or over a mobile phone), anticipating the workday or the evening ahead, even shaving or applying makeup while navigating familiar city routes. This same behavior also explains a great many traffic collisions and missed exits. The "automatic mind" can be shut off (suspended) through the will of the "conscious mind" when critical decisions need to be made, but this isn't always as easy as we might think or wish. Under conditions of information overload, the conscious mind bends to the will of the automatic decision in hopes of easing the burden. If we allow this to happen, the quality of decisions will be compromised by our underconceptualization of situations.

An amusing example at a high level of cognition showing a contest between the automatic mind and the conscious mind was discovered by a cognitive psychologist named J. Ridley Stroop. The Stroop effect challenges a respondent to read the printed name of a color (decoding semantic meaning) when that name is written in a color that may or may not be the same as the color name written in letters. For example, a test may include the word "red" written in green crayon, or the word "blue" written in orange crayon. A respondent is instructed to state the name on the card. At modest speed, this proves to be a difficult task, and error rates can be enhanced with the insertion of other cognitive distractions. Two competing mental processing systems are colliding—identification of the semantic meaning of the written name of a color while trying to ignore color cues. As a result, decision speed, and quality, suffer.

The point to appreciate for group work is that individuals deal with reflections and subconscious observations even as they are concurrently engaged in group decision work. These distractions not only compete for the cognitive capacity of individuals but can also flavor the cognitive response of individuals, particularly when groups are dealing with complexity that overloads individuals' capacity to fit information into their preexisting frameworks. In many group design processes, hunger and fatigue are managed with frequent breaks, continuity in group decision making is ensured through information management practices, and social influence is managed by sharply segregating the cognitive content of the participants from the process control of the dialogue management team. Structured dialogic design additionally liberates individuals from many other individual cognitive traps by promoting dialogue that limits autopilot decision making, individual cost estimates, distorted probability based on individually experienced events, overconfidence of immunity from consequences, comfort in the status quo, interpretations based on the sequence with which events are considered, and individual notions of immovable barriers for exchange or interaction.

COGNITIVE FRAMEWORKS

Cognitive frameworks consist essentially of bins (or objects) and links (or connections). Some frameworks have specific geometries, and other frameworks seem to fill a space like clouds fill the sky. What matters more than their form is how well they work for us.

Education experts tell us that from a very early age, all learning takes place within our individual cognitive framework. We "fit" information into a structure of relationships, making individual changes to our individual frameworks as we move through life. Group learning is challenging, because only rarely do we come together with others to address a complex problem while sharing the same cognitive framework for that problem. The implication is that we need to construct a shared framework upon which we can assemble bits of new information. In practice, the challenge is larger than this, because as we attempt to construct a shared framework, we also will be evolving a shared language that depicts that framework. This foundation building activity is taxing for many individuals, because it challenges both their own individual frameworks and also our individual habits and traditions of using specific words and phrases to express understandings. In problem solving dialogue, language and meaning unfold as a framework is jointly constructed to explicitly represent relationships that the community strongly recognizes. This chapter discusses the background considerations for an orderly and efficient means of constructing new frameworks for collaborative learning. Shared frameworks are the foundation of collaborative design and community-based planning.

INFORMATION AND INFORMATION OVERLOAD

Information emerges as observations. Observations have a context. In the field of information science, an observation is a datapoint, and its context represents "metadata." While the observation might be comparatively easy to track, its associated metadata can be an enormous suitcase of information that is only unpacked when it is necessary to know more about the data. As a group collectively considers a specific observation, the metadata gets unpacked and the observation takes on new meaning. For this reason, in a complex planning situation, any single observation can carry a universe of meaning that is not fully appreciated when the observation is initially expressed. This potentially represents an "explosion of meaning."

In a parallel fashion, complex situations may be characterized by many individual observations. The potential to extract many meaningful observations from a single complex situation represents an "explosion of observations."

A third consideration relates to the fact that in any complex system, observations are connected. Observations can be connected in a great many different ways. Mathematically, we can present a formula for the number of potential connections of n observations. If we consider a set of relationships such that every observation is connected to every other observation, we can experience an "explosion of connections."

All of these explosions threaten to overwhelm us through cognitive overload.

The problem of cognitive overload is so common in our society that we have many sources of advice that all tell us to seize upon simplicity. Occam's razor (attributed to William of Ockham, a Christian philosopher of the 1300s) generally advises those dealing with complexity to accept the simplest solution that fits. Albert Einstein paraphrased this aphorism by saying that "a problem should be as simple as possible, but no more so." Arguing against simplification, political commentator H. L. Mencken is credited with saying that "for every complex problem there is an answer that is clear, simple, and wrong"; and Alfred Chandler has cautioned that "you can't understand (a business) by simplifying it—you have to master its complexity." In the face of a threat of cognitive overload, and in the absence of technology for managing the information, the natural instinct remains that of empowering individuals who promote simplicity.

After the end of World War II, the world experienced an expansion of technical culture that continues today. Tools for managing information overload have been evolving in parallel with the need for dealing with this complexity. Information management technology is not what is limiting our capacity to deal with information overload. Tools exist. Without tools, our information management capacity is limited to our innate abilities to hold observations and relationships in a fixed amount of mental processing space while we manipulate those observations and relationships into new patterns. Our average capacities as human beings are genuinely modest: we can hold about seven objects (the range is seven to nine, on average) in our mind at a given time. This simple truth has withstood the test of time since George Miller reported this finding over fifty years ago. Our average capacities as groups of human beings are distinctly less than our capacities as individuals. Twenty years ago, John Warfield's meticulous group process research led him to proclaim groups are capable of holding and processing no more than three items at once. In complex problem solving situations, groups need to be supported to work through large amounts of information in systematic fashion. This is another way of saying that the power of information management technology needs to be brought into groups at the level with which groups are capable of processing information.

A simple sheet of paper or a flip chart can hold dozens of objects concurrently. We cannot simultaneously process even this amount of information either as individuals or as groups, but we can work our way through this complexity if we embrace a disciplined process based on sequentially making many small decisions which can be aggregated into a coherent systems view. The goal of this chapter is to assure audiences that this technology does exist.

THINKING THROUGH GENERALIZATIONS

Categories, or bins, are the simplest features of a cognitive framework. Categorical thinking is as natural as magical thinking in children. We implicitly construct categories of "likeness" and seek to put new information into our existing set of boxes. We also implicitly teach others about our preformed categories of thought. On the one hand, this is a pragmatic and adaptive way to rapidly respond to complex information. Many observations that don't fit neatly go onto a shelf that we designate for items that are to be ignored. This allows us to rapidly filter out "distracting" observations and concepts. But although this capacity is adaptive in many daily functions, in excess it can disable learning. We will illustrate this with a simple example.

A mother had taken her son to the Brooklyn Zoo one late summer afternoon. As she and her son stood before an area that was home to several tapirs, a small animal scurried beneath their feet. The young boy gasped, "Mommy! Mommy! What is that?" in excitement. The mother responded briskly, "Oh, that's just a squirrel," and then rapidly pulled the boy on to the next exhibit. The mother had a preformed bin for "animals that don't matter," but the son was still in the business of constructing his set of bins for the different ways in which animals do matter.

In the shuffle represented by this story, not only the squirrel but also the small boy lost out. For his mother, the bins of "interesting animal" and "uninteresting animal" were strongly influenced by the attribute of "on exhibit at the zoo."

The ease of living with generalizations easily trumps the labor of constructing new meaning. Creating new meaning involves the mental effort of drawing or appreciating new distinctions. We tolerate imperfect fits as we toss ideas into bins. This is not a human failing. It is a genuine and valuable coping mechanism. Bins do, of course, also underlie some socially unacceptable prejudices that can be socially communicated beneath the level of deliberate thought. The ability to construct bins based upon "likeness" is an early childhood learning skill, and its absence is taken as a measure of learning disability.

Creating bins or cognitive categories through group deliberations is not as intuitive as sharing names of existing bins, but creating new bins together actually is easier than attempting to share a large number of individually preconstructed bins. It is difficult to share preconstructed bins in large groups, because we individually name bins and individually identify and weigh the attributes that we use to construct them. Actually, our intuitive and long-held ways of rapidly sorting related observations into bins can stand as a barrier in a collective effort to recognize similarities. A conscious effort is needed to shed the comfort of the use of preexisting bins and take on the burden of collectively constructing new bins.

Coconstructing bins has both social and cognitive value as groups learn how to think together. Coconstructing bins, even though it does involve mental energy, is relatively "easy" for groups. As a task that is engaged early in the "learning to learn" phase of group design, it dispels any myth that may exist about the group's ability to learn together. For this reason, coconstructing bins has a social value of build cohesion within a group. This process also instills in the group a norm of tolerating "less than perfect fit" of individual observations with other observations in specific cognitive clusters. When a group internalizes its capacity to cocreate acceptable yet imperfect shared cognitive constructs, it recognizes that it could apply this skill iteratively to move more closely toward perfection—as specific needs may require. In complex learning situations, successive approximations of a collective reality that is constructed collaboratively by groups of stakeholders are superior to any static view delivered by "experts," because the group's construct is a living and learning entity that they control. In designing social systems and planning for collective action, successive approximations of reality constructed collaboratively by stakeholders are more acceptable than models of reality delivered to them by "experts."

THE EMOTIONS OF COLLABORATIVE LEARNING

Cocreating cognitive affinity clusters ("bins") is a comparatively simple form of collaborative learning that we often engage beneath the radar of our conscious thought. Rather than making deliberate choices, we often "sense" the harmony of a fit or feel the dissonance of a poor fit at an emotional level. This type of emotion-guided learning has the quality of music. We may feel a relaxation or resolution of dissonance as our cognitive framework shifts toward a new way of ordering our observations of the world. We may feel a suspended tone as we hang in the space between our sense of certainty and confusion. Individually, we fit observations into emerging sets of categories rapidly as pleasure and necessity dictate.

Some among us enjoy the wash of mental emotions and actively seek out new learning opportunities. Others find the uncertainty of an extended learning moment disquieting and—like a cat in freefall—desperately seek to put their feet immediately back on the ground. For this reason, within any one group learning situation, the passion for learning and the passion for certainty need to be mutually honored. Engaging a group in the serious business of sorting observations into affinity clusters provides a gentle ramp for anticipating the mental emotions that come with higher levels of learning.

We cannot, and should not, expect every individual in a group to experience the same mental emotions at any one moment in time, but this does happen at times. For example, the phenomenon of "making a breakthrough" is associated with a relaxation of mental tension and a warm glow of shared satisfaction for the mutual relief that all struggling members of the group share. Such moments are great catalysts for continued learning. Learning situations that combine challenge with relief—and compassion with humor—create a rich fabric for supporting group learning. But getting to this degree of emotional intimacy can be exceptionally challenging if groups gather under a dark cloud of fear, suspicion, or disdain. Still, through a wisely selected sequence of group learning tasks, groups can come to experience the emotional intimacy of shared learning and overcome fear, suspicion, and disdain—if only for the duration of the group learning session.

We have seen this emotional "thawing" in many group learning situations. Most facilitation practices launch group work with an "icebreaker" activity for this precise purpose. Contrived "icebreaker" activities produce token learning as an incentive to catalyze collaborative action, but this approach may be counterproductive if the transparent playfulness of icebreaker activities irritate audiences coming together on tight time budgets to take on serious challenges of a significant social problem. We do agree that playfulness and creativity are kindred spirits; emotional engagement at this level should be gently encouraged throughout the entire collaborative learning process.

CREATING NEW MEANING BY CONSTRUCTING NEW CATEGORIES

Putting ideas into preformed categories relieves the dissonance of the uncertainty in engaging new information, but sometimes new ideas simply don't fit into existing categories. New categories need to be created. Observations are assigned into affinity clusters based upon a combination of shared attributes as well as some uniquely held and differing attributes. For example, it is possible that two items can be held in your hand, be eatable, be juicy, be sweet, grow on trees, and have seeds in their centers— yet differ by being green or pink or having a smooth or textured surface. Depending on the context in which you are organizing information, you might be content to put the pear and the peach into a bin you might label "fruit." Differences in many attributes of different types of fruit might not cause us dissonance. But in some contexts, specific attributes of different types of fruit might require that they be placed in separate bins. For the purposes of shipping fruit across the country, a pear may be significantly different from a peach. You may need to assign different types of fruit into specific bins for "fragile fruit" and "sturdy fruit." Every pattern of categories is dependent on the context for its formation.

Modifying Cognitive Affinity Structures

Cognitive work is involved in abandoning categories for organizing ideas and reorganizing those ideas in a new way. In some internal fashion that may parallel the use of hyperlinks on Web pages, we can store observations in multiple bins and minimize the burden of actively unlearning prior categories. In other cases, more effort is needed to expunge and actively rebuild categories. A case in point can be made with a category of thought in a mythical planet called *Erlerler*.

On Erlerler, Erlerlerians have either one head or two, much as Earthlings may be lefthanded or righthanded. On Erlerler, young two-headed Erlerlerians are told that "two heads are better than one," so they form a bin early in life for "good Erlerlerians" as having two heads, and another bin for other ("bad") Erlerlerians as having only one head. The cognitive bin gets carried forward through life until one day a specific Erlerlerian with two heads finds himself in an extended and frustrating argument with another two-headed Erlerlerian. To his surprise, he finds that his points are understood, and embraced, by a one-headed Erlerlerian who happens to be in the room. As the two-headed Erlerlerian and this specific one-headed Erlerlerian both attempt to explain the perspective to the stubborn and argumentative two-headed Erlerlerian, the way that they all view each other forces a reconsideration of cognitive bins. Perhaps not all two-heads are better than one-heads.

The simplistic information management bins for "goodness" and "otherness" will need to be deconstructed. Its content will need to go elsewhere. The "cognitive prejudice," once discovered, will have to be actively rooted out.

The Erlerlerian example is illustrative of the natural consequence that typically afflicts stakeholder experts as they come into a boundary-spanning, complex problem solving session. In preparation for dealing with a problem, most technical experts tend to organize the information into well-structured, individually defined, preconceived bins. During discussions that challenge the legitimacy of these preconceived bins, stakeholders can become tense, distressed, and irritable under the pressure of the cognitive burden to disassemble some cognitive categories. This burden is not unique to technologies or science but applies to social professions (such as law, business, and political science) as well, for these also can be subjected to the same tension.

Creating Cognitive Affinity Structures

Constructing new bins begins by drawing distinctions that manifest themselves in new categories of thought. New categories arise by lumping observations together, splitting existing categories into subcategories, or fusing categories into new supercategories. When shipping fruit across country, we may happen to have no preformed mental category for fruit that is "sturdy" and fruit that is "fragile." Creating subcategories within the category of fruit seems like a simple solution for handling the dissonance, and, as creatures seeking easy lives, we seize the simple solution first.

Splitting—or refining—categories doesn't always work, of course. When we bump into an object that can be held in your hand, that is eatable, that is juicy, that is sweet, that has a textured surface, and that swims in the water, we will recognize some attributes shared with peaches yet sense dissonance in trying to fit fish into the category "fragile fruit." We have some real mental work to do. We must construct a new generalization by assigning a new category of observation.

One way to construct a new category of ideas is to mentally unpack attributes of pairs of observations into parallel lists. We do this by naming attributes such as physical properties, familiar uses, history, and so forth. We can mentally walk through the list making pairwise comparisons of individual attributes in which we can either tolerate mismatches (when attributes don't really matter) or not (when attributes do matter). We will choose the attributes based on what we feel matters. We can approach this formally, on a highly cognitive level, or intuitively, on an emotional level. The accelerated way to construct a new category is to begin with any two observations and ask for an intuitive/emotional impression of whether a third observation seems to fit or to belong elsewhere. Intuitive responses in this context tend to be sensitive to expressible as well as deeply embedded attributes shared among observations. Regardless of the method selected to test and then discover what idea fits into a specific category or cluster of similar observations, the goal is to reach an acceptable level of comfort with the clusters. As the group moves in this direction, it is continually evolving its understanding of what does, and what does not, constitute similarity. When significant distinctions no longer present themselves to a group, the clustering process has reached effective closure.

In practice, we cannot presume that a sufficiently diversified group addressing a truly complex problem situation shares a sufficient set of related categories to organize important observations by refining their combined set of existing categories. Groups need to engage a process of building categories from the bottom up. Resisting the urge to jump toward familiar categories of thought and apply personally framed labels for those categories of thought will open a group up to collaborative learning. Our experience tells us that a bottom-up approach to building clusters of similar observations results in the discovery of new categories that are distinguishable from the old, familiar set of categories. Discovering new categories has many implications in terms of designing a solution to a previously nonresolvable problem situation.

Building new clusters as a group through an intuitive/emotional guidance method benefits from whole-body involvement. We typically demonstrate the construction process by moving posed observations along a wall into small sets by asking the group to respond with their gut feeling to the question, "Does A belong with B, or does A belong somewhere else?" We expand the process by asking the same question about C. When the group has become comfortable with the process and is responding promptly, we then have the group come to the wall and lift the name of a specific observation off the wall and move it into an existing or emerging cluster. When the ideas have been put into preliminary clusters, we then ask the authors to "walk" through the clusters and reassign their observations if they feel they should be assigned in different clusters. This process is a bit like cooking popcorn—when the popping lessens, the group is converging on a stable set of categories. The affinity clusters stabilizes when the group agrees that the observations are distributed with an acceptable level of harmony and resonance.

Internalizing the Dimensions of the Learning Challenge

As the group then reflects on the structure of clusters, it sometimes determines that specific observations need to be represented in multiple clusters, and that some clusters must exist to represent single ideas. During this reflection, the group is asked to collectively agree upon a label for each of the clusters that it has created. During these discussions, members of the group frequently name specific attributes of the observations that have shaped their thinking. Clusters are named and amended if most of the group agrees with the name or the change and no member of the group is strongly opposed to the name or the change.

Named clusters represent "dimensions" of a design challenge or a solution space. Dimensions are useful to consider for the purposes of being inclusive in individual reflection. Individuals who recognize that they have been looking at a complex problem from a single dimension (or small set of dimensions) will recognize the opportunity of seeing the multidimensionality of the problem situation with equal legitimacy. When groups engage in selecting action options to incorporate into an action plan, drawing from across all dimensions of the solution space will result in a stronger and more comprehensive and multidimensional response to the design challenge.

As a result of constructing affinity clusters, similarities are highlighted— and, by default, distinctions also emerge. As we have stated elsewhere, the structure is highly dependent upon the group's understanding of "what matters." For this reason, the issue of setting forth a clear and consistent definition of "what matters" is essential in collaborative design. We address this specifically through the use of a triggering question.

After affinity clusters have been constructed, members of the group are asked to consider specific observations that now seem most critical for understanding a situation or responding to a challenge.

ESTABLISHING CONNECTIONS AMONG OBSERVATIONS

When a group has assembled observations into affinity clusters, the group is asked to reassess "importance." This is not a matter of "guessing" correctly, but more a matter of assessing preferences from the group. These votes provide a means of identifying sets of observations to consider first when constructing a view of the essence of the challenge. The number of votes that each individual is allowed to cast will vary with the scope and scale of the design challenge, but we do ask that individuals place only one vote on each of the observations that they wish to call forward in the process. In the definition of the problem situation stage, we usually ask people to select their five relatively more important observations. Having members of the group write their names on adhesive dots before they vote can foster compliance with this directive if such measures might be appropriate. After this voting, the design support team counts the votes and reports the tally to the group.

If no individual learning has occurred during the discussion for clarification of the meaning of individual authors' observations, then group voting will result in only one vote (or an equal number of votes) for each of the ideas contributed by the authors' observations that have been gathered and explained. Our experience from the arena of practice tells us that aggregated votes for specific observations indicate that members of the group have come to recognize and agree on the elevated importance of some observations for which they are not the authors.

While the voting is individual, and thus not based on a constructed consensus, the aggregation of votes does foreshadow where some consensus may arise. Unfortunately, many dialogue facilitators declare this preliminary vote to represent a group consensus. As we mentioned in the previous chapter, our empirical studies have illustrated that groups that adopt this preliminary vote as a final vote on importance invariably suffer from what we have called "erroneous priorities." The reason for this is because reflecting on categories does not provide insight into influence, bottlenecks, dependency, and highly dependent but uninfluential observations related to the situation or solution. To get this critically needed information, groups need to construct a systems view.

Systems Views

Complex problems are characterized by many observations and many possible linkages among observations. A shared understanding of a complex problem is characterized by a set of important observations connected in a mutually acceptable systematic fashion. In essence, observations and relations are mapped as nodes, and links among those nodes are mapped into an interconnected network or system. Such systems views are familiar to audiences as network maps, system dynamic diagrams, and cognitive maps. Network maps support an understanding of communication elements and the communication links. System dynamics maps support an understanding of entities or state variables and the flows among the variables. Cognitive maps support an understanding of issues and the **logical connections among issues**. All three of these maps can be constructed by individual technical "experts" and small expert teams, but only cognitive mapping has been used extensively to track the decisions made within large stakeholder groups.

As discussed earlier, cognitive mapping is practiced in two fundamentally different forms: one practice is discussion-based, and the other is decision-based. The discussion-based practice focuses on capturing a pattern of relations as that pattern "naturally" unfolds through a reflection or a discussion. The result is a descriptive map that is used in a variety of dialogue facilitation practices. The decision-based method anticipates, captures, and depicts decisions that have been made as a result of a "structured dialogue." Structured dialogues are used in dialogue management practices to systematically aggregate incremental buy-in for a collaborative action.

While network maps and system dynamic diagrams are largely descriptive (based an existing or proposed physical system), logical maps can capture observations that link physical systems and stakeholder intentions for putting those systems into practice. In this sense, logical mapping is different because it is both descriptive and prescriptive. Decision-based cognitive mapping is appropriate for groups seeking to discover ways that they will collectively solve complex problems or capture elusive opportunities. This approach is familiar in the professional literature under the name "problematique."

Regardless of the decision-based cognitive mapping method that is used, groups who are constructing a systems view for collaborative action should start the mapping process by exploring relationships among observations that have received many individual votes.

Constructing a Systems View

Maps that capture systems views of a group's deliberations are constructed by an individual or team working on behalf of the group. Discussion-based approaches capture and code ideas as they surface and link the ideas with a variety of types of relationships. As and example, a discussion-based approach called "dialogue mapping" enumerates conversation comments made within a group and links them in a temporal sequence. This method involves concurrently constructing an issues map wherein the mapmaker interprets the comments and codes them as either a new idea, a question, a supportive comment, or a detracting comment. The map is presented to the group as a record of ideas that surfaced in the discussion.

Decision-based approaches schedule a sequence of decision making activities and capture and display decisions, but they do not impose any intermediate interpretations on the group's work. Structured dialogic design introduces a focused triggering question, collects labels for observations in response to that question and captures clarification statements about those observations, records the group's assignment of observations into affinity clusters and reports the group's selected names for those clusters, identifies the group's preference for important observations, prompts and records the group's decisions with respect to influences among pairs of observations, and reports the structure of observations and relationships identified and assigned by the group. All steps of group decision making are packaged and provided to each group member—in real time. The logical map is presented as a living document rather than a mere record. Because the group retains the complete transparent record of its deliberation, it can reconvene to update or revise its map without reconstructing the entire deliberative and decision making process.

Dialogue mapping and structured dialogic design both use relationships to connect observations in systems maps which are based on group dialogue, but they do this in distinct ways. Dialogue mapping codes a comment based upon one of four relationships, whereas structured dialogic design selects a specific type of relationship (from a set of several types of relationships) and consistently applies the same relationship for the group decision making. These differences impact the readability of the resulting maps and provide differing input on the structure of the dialogue. One approach (dialogue mapping) is a passive, descriptive approach, whereas the other (structured dialogic design) is a normative, anticipatory approach.

The dialogue mapping product is manually constructed by a facilitator (typically through the use of a graphic interphase). The map includes considerable third-party interpretation of stakeholder observations. The map does not play an essential role in enabling the dialogue, even though it can guide explorations within a dialogue.

The structured dialogic design map is computationally "extracted" from a matrix of decisions that is compiled from a record of the pairwise influence assessments made by the group. This type of map includes only the authentic contributions of the stakeholders in the dialogue. The map does not contain any facilitator's language or interpretations. Furthermore, the map plays an essential role in presenting a systems view of the group's understanding to inform group priorities within the dialogue.

Unique Learning Enhancement (with Structured Dialogic Design)

Pairwise assessment and construction of relationships enriches learning. Structured dialogic design uses a matrix management tool called "interpretive structural modeling" (ISM) to record and prompt relational queries between pairs of observations and to track the results of the majority votes of the group. As a result, ISM allows a group to make relational decisions "in isolation of the full set of other observations" with the capacity to amend the result of the decisions across the full set of observations later. First, a structuring relation is selected (e.g., "Will the success of observation A significantly enhance observation B's prospects for success?"); then, the group is prompted with a pair of observations and a consistent "enhancement relationship" to assess, the group decision is recorded, and the majority voting decisions are aggregated, extracted, and displayed as a map. As a result, ISM "focuses" the group on an exploration of the nature of a single, directional relationship of significant influence. As different voices contribute to exploring the relationships from multiple perspectives the group is frequently presented with different types of explanations of influences as well as differences in the assessed magnitude of influence (i.e., "significance"). ISM directs the group to consider pairs of relationship that might otherwise be glossed over, guiding the group to consider directions of influence that might not be otherwise deeply considered (e.g., the influence of A on B is distinct from the influence of B on A).

The open voting approach associated with pairwise influence assessments catalyzes learning because it helps the group to identify "minority" perspectives. After a vote of yes or no regarding the relation between two observations, individuals who see the situation differently from most of the other participants are first called upon to offer explanations for their perspective. Sometimes a minority perspective leads to a change in a group vote. Individuals from a majority perspective are also asked to explain their perspective, and sometimes these explanations change the views of those who had offered a minority perspective, or vice versa. The goal of group learning, however, is not to change individual perspectives, but rather to explicitly share an understanding of what is perceived within the group. Strongly shared perception defines the most solid ground for constructing action plans. In addition, groups that learn to work together with tolerance of competing perspectives and willingness to attain a deeper understanding of the situation can implement evolving plans that other groups cannot.

Pairwise decision making is essential in situations in which information overload is a serious consideration. Frequently the mental work and discussion time involved in making influence assessments exhausts a group. Design managers need to be sensitive to the issue of participant fatigue, and for this reason the standard recommendation is that complex design challenges always be viewed as multiday events. Rushing decision making stresses group members, because they can come to feel that they are individually and collectively making poor decisions. Groups engaged in extensive decision making can also get trapped in arguing intensely for small differences. This adds to fatigue.

To control the intensity of emotional energy invested in arguing over small differences, the nature of the voting and its impact should be clarified. The preunderstanding that groups hold with respect to voting is that a vote is a win–lose proposition. This tension can be relaxed when groups recognize that voting for strong influence does not lead to exclusion from a resulting map, but rather affects positioning within that map. Maps show strong agreement. The group retains the privilege to creatively and constructively disagree. Disagreement is not expunged from the process. Rather, agreement is placed above and before disagreement. Supermajority voting (i.e., agreement among at least three-quarters of the participants) with the insertion of clarifying dialogue between cycles of voting on contested influence assessments protects a group from the risk of falsely assigning a relationship of influence which did not exist. This reinforces the group's confidence in the strength of the resulting systems structure.

During the process of voting, different individuals will occasionally feel frustrated by their inability to effectively communicate their perception of significant influence for a specific pair of observations. Participants can discover the need for artful stories of their experiences to promote reflection on a comparative assessment. Through these focused and open exchanges, individuals come to understand the group better, and this improves their expectations and strategies for working with each other most effectively. Frequently we see a realignment of original positions on issues—including the possibility of crossing political or ideological boundaries. On one occasion, a member of the Communist party in Cyprus addressed another member of the group from the opposite party as a "cryptocommunist" after listening to his views on a particular issue. The statement humorously expressed the discovery of an unexpected alignment of ideas that bridged ideologies.

In our experience with potentially contentious discussions, ISM generally is not a source of aggravated tension. In discussions that are focused on comparisons between two well-characterized ideas, individuals can find themselves open to being strongly influenced by observations voiced within the group. In contrast, if groups seek to collaboratively define the meaning of an idea itself (without relying on an individual author for an individual meaning), the dialogue can become contentious. This is not a comment on personal animosity (which is not allowed), but rather a statement about the nature of perceptions of situationally understood ideas relative to perceptions of specific relationships. We have found that discussions of influences among pairs of observations is generally far less contentious than discussions of the boundaries of specific observations themselves. ISM enables types of learning not available in alternative dialogue mapping methods, because its pairwise approach engages stakeholders in successive approximations in the construction of their situational reality. This type of learning can only emerge from within the community and cannot be imported through the presentation of expert network maps and system dynamic models. Structured dialogic design is unique among dialogue management approaches with respect to the learning that it cultivates and captures through a comprehensive examination of pairwise relationships.

Reassembling Complex Understandings

During the process of constructing a cognitive framework of shared meaning, information overload is managed by systematically presenting manageably sized decision tasks. Small decisions are designed so that they can be aggregated into a systems view to capture strong group support and engender collaborative action. Structured dialogic design does this by assessing relationships among pairs of observations. The observations are paired with a consistent logical relationship that can reflect a systemic property of the set of observations. Specifically, observations are assessed in pairwise fashion with respect to the influence that they have upon each other. Influence relationships are transitive, asymmetric, and irreflexive. This means that when a group exhaustively conducts a pairwise assessment of influence among a set of observations, the resulting matrix of cross-impact decisions can be run through an algorithm that assembles the observations in a "tree" in which connections are represented by the unifying relationships of influence. This is more than just a huge timesaver. When the pairwise influence assessments are initially collected into a table (a "matrix"), the "structure" of the relationships taxes even the most expert eye. The tree structure of the influence map is immediately readable with only a modest explanation of conventions.

Individuals who lead group design generally recognize that a shared understanding provides a framework and a language for explaining how additional aspects of a problem connect with the strongly held view of the essential structure of the problem. The strongly held view itself is a living understanding. It can be augmented and amended. In practice, collaborative understandings are living understandings and must remain responsive to accommodating insertion or deletion of specific observations. Structured dialogic design lends itself to this type of continuous learning and continuous self-editing of the group's cognitive map.

REFLECTING ON COLLABORATIVE LEARNING

When individuals reflect on a framework, they look for objects on the map that are bottlenecks, or that are highly dependent upon other objects on the map, or that themselves have some powerful influence of specific objects on the entire system of connected objects. In effect, during reflection, individuals "walk" multiple paths through the set of connected issues and internalize the sense of interconnectedness that a group has identified. The map is a reminder of the dialogue that was shared and is also a prompt for a possible future dialogue. The reflection may prompt a participant to name missing pieces of the map and may lead the group to reconvene to amend the map by adding in those pieces. Individuals also may choose to individually consider how their personally preferred observations might be linked into the core structure of the map that the group has created. In effect, individuals reflect on what the group has come to recognize as the "group view" and then may independently come to understand their own issues in the context of their view of how those issues connect with the group understanding. The individual learning reaches beyond the collective learning, because individuals augment the collective understanding as they extend that understanding to reach deeper into their individual worlds.

Sometimes a new collaboratively created cognitive framework strongly conflicts with an individual's personally held logical framework.

Depending upon the magnitude of the conflict, some individuals may find this discovery painful. Experts are subject to this form of cognitive pain. The pain is combined with the fatigue of the "mental gymnastics" that may have been attempted in order to envision a harmonic fit of the old and the new frameworks. This does not mean that the new framework is unappreciated. It simply means that adjusting to the new view of the world is personally difficult. One participant has described this phenomenon as "mourning the death of your old worldview." Another participant, who happened to be a psychiatrist, described the mental gymnastics as a "cognitive striptease" because of the need for the authors to reveal their thinking in an authentic way.

Individuals can also mourn the close of the collaborative learning program itself—which is to say that they feel the loss of the intimacy that they have shared within the learning group. We are sensitive to the fact that in strong command-and-control organizations, collaborative learning events are initiated only around specific problem solving or opportunity capturing needs. Individuals who participate in these events experience the form of authentic participatory democracy that happens to be incidentally essential for the success of the design program. At the close of the program, they can grieve the loss of the environment. It is also possible that within the comfortable intimacy of a collaborative learning environment, some individuals may become a bit too candid for their own good when they return to a hierarchical organization structure after the close of the collaborative learning session. Sociologists recognize that while minority opinion is a valued source of learning, it also can be a source of social marginalization in cultures that routinely reward groupthink. We believe that these risks are not unique to any collaborative learning environment, but we are sensitive to the fact that the intense use of open voting and deliberation in our practice heightens distinctions, and that clear, strong distinctions accelerate learning.

In the best of cases, new shared understandings open up new opportunities. This can be exciting, but it also can be a source of stress. Excitement about the opportunity to reach a goal might trigger a footrace of uncoordinated action. In our experience, however, individuals within groups that have jointly framed new understandings and discovered their cohesiveness as a learning community are predisposed for collective action. The experiential value of shared learning may be very strong social cement. Steven Covey recently parsed the essential drives of humanity into a drive to live, a drive to love, a drive to learn, and a drive to leave a legacy. A community that shares a powerful collaborative learning experience may form enduring interpersonal attachments. This prediction is consistent with our experiences in over forty years of supporting collaborative learning in communities of many types and in many nations.

Thomas Fetterman, the vice president of Bryn Gweled Homesteads, described his impression of structured dialogic design this way:

> I am a 15 year member of Bryn Gweled Homesteads, founded in 1940. We are the intentional community discussed. There are currently 74 families living in owner built homes who share the ownership of 240 acres of woods. The sole intention of our community is to be good neighbors to one another.
>
> A schism developed in our traditionally harmonious nature when it became evident that our over abundance of deer has caused over 70% of our members to be infected with Lyme's Disease. The deer have also destroyed the under story of our woods and caused multiple car accidents.
>
> When there is an emotionally charged issue like the culling of deer, we require a super-majority written vote of 2/3rds or better to initiate action. Mr. Christakai [*sic*] is a member and resident of our community. He graciously volunteered to engage the community in a structured dialogic design process workshop. The results were so enlightening and revealing that some time later our community hired him to host a second SDD workshop.
>
> These two SDD workshops were pivotal in resolving this deeply emotional issue. Our community subsequently created a three part strategic plan that won an 80% super majority vote. Our plan is now being implemented successfully. The SDD workshops also fathered an ongoing ad hoc committee to help us all improve our decision making abilities. This in turn has encouraged less active members to participate anew.
>
> Our community harmony is now greatly improved and getting so much better all the time! (http://www.amazon.com/gp/cdp/member-reviews/ AQ744P1Z2WHP5/ref=cm_pdp_rev_more?ie=UTF8&sort%5Fby=MostRecent Review#R5P58O66C8DWL)

THE FINAL WORD

Categorical thinking is powerful, yet also constrained by the existing collection of categories. Conversely, the process of clustering and constructing new categories within a group is important in building shared frameworks, because it forces individuals to reconceptualize their preconditioned categorical thinking. This opens group members to new structures of thought based upon the group's collaborative learning. Affinity clusters effectively represent distinct "dimensions" of the design challenge. Explicitly identifying multiple dimensions of a design challenge can alter the way that individuals perceive specific observations.

There are downstream planning capacities that are specifically enabled by clustering, too. In the solution phase of collaborative design, the strongest assembly of options for action in an action plan will generally be drawn from across all dimensions of the action options.

Collaborative learning is a deeply personal, yet also transparently social, experience, and it carries a rich array of emotions. When citizens see their communities from within an SDD workshop for the first time, they experience a "cybernetic embedding" whereby the otherwise "atomistic behavior" of individuals that is usually based on a simplistic understanding of their complex situation is transformed into a different mode. We have heard this echoed by statements such as, "I couldn't believe it. There were individuals in that room who never behaved that way in public before. I still don't really believe it."

This behavioral mode exhibits humility that is based on the understanding of new complexity, as opposed to the arrogance often founded on the false confidence of simplicity. By "cybernetic embedding" we mean the collective immersion and appreciation of the group by the group. In these situations, the tone within the room moves from a "telling" mode to a "pleading for understanding" mode. Speakers who simplistically expect to be believed and obeyed find themselves pleading to the group for collective understanding of the points that they are making. This conditional group norm emerges because the need to trust each other promotes a public intimacy within which one's strength is measured by one's capacity to be concerned for the thoughts of each other. Eventually, the only power that counts is the power of logical explanation.

There is a functional parallel with cybernetic embedding in collaborative learning environments. Greek tragedy uses "silent catharsis" to engage audiences participating in the unfolding of a play by individually shedding psychological burdens and becoming liberated to embrace new feelings and roles. In the SDD sessions, the cathartic release is more explicitly shared through empathetic dialogue among the participants. The empathy is not necessarily directed toward the perspectives of an individual speaker but rather is directed toward the essential need for each speaker to be understood. This shared need for understanding each other deeply—which, for many participants, may be experienced for the first time in a group learning experience—becomes a shared bond and further promotes the emergence of public intimacy.

SECTION II

THE PRACTICE

"Talent wins games, but teamwork and intelligence wins championships."

Michael Jordan
Sports icon

"A different world cannot be built by indifferent people."

Horace Mann
Philosopher

Note: The events and situations discussed in this narrative are fictional. They draw upon real situations that have been assembled in a composite for the purposes of providing a rich learning opportunity, but any resemblance to words or actions of real individuals is purely coincidental.

CHAPTER 6

THE PHONE CALL: WORKING WITH SPONSORS OF COLLABORATIVE LEARNING

"Opportunity doesn't knock, it only presents itself after you beat down the door."

Bill Cosby
Comedian and educator

Phones do not ring as frequently as one might expect in many specialized consulting practices. Yes, of course, we do call out to check in with our referral networks. A lot of this is done with snippet e-mails—never too much to burden a friendly reader, just a simple tug on the thread that links us. And face-to-face discussions remain critical to opening new doors. So an incoming call is always a source of excitement. It almost always represents a "lead" from someone who genuinely understands the capacities of the specialty consulting firm.

One fine morning—and when this happens, it is always a fine morning—the phone rings. The conversation goes something like this:

The Talking Point: Creating an Environment for Exploring Complex Meaning, pages 83–92
Copyright © 2010 by Information Age Publishing

THE CALL

Our Voice: "George, it is great to hear from you. We've been thinking of the folks at the institute and wondering how the project has been progressing. How can we help you today?"

Caller's Voice: "We are exactly where we expected to be with the project at the institute. But something new has come up and it seems to be right down your alley."

Our Voice: "Great—you know what we do as well as anyone, so what's up?"

Caller's Voice: "Well, we have a partner who is heading into deep water. They have been struggling for years with an important mission and limited success. Now they see a huge opportunity, but it also has a huge risk. They cannot act on this alone, and they know that there is a lot of explaining that would need to be done. They don't have the time to spiral round and round building up confidence and commitments one by one until they have the buy-in that they need from the partners who must work together. I have suggested that we use your process and rapidly build the understanding that we need so that a collective decision might be made. There is no real conflict here, just a whole lot of moving parts and a really significant commitment of resources."

Our Voice: "Tell us a bit about the sponsor. Are they genuinely ready to have a group collectively design a way to move on the opportunity?"

Caller's Voice: "Yes, they have a big-picture idea, but they don't have an action plan. They know the roles that some of the partners are ready, willing, and able to play, but they don't know how all the related interests will come together. They don't want to start with a small set of partners first, because they feel that this might make some of the other partners feel like second-class citizens. All of the partners are going to be playing critical roles in their own ways if this is going to succeed."

Our Voice: "It seems like you are discussing what we call a "partners forum" that can serve as a foundation for project planning. If the partners can get the issues that they need to address sorted out so that their individual and collective risks are recognized and managed, then they will be on a firm footing for hanging together to put a plan into action."

Caller's Voice: "You've got it spot on! This project is going to have to run for years—for longer than anything that the organization has ever attempted in the past. I already know a fair number of the key players, and it is clear to me that the project is going to run into significant costs, even for the high rollers in the partnership. Everyone is going to need to know—and also genuinely believe—that they are in this together—even as we go forward to sort out exactly what 'this' happens to mean in operational terms."

Our Voice: "When can you bring us to talk with the sponsors of the project?"

Caller's Voice: "I was hoping you'd ask that. Can you come to my office next Thursday around 11:00? We'll talk a bit, continue over lunch, and then let us see where we get in the early afternoon?"

Our Voice: "We're on. I will bring my lead project manager with me. See you Thursday!"

WHAT HAS HAPPENED

We have just received a call from an individual who is playing the role of what we call a "broker." Brokers are individuals who understand both the specialty consulting methodology and individuals who would be making use of that methodology. It is—and yet it also is not—a salesman role. The broker scouts for the match between consulting methods and community needs. Brokers are respected by groups that they serve because they have a best-practice view of the world. Their credibility depends upon setting up connections that get the job done—particularly when the job seems impossible. Brokers are never at financial risk for the execution of a design project, but they do put their professional reputations on the line every time that they make a recommendation. For this reason, it is not surprising that many brokers have, at some time in the past, directly experienced the SDD design methodology in a real-world application and thereby convinced themselves of the merits of the approach.

It is difficult to predict when and where future brokers will emerge for any specialty design practice. Sometimes an organization will see the value of embracing a specialized design methodology to create competitive advantage and will reuse the approach frequently. At other times, the option to apply the method will be held in reserve for occasions of great need.

Complex, information-intensive companies (e.g., pharmaceutical companies) have been using the approach for years. As complexity increasingly overtakes more of our corporations and civic organizations, and as complex multiparty agreements need to be forged to smooth acquisitions or to engage new opportunities, the need for specialized design approaches will continue to rise. There is, of course, also a bit of a catch-22 in the diffusion of any innovative process into a global arena. Until you have a sufficient body of skilled practitioners offering the design method, you cannot offer the service efficiently at global scale—and until you have built up a large base of design method users, you cannot coax the talent that you need into the practice. Lead design firms offering the service can find themselves facing a formidable marketing challenge in trying to convey an understanding of the merits of their approach. This is because *all group processes are an experience*—the challenge in explaining a group process is like the challenge of explaining the experience of riding a bicycle. You can point to the outcome, but you cannot point to the process as an experience. It is, of course, precisely for this reason that personal referrals (from "brokers") are so important to innovative processes.

Some days are just full of sunshine. Shortly after our first call, we get another. This call unfolds as follows:

ANOTHER CALL

Our Voice: "Peter, How are things going in Atlanta? It sounds like you folks are up to your ankles in alligators with your water shortage these days."

Caller's Voice: "That is exactly why I am calling!"

Our Voice: "Well, we do work an occasional miracle, but we can't promise to make it rain."

Caller's Voice: "My bet is that you can. I have got a group that is desperate to get the region to rethink the way that it is managing water resources. It is a great opportunity for you guys. It is just what you do."

Our Voice: "Saving the planet is certainly part of our mission. What do you have in mind?"

Caller's Voice: "Well, I have two dozen folks from real estate development companies, water resource technology companies, environmental groups, and a range of state and local government agencies. I have been telling them about your design methodology and while they are skeptical, they are interested. I have told them that I would call you and ask for a demonstration. What can I tell them?"

Our Voice: "I understand. They are seriously looking, but they don't know where to place their faith, or their bets. We can tell them where we have helped similar groups make comparable breakthroughs in the past. They can call up some of these participants and get their responses. Will that build the confidence that you feel they need?"

Caller's Voice: "Actually, I was hoping that you might get a small group of them to sit down and run through a short experience—a simulation of some sort—so that they can understand the mechanics of the design process."

Our Voice: "We could convince them that we have a cool methodology. In the past, however, we have found that groups are not comforted by understanding a methodology until they have been reassured that it will work with their unique situation—both the problem that they have and the group that they will be working with. Demonstrations don't take into account the significant work that goes into preparing for a design session. Also, demonstrations have the disadvantage of engaging the players in roleplaying, which is an artificial situation. When we try to demonstrate a design methodology without working through the preparation for the design activity, participants have every reason to feel uncomfortable about the fit. There is a risk that we would create a superficial understanding of the mechanics of the method and at the same time create a misunderstanding of how the method is fit to a group of participants and situation. Your project team could come away with a false impression that "now they understand the methodology" and still don't feel comfortable with it. In our experience with design management, every situation is participant-dependent. They are simultaneously the observers and the experiential owners of the problem. We have learned that when participants know that they do not own a problem, they know that they do not collectively own the solution they codesign either. If participants walk out of a structured dialogic design session without feeling that they now coown a problem, a solution and an action plan, then the effort will have been wasted. We can't waste a community's time—there is just too little collaborative planning time left to all of us these days."

Caller's Voice: "So what is the best way forward?"

Our Voice: "Let's get together with the key parties who will sponsor the design session and talk through the big picture. This will include a discussion of the method along with the reference accounts that they will need. If they want to begin with a "small project," that is okay—a small project is different from a demonstration, because even a small project will have a real world impact. Without the need to make the connection with their real world problem and solution, we will be spinning everyone's wheels. And if we bring them through the rigor of a design session without delivering a solution, they would—and should—wonder about our ethics. Do you see what I mean?"

Caller's Voice: "I guess so, but I am not sure why demonstrations don't work for you guys. You have a *great* methodology."

Our Voice: "Yes, you already have experienced the methodology several years ago in the context of dealing with a real problem that you coowned at that time. And for this reason you could genuinely appreciate the value of the methodology. If we are not real, we can, at best, hope to be cute. But then we ask our participants to work too hard for an outcome that is only cute. Participating stakeholders don't want to work hard for something that they cannot put into use. We cannot begin a relationship with our clients by giving them something that they will not genuinely value."

Caller's Voice: "Okay. When you spell it out like that, I get it. Let's get a date on the calendar when you can come down. I will check back with you in a day or two. In the meantime, keep dancing for rain. We need anything you can send our way?"

WHAT HAS HAPPENED

It is not unusual for folks to ask for a sample. If we were selling ice cream, we would certainly offer the pink spoon for a taste, but our real life isn't so easy. We are offering something other than dessert—think of the solution that we are bringing to communities as a bit like a medicine. It isn't quite "hold your nose and swallow," but it also isn't "try a sip, and then if you like it, try enough to actually make a difference." Let's face it—serious design work is serious work. We cannot land safely if we only open a parachute 15%. Only the authentic experience is the authentic experience.

It isn't easy being both an emerging practice and also a rigorous practice. Yet this is where we are at the cusp of the new millennium. Creating a "safe place" for sampling an authentic experience means inviting an "observer" into a real application. This can be done under some extraordinary circumstances. The special conditions will be related to the acceptance of an "observer" by a community that is engaged in a design project. In general, if a person doesn't have a role in either dealing with the content for a community design as a community participant or dealing with the process of the design project, then they don't have a legitimate reason to be in the project—and their presence can be a significant distraction to the members of the community. When communities get together to design solutions to significant problems, they are not "on display." Yes, their deliberations are carefully recorded, and their decision making process is fully transparent—but where sensitive issues need to be openly discussed to enable shared understandings and breakthroughs, design processes need to protect candor and ensure trust. Individuals who are seriously committed to understanding the design methodology—and who may themselves become practitioners—are typically invited to take on specific roles as members of the design management team.

THE LUNCH

Many solutions to important problems begin over discussions around a meal. The symbolism of sharing sustenance may play a small part in the mutual purpose of the discussion. We have had many meetings over light lunches, and the general structure is that a party who knows what we do based on their experience (someone who might be seen as a broker) makes an introduction to one or more individuals who have the capacity to convene a community into a problem solving session (which is to say that they can "sponsor" a design event). Introductions generally lead into the following flow of thought:

Broker's Voice: "This lunch is long overdue. I have seen your group struggling with its efforts to find a way forward for—what—almost two years now?"

Sponsor's Voice: "Well, it isn't for lack of desire. We keep bashing into ourselves. I think that we have what we need to solve the problem, but we can't seem to pull ourselves together. Our discussions get really heated. Yes, we do cool down—and I have to admit that we have succeeded in remaining friendly with each other—but the frustration is eating away at our morale. If we don't go forward, we certainly will be slipping behind."

Our Voice: "You are not alone in your struggle. It sounds like you are experiencing what we call 'a collision of good intentions.' This typically happens when folks don't fully share an understanding of the larger problem they are collectively trying to solve. When people see only part of a problem, they design their solutions to address that specific part of the problem. You want your group to have confidence in their vision for solutions, so it is painful for them to let go of a solution that seems so right from an individual perspective."

Sponsor's Voice: "This sounds like us. We have some very strong personalities. We are a community of experts. No one wants to be the guy without answers or without a plan. We actually have exactly the type of individuals that we could most hope to have. And now we are just beginning to consider the possibility that we might start to lose a few of them. This would be very bad for us."

Broker's Voice: "Well, this is why we are having lunch. You really don't have the time to walk through extended cycles of planning. You need to step out of your routines and hammer this out in a way that is going to make people feel that they belong to each other. This is the result that fell out of the partner's retreat that we held at the foundation last year—and, in very large measure, our success was critically dependent on the process that we used. So today you get to meet the team that worked the magic for us."

Our Voice: "Thank you. And, yes, the partner's forum was a typical success. I don't mean to diminish it in any way—that would be inappropriate. What I mean to say is that when groups find a really effective way of working together—and when they genuinely do want to work together—they do connect with the structured dialogic design process. Often they point to us as if we were gurus or magicians. It is natural to think that we did something heroic. Think of us as a team that drives the taxi. Your community tells us "take us to the hospital—we're having a baby, and we don't know which hospital we want to go to." We manage the mechanics of the trip. Now, if a community has never been in a taxi together before, they think of the experience as a magic carpet ride. They do have to hold on, but they soon see the progress that they are making. We are more mechanics than we are magicians."

Sponsor's Voice: "Well, this may be just what we need. Clearly we have something that is broken, and we can't afford to sit back and see if it will mend itself. Your taxi ride comes highly recommended. Let's put a package together and try the new approach. At this stage, the risk of doing nothing is far greater than the risk of trying something that isn't familiar to us. What is the next step?"

Our Voice: "We will need to understand the context of your challenge so that we can offer advice on the diversity of perspectives that will need to be included in the dialogue. So we're going to do some background work that will result in a very concise report—a 'white paper' on your current situation, if you're familiar with the term. And we'll then work with you to focus the discussion with a precise trigger question that we can't help you frame without some additional background work. We don't have the authority to convene your community, so we will need to work with you to schedule the design session and invite—really, 'recruit' is a better word—the specific participants who must bring their perspectives to the design. We do this by working with someone who knows your organization and who has an intuitive or experiential understanding of the mechanics of democratic design."

Broker's Voice: "I guess I can see where I might be fitting into this picture. Yes, I've seen both sides—the challenge and the design method. If we're going to go forward, I'll play the 'broker' role for this project."

Sponsor's Voice: "If you can manage the interface, that would be great. I can see that this is a complex situation with a lot of moving parts. I have to admit that I get nervous when there are a lot of moving parts—it means more opportunities for a part to go wrong, and then we'd have a real mess on our hands."

Our Voice: "You're right. The planning process is critical. If planning for the design event is poor, no one can expect to have an optimal design. We have over three decades of experience in planning collaborative design sessions. We will bring this experience to your support. Once we are in a design session, then all of the project risk is fully controlled. I say this because the methodology has consistently helped groups attain design goals, and it does this within the schedule of the design session. Unless lightening strikes our design room, all of your risk is in the up-front planning for the design session."

Sponsor's Voice: "How soon can you start?"

Our Voice: "We'll put a scope of work in the mail tomorrow, and we can start pulling together a design management team next week. We'll need about a month to construct the white paper, and we'll be working concurrently with our new broker and old friend here on the stakeholder analysis for the design session. Allowing time for participants to schedule in the event, we can expect to launch a design session for forty to sixty participants with about forty-five days' lead time."

Sponsor's Voice: "Okay. Let's take a look at the numbers and pencil in a date. This lunch is on me."

WHAT HAS HAPPENED

A sponsor has acknowledged that his community has been dealing with a persistent, complex problem, and that the consequences of continuing to leave the problem unresolved are rising. This defines a threshold for trying something different. Collaborative design is a costly process, because large, real dollar costs are involved in pulling a community of important participants out of their daily routines and into a structured dialogic design session. The bonds of informed trust need to be strong between brokers and sponsors so that a broker can assure sponsors and participants that any risks unique to the community are understood and will be controlled. With the combination of a respected broker and a willing sponsor, the opportunity for hosting an innovative design session moves one large step closer to reality. In principle, an agreement to go forward was established. Projects will differ in terms of scope of work and cost structure. Some situations will need extensive background research; others will not. Some situations will have a well-characterized slate of motivated participants, but others will require extensive recruitment.

THE FINAL WORD

Doors are opened for first-time use of innovative design processes by individuals who have been part of a related design session in the past. Based on their successful experience, they become advocates for the use of specific methodologies. This is a social marketing phenomenon. Reference accounts are helpful, but a critical feature is a bridge of trust among individuals who share and solve significant problems. It is through a sponsor network that design innovations can diffuse most rapidly. New sponsors will have concerns about "leaning" on an unfamiliar process. Ultimately, sponsors need to trust the judgments of others. Sufficient use of an innovative process within an organization or a community makes it familiar, and is more readily put to use for new applications.

Passion for the process is essential, but it also is not sufficient to ensure diffusion. It is the community's desperation for a solution—not their interest in the problem itself—that leads members to try new ways of solving problems. And it is trust in the wisdom and sincerity of past users of a process that ultimately holds the door open.

CHAPTER 7

THE DESIGN MANAGEMENT TEAM: FRAMING THE SCOPE OF WORK

"You can't understand a design project by simplifying it. You have to master its complexity."

Alfred Chandler
Professor, Harvard Business School

"A problem clearly stated is a problem half solved."

Charles Kettering
American industrialist

Design management teams are groups of experts with the complementary skills that are needed to implement a specific process for managing a design project. This assembly of process experts is distinct from the gathering of designers themselves. Designers are stakeholders in the design product. In a collaborative design engagement, these stakeholders will contribute specific and diverse expertise through their participation in the dialogue.

The Talking Point: Creating an Environment for Exploring Complex Meaning, pages 93–112
Copyright © 2010 by Information Age Publishing
93

The design management team will create and sustain a productive environment for collaborative design.

In complex design challenges, designers and design managers hold distinct roles. In low complexity and familiar design challenges, senior designers often concurrently provide design management oversight as well as design content knowledge. When the teams are dealing with high levels of complexity that spans disciplinary and other knowledge boundaries, there is a very real risk that one designer's personal preferences may be perceived as dominating the views of other designers. This can be a problem when the designer team needs to work collaboratively to design and implement a plan.

Authentic collaborative action can be cultivated with equity but can rarely be forced through the influence of power. For this reason, sponsors of design work typically contact us when they are dealing with a boundary-spanning, complex design challenge for which implementing a solution will require coordinated and collaborative action. The neutrality of the design management team plays an important role in reassuring designers that there is no preconceived "correct" or "favored" design solution. Appreciating this distinction of roles liberates designers to broadly consider a variety of options and to invest personal energy in sharing their perspectives. Openly and candidly sharing diverse perspectives minimizes the risk of incompleteness and underconceptualization of the design challenge. The design management team needs to share the commitment to create this unfettered environment for the designers.

Just as designers manage only the content, the design management team manages *only* the overarching decisions related to achieving a design sponsor's goals and enhancing the efficiency and effectiveness of the design process.

Design sponsors frequently have the mental image of "facilitators" when they first envision a design management team. Although facilitation is an art that relates to keeping groups of people on task, the design management team has larger responsibilities that include ensuring that the knowledge base of the designers will be captured and presented in ways that favor flexible graphic representations of the information into an emerging design. Beyond enabling technology for managing information, knowledge, and wisdom, the design management team is responsible for ensuring an appropriate design environment and launching activity. Much as a billiards player will approach a rack of balls for the critically important "break" that signals the launch of a series of critical tasks, a design management team plans for a sometimes fragile and always critically important launch of a complex design project in which a mess of interlocking issues needs to be isolated, sorted, and reassembled by the designers.

METADECISION MAKING AS A DESIGN MANAGEMENT SKILL

The familiar roles of a design management team includes scheduling a series of knowledge management tasks, pacing designers as they progress through these tasks and generating a flow of work products that speed and ease the burden of managing complex information and knowledge. In a complex design challenge, where new knowledge is rapidly generated and assimilated into the design, the process requires as much science as it does art. The science is thoroughly detailed, documented, and validated as "generic design" (see the work of John Warfield, Alexander Christakis, and colleagues). The art of our design practice is found in the mastery of the skill of working with individuals as they interact in groups with clarity, humor, strength, authenticity, and humility.

The less familiar role of the design management team includes guiding the overarching decisions of the design project—defining boundary conditions and defining the rules for organizing design ideas into a coherent product. Formally, these are "metadecisions." These are the decisions that evaluate the number and diversity of designers at the table, assess how the billiard balls appear to be stacked against each other, and find the language appropriate to launch and sustain the focus of the design project.

All sponsors of highly complex design projects share a fundamental dilemma—they cannot simultaneously stay within a world of familiar meanings and expectations about the future (normative boundary judgments) while enriching their design through the vast array of possibilities (ontological boundary judgments). Individual designers navigate these boundaries in their own individual ways, and with their own partial or fragmented understanding of the whole system of issues inherent in the design challenge. Groups can provide this larger systems view, but while groups are much wiser than individuals, they are not as adept at thinking and conceptualizing collaboratively.

The design management team supports the process of dealing with these metadecisions in advance of the group design activity itself.

ANTICIPATING THE CONTENT

The lead contact on the design management team sustains the communications with the sponsor. This is a relationship of exquisite trust. Sponsors put far more than dollars at risk as they trust their community of designers into the hands of a process that they themselves may not fully understand. This being the case, the lead on the design management team needs to communicate everything that the sponsor must understand while also not overburdening the sponsor with tactical details.

The key points that need to be taken from the sponsor include the nature of the arena for which the design will be constructed (e.g., health care networks, biomedical devices, wellness campaigns), the "stage" of the design project (e.g., defining the full scope of the challenge, developing a strategic action plan, implementing a project based on a collaborative design), and the expected dimensions of the project (e.g., the number of distinct perspectives that will need to be engaged).

The contact lead on the design management team assembles a team with the skills needed to capture the language of the designers and to support the specific stage of design activity that the designers will be engaging.

ANTICIPATING THE PROCESS

In any design management consultancy some decisions are built into the nature of the practice. In a dialogue-based design process, the ease with which unfamiliar ideas surface, become clarified, and enter into an emerging pattern of understanding depends upon the number of participants, the process used to manage the information and knowledge produced, and the efficiency of the design management team.

As participants engage in dialogue, ideas will be shared and captured. Participants will reflect on captured ideas and make connections and distinctions. The group's connections and distinctions will be captured and displayed. And participants will reflect on these connections and distinctions and discover patterns. The patterns discovered by the group will be interpreted by group members, and these narrative interpretations will give rise to new meaning. The cycle may be extended to generate new ideas, connections, and distinctions—all of which can augment the group's patterns. The flow is paced to ensure clarity and full participation and is sustained until the group has established a comprehensive view of a core structure of ideas that the group agrees are the essential elements to address or to incorporate into the design.

In our practice, simple rule-of-thumb heuristics apply to determining the size of the design management team needed to support a specific design project: an assembly of twenty-five designers working across institutional, disciplinary, or individual boundaries will require one idea recorder, one work product production manager, and one dialogue manager. In this team, one member must additionally play the team leader role in managing the bridge to the sponsor, and one or more members must additionally manage framing the scope of work, conduct preparatory research, and identify the triggering question for unpacking an understanding of the design challenge.

FRAMING THE SCOPE OF WORK

Design activity consists of sets of tasks that are applied in phases and stages. In professional consulting companies, these tasks are typically highly codified. Codified processes lend themselves to systematic analysis and continuous improvement. One metric of a codified design process is the time that tasks take based on the size of the group engaged in the task. One member of the design management team will generate a cost estimate based on tasks that will need to be completed and historical task performance times. The phase of the design process, the size of the group, and the urgency or lead time will factor into the costs. Travel and expenses will be written in as a not-to-exceed line item.

The tasks in a design management project do depend upon the phase of the design work. When a design project is initiated at the phase of defining the full scope of the challenge (which is a requirement for our practice), the scope of work will contain provisions for constructing a white paper to corroborate (or extend) the sponsor's understanding of the required design participants. The white paper typically includes a stakeholder analysis. Stakeholders are identified in an iterative fashion, beginning with named individuals or job titles that are contributed by the sponsor. The design management team will budget for this research task, and costs will be driven by the number and nature of interviews (i.e., telephone versus face-to-face with travel costs). Interview subjects are typically asked to name individuals who they feel may have additional views on the topic, and this may expand the scale of the research. The study is continued until five interviews in distinct segments of the field fail to generate any new perspectives. At this point the findings will be synthesized, categorized, and reported without attributions to any specific authors. The design team will, however, compile a list of individuals who have expressed unique perspectives for poten-tial inclusion as designers. The sponsor will make the final decisions on expanding the design team.

Based upon the arena of design, the cost estimator for the design man-agement team will either recruit an internal researcher, who has expert understanding of the vocabulary and practices in the specific design arena, or will identify and contract an external expert for the task. Stakeholder analysis for complex design ranges in cost from $20,000 to $30,000.

Within the group design session phase of a design project, time and costs are highly predictable and are driven by the number of designers participating in the group work. In our practice, an additional project team member must be engaged when more than twenty-five designers are working together, and another project team member must be engaged when more than thirty-five designers are working together. Cost per participant falls as the size of the group approaches our preferred cap of fifty participants. Our method has been used successfully with design groups of several hundred (e.g., with a Forest Service project involving 200 stakeholders), but this special use requires recruiting and training a large design management team.

Once a cost estimate for a scope of work has been prepared, the design management team leader discusses the estimate with the sponsor. New sponsors typically want to understand what drives the cost of the design project and will generally seek to limit cost. This usually leads to a candid and healthy discussion. If the sponsor sees the design management team only as a facilitation practice, then they will want to see the work priced on par with conventional facilitation practices. In such cases, we are happy to make referrals to independent facilitators, although without claims for outcomes.

While the design project sponsor is reviewing budget issues and possible additions to the designers group, the design management team leader is telegraphing the potential engagement to possible design management team members. In many cases, once a sponsor has decided to move forward, they will want to move rapidly. When the sponsor has made a final decision about the scope of work and proposes a launch date, the design management team will be ready to submit a contract proposal that will include a finalized "bulletproof" statement of work.

PUTTING KEY ROLES INTO THE SCOPE OF WORK STATEMENT

In our practice, eight or nine key roles are needed to implement a boundary-spanning collaborative design work plan. Three key roles exist on the sponsor side, and five or six key roles exist on the design management team side. In many cases, a single individual can play multiple roles, but, as in any major production, a leading role is best protected by including individuals who are understudies or who have cross-trained in multiple key roles.

Design Project Sponsor Side

The sponsor organization's functions include the sponsor role, a broker role to manage recruitment and retention of the designers group, and a logistics role to secure, provision, and manage the design session facility. It is critically important to specify these roles in the statement of work along with a clarification of what is involved in those roles and specific individuals who will be responsible for overseeing the performance of the roles.

1. The Sponsor Role
   The sponsor has an essential role in establishing and ensuring design project continuity. Sponsors universally share a knowledge of a problem

situation that requires the attention of a community of stakeholders. In some cases, sponsors may have an idea for how the community might go about solving the problem. And in some cases, sponsors have expectations for how the community will address a specific problem. These three distinctions also parallel four stages in group design work:

1. Problem definition
2. Alternatives design
3. Action planning
4. Implementation

In some cases a sponsor will "leap" over the use of collaborative design to work through stage 1 or stages 1 and 2 and will seek help specifically with stages 3 or 4. In our experience, this doesn't work out well for the sponsor whenever authentic collaboration is required to implement an action plan. The general reason why imported action plans fail to mobilize strong collaborative support for highly complex problems is because participants have nagging concerns that some important dimension of the complex problem situation hasn't been appropriately conceptualized. The concern is for the "we don't know what we don't know" formal Type IV category of errors. Groups tend to collaborate deeply only after they have "discovered" (i.e., designed) an action plan based upon a jointly framed understanding of what needs to be addressed. Our design methodology requires that we begin our design activity with a jointly framed understanding of the problem situation. The sponsor's role is thus to strongly adhere to a sequence of framing the problem situation, designing alternatives, converging on a collaborative action plan, and then implementing the action plan collaboratively. We have learned from many years of practice that when stakeholders do not own the problem, they do not own the solution, even if the solution designed by others is the right one.

For example, if we want to fix the high dropout rate by young people in our schools, we need to bring students to the table and ask them, "Why are students dropping out of school?" Only by engaging them in defining their own problem from their own perspective is there hope of making progress in resolving this mess. If we do not help them own their problem, they will not own any solutions that are designed by other stakeholders, such as parents, teachers, administrators, and the like.

A sponsor typically supports the launch of a design project by making a statement that reminds all participants of the importance of the work that they will do. This statement is followed by a second statement that puts a specific charge to the group. This charge is presented as a "triggering question" that will continuously guide the dialogue and deliberations of the group of designers. It is a critically important statement, and it cannot be made with any authority or legitimacy by anyone other than the sponsor.

The dialogue manager of the design management team works closely with the sponsor to frame this trigger question. The trigger question will capture the design mission in terms of opportunity, need, and timeframe and will be absolutely clear to all participants in the design session. In practice, the design management team displays the trigger question as the sponsor reads and explains it to the participants. Participants will be asked if they fully understand the trigger question. Some discussion may follow, and—if meaning needs to be clarified—the sponsor may choose to modify the trigger question in some way in response to comments from the participants. In our practice, *only* the sponsor can alter the triggering question, and this must happen *only* at the launch of the design session.

A story from the arena might help illustrate this point. About ten years ago, a pharmaceutical team was working on designing a new drug for the treatment of Alzheimer's disease. The CEO of the company, in collaboration with the broker and the design team manager, had framed a triggering question that was focusing the designers on designing a strategy to complete the development and marketing of the drug in three years and generate $60 million revenue the first year after entering the market. When the triggering question was presented to the designers, the CEO and the broker were not present at the design session because of a company emergency. Another member of the team was selected to explain the triggering question and to answer questions of clarification. The designers proceeded to ask the substitute broker questions that were very antagonistic and sarcastic. They clearly did not want to engage in responding to the triggering question, because they did not like the time horizon and the requirement to generate $60 million revenue in the first year. The dialogue manager took a break and asked the CEO to come to the session. The CEO visited the designers' session and explained the rationale for the triggering question. Only after the explanation and the charge by the CEO were the designers ready to engage in group work and produce the desired strategy in response to the triggering question.

The most difficult task for some sponsors is the exit that they may need to make as the mission of managing the design session moves into the hands of the design management team. In instances in which the political power of the sponsor is profoundly recognized by some or many of the participants, the presence of the sponsor in the design session may lead to some posturing or some loss of authenticity in deliberation of issues. When a sponsor blesses and launches a design activity and then physically leaves the session on schedule, this signifies trust in the participants and the process that they are using. While this may be appropriate or even necessary in some instances, there are other instances in which a sponsor is a member of the community of stakeholders for this issue, but during the deliberations of the team he or she does not exert more influence than any one of the designers. When the sponsor is a "peer" within the stakeholder community, he or she is able to join a seat at the table with his or he peers and will resume the role of the sponsor only by physically moving from a seat at the table to address the community at—or above—the level of the design management team.

The power of sponsorship is essential. The presence of the sponsor is powerful. If a sponsor can temporarily shed all of his or her vested power, he or she can enter the peerage of the collaborative design community in accordance with the transformative leadership style, as discussed in Chapter 3. Sometimes this is valuable to do; sometimes it is not.

2. The Broker Role

Brokers introduce and engage designers into design sessions. This role can be quite troublesome if it is not taken very seriously. A broker's failure to get *all* of the designers into the design session for the entire design session can cause a critical gap in the perspectives that need to be discussed to ensure a robust design. When brokers cannot be guaranteed to get all of the individual designers to participate, some redundancy needs to be built into the participant list. This redundancy has a cost that is factored into the statement of work as a means of avoiding underconceptualization of the design challenge due to missing design perspectives. In some instances, a sponsor wishes to engage a community of designers that he or she cannot compel to participate in the design. In this case, a broker might be engaged from a neutral authority with an even higher civic standing (e.g., a senior elected official, or a director of a community development foundation, or a church leader). When a sponsor appeals to a highly positioned community leader to coax designers to participate, the sponsor may additionally need to provide that community leader with a "cobroker" who will manage the logistics of telephone appeals and reminders—including direction and answers to the invited designers' questions.

Brokers recruiting designers in to a design sessions are frequently asked to provide participants with instructions that define expectations of the participants. Frequently stakeholders are uncomfortable approaching a design activity without reflection on what the final design product "should be." For this reason, the white paper exploring the range of perceptions in the specific field of design is distributed by the broker. The white paper includes a synopsis of varied views of the design task along with a summary of the scheduled design session and the method that will be used. Most designers are happy with this as a preparation for the design dialogue. In some instances, individual designers will push back against a design process—sometimes out of concern for the integrity of the process but also sometimes as a means of asserting a reason to refrain from participating. In these instances, the broker can schedule a call from a member of the design management team to more fully explain the methodology in an effort to "buy" the designer's participation.

The broker's work engaging designers is not easy. Complex design sessions require detailed and slow deliberations. To ensure clarity of complex ideas, their complexity has to be "unpacked" by their authors into digitized bits of understanding. This is done by stating *single* ideas in the form of a brief title, then augmenting that title with an explanation during a clarification step of the idea generation process. And to ensure a comprehensive approach, the digitized understanding from many unpacked ideas has to be "worked" into a new structure through group deliberations. This is a long day of continuous group work. Participants *must* arrive on time and remain completely focused on the design task during the full period of dialogue and deliberation. For a first-time participant, this is rarely an appealing invitation. Every senior design participant has been trapped in an extended and painfully unproductive group design project at some time in his or her career. The broker's task is to convince participants that this time, it will be different—and to then extract a solemn pledge of participation. Breaking the habit of participating in wasteful and unproductive group work from past experiences is not an easy task for the broker to accomplish.

Brokers sometimes need help from the design management team to provide feedback to particularly difficult designers. When a broker is having a difficult time recruiting designers, the need for coaching and support from the design management team can raise the costs for the design management team. As a result, the design management team is highly incentivized to work in a very supportive way to ensure the success of the broker.

At the end of the day, the individual who has successfully played the broker role harvests a windfall profit of connections in the social network of the stakeholder community. Brokers generally find that because of their efforts in contributing to collaborative design, they are offered career advancement opportunities. Fortunately, when brokers have moved upward in their careers, they generally remain open, even attracted, to future opportunities to replay the broker role—with added skill and confidence. In many instances, brokers seek training in the design management method that we use. This is a favorable situation for our type of practice, because every proficient practitioner of the design management methodology is also a potential partner on the road as the demand for complex problem design management service continues to grow. In fact, one of the authors of this book (Tom Flanagan) started his practice in the arena of design management by being the broker for a biotechnology design project in 1996.

3. The Site Logistics Role
Event coordinators are familiar with the role of managing site logistics. While this role is identified as being distinct to the broker role, many event coordinators are familiar with managing both the participant side

and the facility side of the equation. The reason that a strong distinction is made between these two roles in collaborative design sessions is due to the fact that, unlike an event, when guests simply might be "invited," the specific need for key individuals in a design program requires skills that can convince prospective participants that they have been "recruited."

The site logistics are important for reasons that are discussed in more detail in subsequent sections of this book. In brief, participants engaged in complex design sessions will be doing a considerable amount of mental work. Their physical needs and comfort are important in enabling them to stay on task with the mental work. Groups are managed to a high performance level when arrangements are made to avoid their threshold for information overload. While the tools and techniques that we use are specifically designed to manage and control information and cognitive overload, individuals who feel physically uncomfortable, distracted, or fatigued cannot perform together as a team of designers. The entire team effort in a collaborative design is put at risk when shortcuts are taken that compromise the performance of each and every designer.

Design Management Team Side

The design management team's functions include the **dialogue management role**, a **project management role** to coordinate activities within the design management team and between this team and the sponsor's organization, a **recorder** to manage the flow of ideas from participants into electronic archives, a **productions manager** to produce real-time work products as well as preparatory and follow-up documents, and a **stakeholder researcher** to survey perspectives in the field of practice and identify individuals who represent distinct perspectives. Overall quality control for the performance of the design management team falls to the individual who is managing the direct relationship with the sponsor. Frequently, this individual is also the dialogue manager, although this role easily fits within the sphere of the project manager.

1. The Project Manager Role

Project managers have primary coordination roles, and to enforce coordination, they may also have considerable authority within the design management team. The project manager is likely to interact directly with all individuals who have roles in the design project, with the possible exception of the sponsor (who may interact directly with a distinct member of the design management team). The project manager is appointed when the scope of work is attached to a service contract for the project. The project manager is responsible for the timely completion of all of the tasks named in the scope of work and may take on added contingency tasks within the design management team side of the project. This role may be held in addition to roles that are involved in supporting a design session itself.

2. The Stakeholder Researcher Role

When a design project is initiated at the phase of defining the full scope of the challenge, the design management team assigns a competent content expert to conduct a survey of perspectives in the field of application and to summarize those findings in the form of a white paper. This work provides risk control for sponsors as design groups are finalized and provides a backdrop for the design session for participants seeking added details about the project. The survey and analysis work is intended to define the questions that seem typical of what may be discussed during the design session. Purposefully, the document opens more doors that it closes. This may be uncomfortable to some readers, who will expect the research to point toward conclusions. With the design philosophy that we espouse and practice, foreshadowing possible whole-system conclusions (even if accuracy and comprehensiveness in this effort might be ensured, which is very unlikely by the nature of the design challenge) would be counterproductive to authentic collaborative design. For these reasons, the scope of work should explicitly state that the white paper is intended to suggest *only* those types of questions that might arise in the course of a group design dialogue on the nature of the challenge that the group is confronting. The individual who prepares the white paper may be present during the design session, but it is important that this individual avoids presenting himself or herself as an advocate for any of the views represented in the white paper. The stakeholder researcher may be a subcontractor of the design management group rather than a direct member of the design management team.

For example, within the context of a product development project, an individual who was new to the SDD methodology was charged with the responsibility of the broker in terms of identifying and convening the stakeholders. The process was iterative, both in indentifying stakeholders and also in refining the new broker's "pitch" for getting commitments to participate from the stakeholders. What made this particular project challenging was the fact that the broker was calling upon participants who lived in the United States, the UK, the Republic of Ireland, and Northern Ireland, and who were working in fields as diverse as biochemistry, electrical engineering, clinical medicine, health care administration, diabetes management, diagnostic equipment manufacturing, and new business development. Participants would need to make a commitment to travel to Belfast, Northern Ireland, and spend two days in a planning project—with the added political tension related to Protestant–Catholic collaborations during what has come to be called "the Troubles" in Ireland.

The participants were promised that their interests in finding a way to bring improved diabetes diagnostic capabilities to primary care physicians would be woven together tightly with the interests of others, and that the method that would be used would be unlike any method that they had experienced in the past. And, yes, a corporate sponsor would pick up their travel costs and serve as their hosts. The broker would make these promises, build a convincing case for the high caliber of design skill and participation in the event, and remain in touch to dispel any second thoughts that might prevent recruited participants from actually participating. The broker worked closely with the SDD project team to identify both a primary and a secondary stakeholder for each type of perspective that was needed in the design project, and remained in this role until the participants had crossed the threshold into the design room. In this particular case, a decision was made *not* to develop the new product resulting from the group's design (based upon corporate focus and priorities), but the broker received impassioned phone calls from the participants asking if there might be any way to carry the work forward. The intensity and persistence of the calls convinced the broker that the design process had actually transferred ownership of the design to the participants, and that negotiating prices to continue the work would likely have been only a modest problem. The participants had been converted into a tight product development team in only two days. This revelation prompted the broker to begin forging plans to develop his skills to practice the SDD process.

3. The Dialogue Manager Role

The dialogue manager role may be played by multiple individuals on the design management team during any design session. It is not unusual for the individual on the design management team who established the direct connection with the sponsor to play the dialogue manager role in subsequent design sessions. Groups tend to form a relationship of compliance and trust with the dialogue manager who opens the design session and first serves as the custodian of the norms of the group. For this reason, any change in the individual who plays this role must take great care to remain consistent in respecting the norms in effect. The norms used in our practice are essentially those described in the literature for interactive management (see Alexander Christakis and John Warfield). The key to managing a highly creative group focused on an important and challenging design activity is to be clear, consistent, compassionate—and humorous. In our practice, we call dialogue management "the dance"—in part out of our own sense of theatric engagement, but also out of respect for the serious but less obvious work that is being done concurrently by our other design team members.

The dialogue manager is capable of conducting structured dialogue with a broad variety of content stakeholder experts from different disciplines and cultures. He or she is able to retain his or her neutrality in terms of content knowledge, while at the same time retaining and enforcing his or her expertise in terms of the structured dialogue process. However, even though the dialogue manager is "content neutral" by virtue of the fact that he or she is not an expert in the field of the community, some communities will insist upon an individual skilled in their practice to play the role of leading their dialogue. For example, when a group of nephrologists were working on designing a strategy for improving the provision of services to patients with chronic kidney disease, they objected because the dialogue manager role was played by a person who did not have an MD degree (Dr. Alexander Christakis). After taking a short break, and in consultation with the sponsor, it was decided to change the role of the dialogue manager and assign it to a member of the design management team with an MD degree, who was also an expert in the structured dialogue design process. After this change, the whole climate of the design session with the group of nephrologists was transformed to a very productive dialogue and deliberation on the issues. The medical doctors became very appreciative of the role of the dialogue manager once it was played by one of their kind. Dr. Alexander Christakis, who happens to have earned a PhD in theoretical physics from Princeton and Yale universities, was rejected by the medical doctors in playing the role of the dialogue manager for this situation.

4. The Recorder Role

The recorder role involves managing display equipment and capturing the explanations of the ideas as proposed by the authors and the discussion for their clarification during the dialogue. The recorder works closely with the dialogue manager and provides a pacing function for the group. For example, when some individuals in the group begin to overload the group with many ideas delivered in rapid sequence, the recorder is the human processing element that the dialogue manager relies upon to indicate that more is being said than can be captured and that precision is advisable during the group deliberation. Through an appeal to the group for mercy for the recorder sitting in the back of the room, individuals who are given to oratory and proselytizing speech generally adjust their statements to more succinctly telegraph their meaning. The recorder captures and displays these statements, demonstrating that every word from the authors and the participants during the discussion for clarification of meaning is respected and captured.

Early in the process, the group recognizes how information is going to be captured, and they establish the norm of communicating in short, pointed statements. The recorder speaks to—and responds *only* to—the dialogue manager, so even if a participant addresses the recorder directly, the recorder waits for the dialogue manager to instruct them to speak. Responding only when instructed to do so reinforces the role of the dialogue manager as a controller and reduces the activity of dialogue capture as a distraction from the deliberations among participants. It should be noted that the recorder can be a source of distraction if the recorder is not familiar with the language of the design arena and frequently misspells or misinterprets the participants' statements. For this reason, the role of the recorder is very difficult. It requires the capacity to capture the systemic essence of the meaning of a proposal by a designer. Some of the best recorders, in our experience, are people with training as generalists, such as journalists or systems thinkers. Sometimes, as discussed earlier in the case of the World Health Organization project, the person responsible for researching and producing the white paper is uniquely qualified to play the role of the recorder because of his or her familiarity with the content language of the domain.

5. The Production Manager Role

The production manager produces all of the electronic displays and hard copy documents of work products generated by the stakeholder researcher, by the participants in the design session, and by the design management team in follow-up reports. With design sessions, the production manager is producing real-time documents and is continuously updating wall displays for the participants. The role requires tight coordination with the recorder and with the dialogue manager. This individual is constantly running between printers, copiers, wall displays, tables, and computer hardware. Seamless production depends upon complete mastery of production equipment, with contingency plans in place for failure in any system. This is a no-nonsense position where the design management team fully impresses the participants with continuous evidence of the progress that the group is making. This evidence of progress is most critically important during the less familiar steps in the stages of the design session, during which participants can be at risk of feeling confused as well as exhausted. The production manager serves to remind the participants that even in the deep dark of a moonless night, they can feel the progress of the ship by the race of water against the hull.

The production manager has a key direct connection to the site logistics role within the sponsor organization. The design session site must comply with the requirements of production to ensure that work product will flow on schedule. Even the project manager cannot sign off on site logistics until the production manager has been satisfied.

6. Optional Roles

The design management team sometimes will have the opportunity to bring in assistants for the production manager (e.g., an individual to assist with updating the wall displays) and the recorder (e.g., an individual to capture text from alternating speakers). The design management team also may occasionally bring a process auditor into a design session to collect data on design metrics. In some occasions—and *only* with approval of the sponsor—the design management team may invite observers to sit with the design management team for the purposes of learning about the methodology. Assistant, auditor, and observer roles will not be represented in the scope of work statement unless they are specified to play those roles by the sponsor.

BALANCING ROLES AMONG INDIVIDUAL TEAM MEMBERS

Experienced design management team members can "cover for each other" much like a well-drilled sports team. With experience, a production manager can spot or anticipate a crisis for a recorder and take actions to neutralize the problem. A dialogue manager can introduce a pause or a break and then jump into production mode to get the team back on schedule. A recorder can use a pause in dialogue to update wall displays in support of a production manager. In a well-tuned team, no task is beneath any team member, and all team members seek to train themselves to fill in for all essential tasks should the need ever suddenly arise.

Because structured dialogic design is a well codified design management practice, opportunities exist for individuals from different SDD practice groups to share resources for special engagements needing significantly expanded design management teams. Even with a shared basic process, stepping onto a basketball court with a world-class talent challenges all practitioners to catch up to each other's game. When a design management team is being pulled together, the project manager will seek to tap the talent that is both strong in the specific key role and also versatile and able to handle unexpected contingencies.

It would probably interest some to realize that the most difficult position to fill on a high-performance design management team is the role of production manager. In large part, this is because too few individuals seek to make this role a focus of their practice—even though the steadiness of the work (production is part of all phases and stages of a design project) and the intensity of the work (production is a well-compensated part of every design session) remains the smart choice for individuals seeking to maximize their time spent in the practice of design management.

While the point is made about the value of cross-training, there is a specific instance within which we strive to isolate roles: the dialogue manager role should be distinct from the stakeholder research role. The reason for this is because we wish to be explicit in assuring all designers that the dialogue manager (who is the most visible member of the team in a design session) is indeed truly neutral with respect to design requirements. If a dialogue manager becomes extensively engaged in content discussions with some individuals in the design group, then other members of this group could perceive such familiarity as personal favoritism.

INTERNAL DISCUSSIONS IN THE DESIGN MANAGEMENT TEAM

When a project manager is pulling together a team for a major design engagement, the conversation is likely to flow something like this:

Jack: "Good news, Chris, we will be working together again in Geneva. We just got the nod to submit a contract proposal based on a preliminary scope of work for an online education design project with WXYZ."

Chris: "Great—who's on the team, and when do we travel?"

Jack: "We've got Aleco for the dialogue manager, and we're counting on you for recording. Mary is stepping forward for production."

Chris: "Wow. That's a big step up for Mary. I haven't worked with her in that role. I don't know if I'm the best one to ensure a backup for her."

Jack: "Yes. We were concerned about that, so we've got June to agree to come along and run interference for her. June trained Mary and would have been a natural here, but June can't manage the bridge with the WXYZ logistics point person."

Chris: "What do we know about that link?"

Jack: "Mary made the direct contact. She thinks the bridge will carry us. Their point person has managed a number of events using the more conventional forms of group work. Mary's concern was that WXYZ may not appreciate how hard we work our designers. They will be putty by the close of the first day, as usual. Mary says we look good to go."

Chris: "Is WXYZ going to be passing the ball back to us on the recruiting side like we saw with the folks in Ohio last year?"

Jack: "Not fair! That last-minute glitch popped up when the Ohio group's broker got the flu. Yeah, it could happen again, but not likely. I've already spoken with my counterpart on the other side of the pond. His name is Karl, and he seems really interested in discovering what we are all about. He's crystal clear that we will be offering his folks something different, and they are hungry for something new. I think he can sell the idea of coming on board. The venue is slated for a lakeside resort at the close of the fall season, so we'll have the participants all to ourselves once they arrive."

Chris: "Is the sponsor steady?"

Jack: "Yes, from what Aleco tells me. I haven't met the sponsor. Aleco says he was referred to us from the communications project that he did with the FDA two years ago. It seems the sponsor has some very close links to the back office over at the FDA, and while the technical folks there don't know quite how it happened, they say that their project has been unbelievably smooth."

Chris: "Success breeds success, eh? Count me in. Geneva in the late fall seems like a good plan. Let me know if this gets bumped, because I'm looking at a 'maybe something' with Tom down in New Bedford around that time, too."

Jack: "Okay. I'll send you a copy of the statement of work."

Chris: "Just out of curiosity, do we have a triggering question yet?"

Jack. "We're just thinking in this direction now. We have a proxy. 'What barriers will we need to address in the next five years to open up a market for a global health curriculum?' Actually, it's a bit complicated, because the sponsor needs to get a confirmation on the big picture from his partner a BlaBlaBlu media. We're in that triangle situation where our sponsor's client is our client, too."

Chris: "Sounds like that pharmaceutical company project from a decade ago! Who's doing the background research for us on this project?"

Jack: "We'll probably use Tim again if he's available. He and Gayle are working with wiki technology to enable surveys online. The direct phone calls are still most important, but Tim is now using a voice over IP system that he says will keep his costs low. He's keen on the topic, and he has a gift with words."

Chris: "Good—I'll want a draft copy of his white paper to scan for language, too. I don't want to be surprised with new terminology in the middle of a design session, and from where I'm standing, the field is continuing to bubble with new technojargon."

Jack: "I hear you. Let's connect next Thursday for an update. The statement of work should be in your e-mail already. Cheers."

WHAT HAS HAPPENED

An experienced practitioner has just been recruited into a virtual team for an international design management project within a familiar domain of practice. The newly recruited member has run through a checklist of concerns and confirmed availability. The new member will be a recorder, he and wants to have a quick doublecheck on the language in the online education and global health world that is captured by the researcher who will be doing the stakeholder analysis. The new member also wants to clarify his comfort level working with a team member who will be serving in a new role on the team. Next Thursday, he will call back after reviewing the scope of work statement for a final check-in as the project goes to contract. As he was ending the call, he asked about the status of the triggering question. In asking this, he was also asking about the status of the relationship between the sponsor and the dialogue manager. If the sponsor already had strong feelings about the specific triggering question, the results from the stakeholder analysis might generate a bit of tension. It isn't clear that this would be a problem, but in this case, the question surfaced a complexity that relates to the sponsor's challenges in representing the interests of a third party. The sponsor wants to be sure that the design project serves and pleases this third party, so in this particular case, the challenge of framing the triggering question will become a three-way negotiation of shared understanding.

THE FINAL WORD

A design management team is a precision piece of equipment that can be pulled together from varied sources when each team member has been individually certified in a specific role in a well-codified methodology.

When a design management team is pulled together, a division of labor still exists between the design management team and the sponsor organization. Coordination between the sponsor organization and the design management team becomes a shared responsibility, but the central coordinating role exists within the design management team.

Readers who reflect on the distribution of the roles we have identified in design management for complex, boundary-spanning problems may feel that a team approach is excessive. We have sought to argue that a team is needed to assemble complementary skills, and also to isolate the incompatible functions (i.e., stakeholder survey and analysis and design session dialogue management). Doubtless there will be individual design professionals who have confidence in their capacity to manage the entire process directly and independently.

As design management practitioners, we believe that all individuals are capable of managing design under some conditions, and that some designers are quite capable of managing design under some highly complex conditions, too. The challenge that a designer must master when moving from the designer role to the design manager role is to establish and convincingly communicate his or her personal neutrality in influencing the emergence of the design. By this we mean that a designer who imposes his or her individual power on a group's design through the role of design manager risks distorting the power of the group's collective wisdom. When group members in a collaborative design process sense that the design has been distorted, they lose the will to invest their resources in implementing the design.

From many years of experience with design management teams and design work in a variety of settings, we have come to the conclusion that **when the stakeholders do not fully own the problem, they do not own the design solution or the plan of action**. The implications of our design philosophy are immediately grasped and embraced by some sponsors and rejected by others.

CHAPTER 8

THE PARTICIPANTS: STAKEHOLDER IDENTIFICATION AND RECRUITMENT

"You can tell whether a man is clever by his answers. You can tell whether a man is wise by his questions."

Naguib Mahfouz
Egyptian writer and Nobel Prize winner

The dialogue management team has gathered to discuss "who's who in the zoo." This is both a playful time—because it is a time for creativity—and also a very serious time. The team knows that it may be spending several weeks struggling to get the finalized list set. The process begins with a reflection at 30,000 feet.

THE FIRST PASS

Team Leader: "Okay, here it is. We have a contract. Our sponsor, George Bennet, wants to get a community view of how the new universal health care coverage is going to ensure health and wellness in the region. He's not

The Talking Point: Creating an Environment for Exploring Complex Meaning, pages 113–120
Copyright © 2010 by Information Age Publishing

saying that he has specific doubts about what the program is likely to do, but he *is* concerned that he may not be anticipating some of the needs that slip through, and he wants to find ways to make the program as successful as possible."

Team Member 1: "So he's already thinking of patients and health care providers, right?"

Team Leader: "For sure. The primary players are always the 'usual suspects' and get considered immediately. He is thinking of hospitals, neighborhood clinics, and individual or group practices and their respective doctors, nurses, and administrative support."

Team Member 2: "And information technology folks?"

Team Leader: "He didn't mention them specifically, but I'd say—most certainly. The sponsor is concerned about the flow of medical information across care providers as a quality of care issue."

Team Member 1: "Does he have a specific demographic in mind for the patients?"

Team Leader: "This is one of the areas where our work begins. The general idea is that the universal care coverage is a safety net for the poor, although it is a program that will serve us all. Some affluent users will surely go beyond any safety net that is offered. The sponsor is not concerned about how the safety net could be better so much as he is about how much we can really hope to get done with the current plan."

Team Member 3: "Does the plan cover all kinds of clinical care? Does it cover alternative medicines? Does it include fitness centers?"

Team Leader: "This I can't answer yet. We'll have to look at the plan to see what is covered. I *am* interested in knowing how far the plan might go in supporting wellness. If we don't work on the disease prevention side of the equation, the people will continually be needing health care. I imagine that a great deal of money could be spent on some wellness care without clear payback, so I do expect that when we look into the plan we will get a clear view of who they have identified as their targets. As always, we need to think outside of the box here. There are likely to be some unrepresented voices from the community. We will have to think about how to bring such perspectives into the dialogue."

Team Member 2: "We have demographic dimensions to this, too. Do we have a handle on the organizations in the community that represent distinctly the various segments? Are there gaps?"

Team Leader: "And that's why you get your paycheck! We have to pull together a draft view, and then we'll run it by the sponsor and get advice on who we should engage in the community to help us doublecheck the list. We have been asked to check in with Vic Moro, who led the regional hospital network, and also with Val Mason, who has been leading the Healthy Cities campaign, so their thoughts will get us into motion. Take a look through the high-profile news sources, too, just to see where the media is finding the strong voices. Our first task is to generate some lists. So if everyone's got the big picture, let's get to work."

WHAT JUST HAPPENED

The project team has taken a general view of the stakeholder candidates. The sponsor of a collaborative design project is generally wise enough to appreciate that if you ask the same individuals the same questions in the same way, you are likely to end up with the answers that you already have, especially if you use conventional approaches. In a sufficiently complex situation there tend to be perspectives that happen not to have been included. At the same time, there can be pressures for some perspectives to be "overrepresented" in a design session. The project team's first goal is to concern itself with the perspectives, and not with the individuals who would speak for that specific perspective. Since a community cannot "balance" the voice of its individuals without including all individuals, a community dialogue needs to focus on balancing the perspectives. The sponsor, for example, may happen to feel that a dozen individuals in his or her organization should participate. The project team's first task is to define the range of perspectives for the sponsor so that the sponsor can appreciate the need to diversify the voices in order to include a richer range of perspectives. It would be foolish (risky at the least!) and also premature for the design management team to begin identifying individuals essential for a dialogue before they have addressed the issue of the range of perspectives that need to be included. This task typically involves looking at the community a bit differently, so the experienced—yet also not habituated—eyes of the design team add value in suggesting possible perspectives to include.

A SECOND TAKE

Team Leader: "We are making progress. We have lists of individuals and organizations from the sponsor, as well as from two individuals who have been working in the community from differing angles. We have about forty names."

Team Member 3: "And we have another twenty-three names here. I pulled these names from sources that found their way into the news over the past year-and-a-half."

Team Member 1: "I have a take on the community from Tom. He is naming organizations that he expects to be involved. He told me that he had done a scan of organizations involved in health and wellness in four related communities, and he guesses that we will have similar organizations here."

Team Leader: "That's good. We may find some of those overlooked voices that will give the group an opportunity to have some breakthroughs in how they see their situation. Let's compile the list based on organizations and the folks in the community who they serve."

Team Member 2: "I have a start on that based on the sponsor's list. He actually did make a clear effort to reach beyond his own organization with his suggested stakeholders. I have thirty-four individuals who come from twenty-eight distinct organizations, and the twenty-eight organizations are falling into fourteen types, but the list does read a bit like a catalog of clinical specialties that you'd expect to find in a hospital: emergency room, obstetrics, cardiology, internal medicine, orthopedics, oncology, and then on to practices like nutrition and physical therapy. We have the paramedics, but we didn't see anyone who was named as a physician assistant or a nurse practitioner. And we did have four individuals who were health care administrators. My guess is that we're going to have a very long list. Probably as long as the National Patient Safety Forum last year."

Team Leader: "Yes, we probably will, but let's not worry about that yet. We'll probably find that some of those health care administrators were once practicing medicine themselves, and with the depth of their experiences, perhaps some of them will be able to cover two or three of the bases for us. Let's combine the lists and then see if Tom's research identified any perspectives we don't currently have in our master list."

[a short while later]

Team Leader: "Fine, now we have a good start. I think we're going to need some expert input to confirm whether different cultural or ethnic groups in this community have different health needs and practices. We could be dealing with a lot of cultural segments. If the needs and practices differ, then their perspectives on the health coverage plan are likely to differ, too. Let's discuss this with our sponsor and community advisors. If we can't get reliable expert input, we may need to go into the community and do some survey work to confirm our understanding of the stakeholders."

Team Member 2: "Will we bring the sponsors and the advisors our raw list?"

Team Leader: "Good point. No, let's put the list into a framework first so that they can begin to help us map the stakeholder types. We are going to be challenged to bring together the broadest possible range of diverse perspectives, but we still have to stay within the sponsor's budget. We need to plan on filling thirty seats at the table. Let's map our stakeholders into a "power in the community" and "interest in the problem" matrix."

Team Member 3: "I'd guess we'll want to include the 'formal legitimacy' feature, too. I'm not saying that the ad hoc voices shouldn't be considered, just that we might be well served to agree that we recognize them as such. Some ad hoc groups are highly influential in shaping attitudes and practices in a community."

Team Leader: "I suppose you're right. While we can be entering into some emotionally deep water, you're raising a good point. I'm a bit concerned about overwhelming our sponsor and community advisors with the analysis. I'd actually like to get a handle on dormant or latent interests in the stakeholders—those parties who might become active in responding to the situation if they are brought into this discussion. We may have to tap on those windows with some interviews as we get under way."

Team Member 1: "We have a lot on our plate here. I think we should work up the stakeholders with a repertoire grid on our end of the table so that we might construct a profile of potential latent interests. Someday maybe we'll find a sponsor who can work with us directly at this level."

Team Leader: "You're too optimistic, I think. We have our hands full explaining the merits of structured dialogic design as a research and action planning tool; if you open the door to the deep methodologies of stakeholder analysis, you'll blow them away completely. I agree with you though—let's run a repertoire grid analysis internally, and let's put a Venn diagram on the table to map different groups' sense of urgency, their resource power, and their positional legitimacy as formal leaders in the community. This will provide a shared view of the lay of the land."

WHAT HAS JUST HAPPENED

The project team has decided on an approach for segmenting stakeholders into stakeholder classes. The collaborative mapping approaches are well validated in the literature, even though they are likely to be unfamiliar to the sponsors. The team leader is cautioning about getting "too technical" with the sponsors. There is a diminishing return for the cost of bringing individuals through exacting analysis of their own subjective assessments. It is practical to bring a group through an analytic process, because it will help identify mischaracterizations and reduce ambiguity around similarities and differences in stakeholder perspectives. The task will also prepare the sponsors and community advisors to recognize the essential need to bring (recruit) some additional perspectives into the dialogue as well as the need to choose sparingly from among closely related perspectives.

RECRUITING THE PARTICIPANT LIST

Team Leader: "Today we need to put names to perspectives, but first we must define the essential perspectives to bring into the dialogue. This is a difficult process, and it is also an iterative process. As we find some individuals who are unwilling or unable to participate, we'll need to go back to the drawing board and find a comparable substitute. If we leave gaps, the group design product will be incomplete. If we leave too many gaps, the product will be more than incomplete—it will be flawed. We have to do the best we can, recognizing that we can do much better than has been done before and still fail to satisfy everyone's hopes. If we cannot bring the perspectives together for the entire design process, we need to step back and acknowledge that the community is not ready to solve this problem together. Remember, we are all guided by the law of requisite variety—compromising the necessary variety of perspectives that we include in our dialogue creates the serious risk of underconceptualizing the design product."

Sponsor: "Yes, this is understood. Your team has already gone to a lot of work so far. We have a great understanding of where to find the perspectives that we need to pull together. How do we sell this to our participants?"

Team Leader: "I think that many of the participants will recognize that they have a lot that they can learn from getting together. Some participants will need to be told that this is a powerful learning opportunity. A few may feel that the group will dominate them, and they may need to be reassured that they have been invited into the discussion precisely because their voice needs to be heard more clearly within the community. We are going to have to lean on the network of trust that our community advisors have constructed. They will have to make the calls."

Advisor One: "I do know where some of the difficult sales are likely to be. Getting a commitment of a day-and-a-half for a meeting is going to sound like an invitation to a root canal for some folks."

Advisor Two: "I know that some of the parties I approach will want to send in a delegate. They could come, but they won't join the party without some high-level fan fair. It would almost take the governor himself to get them to come for the duration."

Team Leader: "It may not be such a bad idea to work with their delegate in this instance. We certainly would not do this if we were developing an action plan that would require a major commitment from an organization. In this specific case, we can work with a knowledgeable representative from the institution that needs to be heard. On the other hand, is it impossible to ask the governor to send some letter inviting participation in an event that will be coming back to his office for consideration?"

Advisor Two: "I hadn't thought about that as an option. I do think that I could get some "please participate" letters from a few of our congressional leaders—they are looking for a street-level view of health care coverage plans for discussions that are taking place at the national level. Maybe the governor would help us with the recruitment. I'm sure the mayor is on board, and our state reps will be happy to help out. Let me look into this."

Advisor One: "Tell us again, what do we say to the folks who are **not** coming to the party?"

Team Leader: "Well we should first remind them that their input has been added into the "white paper" that our team constructed through our interviews. This will let them know that they haven't been left behind. Next, you can tell them that with the space that was available, we had to make some difficult choices. Finally, you can do what many managers do—you can blame the consultants for insisting that we draw the line the way that it was drawn. You can tell them we used some powerful computer tools and that you tried hard to open the door, but that the consultants kept insisting that the bus was full. This will get them a bit angry, so you can then also invite them to be a reviewer for the finished report. We can promise that as long as they do not attack any person or organization in a way that identifies that person or organization, we will include their full comments as an appendix to the document. They will have contribute twice—once in preparation, and then once again in review. And they won't have spend a day-and-a-half getting that root canal."

Advisor One. That sounds reasonable. How will we get their response into the document?"

Team Leader: "They can e-mail their review to our team, along with the contact information for the author of the comment. Our team will confirm that the author of the document is the authentic author, and then we will append the document with the review and the author's name. We could also launch an ongoing learning community using Internet technology, if enough of the community can get online. This doesn't work so well with elderly generations, but the times are changing. You'll have to tell us if this will work for the group. We do recommend continuous online support for community groups that are going to be engaged in a series of collaborative projects over some extended period of time. For now, let's focus on the hard copy approach."

Advisor Two: "All right, then. We have a date and a location, and now we're ready to beat the drum and start the parade. We understand that if we can't get a confirmed yes, we'll go with an alternate participant, even if that alternate is from a different organization. If I can get the celebrity letters, I'll let you know. For now, we have the cover letter from your sponsor and the white paper that you prepared, so I guess it's time for us to hit the streets."

Team Leader: "The parade has already begun, then. Our project team will be on call at all times to deal with any glitches. We've discussed all the common problem areas. Once we've got the participants into the planning room, we're on solid ground for the rest of the project. Our preparation deals with all of the ambiguity. Once we're engaged in the design work, the process will pull itself forward."

THE FINAL WORD

Stakeholder mapping is a complex process, and—although rarely perfect—can be significantly improved by formal analysis. In projects that have far-reaching consequences, specific challenges relate to establishing how to bring the voices for the future generations into the dialogue. When project teams sense or confirm a gap in the composition of stakeholders, having a formal analysis can be an effective way of "selling" inclusion of additional stakeholders to the sponsors.

The stakeholder mapping that was selected by the design management team in the example presented here is not intended to represent a full consideration of mapping dimensions for stakeholder analysis. For example, mapping the extent to which a "group" is impacted by the situation, impacts the situation, or is concurrently impacted by and impacts the situation adds more complexity to the analysis. The rigorous analysis proposed by one of the team members is the appropriate approach, but a special case is likely to be required to "buy the time" that is needed to have the sponsor and his or her community experts complete the analysis. While the analysis is profound, its meaning is directly proportional to the complementary pool of knowledge that is engaged in conducting the analysis. When heavy-hitting analyses are conducted at surface level, those findings must be presented as suggestions only. The design management team is planning to use powerful methods through the application of their acknowledged limited understanding of the community to raise some suggestions that may enrich the quality of the project.

Community advisors are playing a "broker" role in this project. In other projects, specific individuals take on the broker role. There are not a lot of logistic responsibilities for a broker, but success depends on the extent to which the broker is successful in "buying time" from the participants. In some occasions, individuals who do not understand why their perspective is important may need to be offered a "stipend" to attend. In complex situations, this is not necessarily desirable, because the highest-quality participation always comes from individuals who understand why sharing their perspective is important for their own efforts.

Sometimes the design management team is asked to play the broker role. This is rarely effective. The design management team—and the lead dialogue manager in particular—needs to preserve objectivity so that during a design session, all participants will recognize that the design management team is managing the *process* only. It is critical that design managers respect the authority of the participants to own all of the *content*. If a design management team is engaged in the effort to recruit, draft, entice, or coddle any essential perspective into the design session, the design management team risks being perceived as "favoring" a specific voice in the community. If the design management team is not recognized as fully impartial at the level of personal connection to each and every participant, the entire project may be perceived as having been compromised.

CHAPTER 9

THE LEARNING ENVIRONMENT: SETTING UP A COLABORATORY

"Communities of the mind are collections of individuals who are bonded together by natural will and a set of shared ideals."

Thomas Sergiovanni
Educator

"The challenge of discovery lies not in seeking new landscapes but having new eyes."

Marcel Proust
French novelist and critic

There are two critical tasks (beyond meeting room logistics) that are prerequisites for an effective learning environment: one is orientation of the participants with respect to the subject, and the other is framing a triggering question that will guide open and focused dialogue. In the following pages, the dialogue management team is discussing a nontrivial problem that has just surfaced as they work to ready the learning environment. The invited participants are reluctant to commit the time that is needed to come together and construct their shared understanding. The reluctance does not relate

The Talking Point: Creating an Environment for Exploring Complex Meaning, pages 121–132
Copyright © 2010 by Information Age Publishing
121

specifically to their individual ability to take the time to come together, even though everyone is busy and struggling. The community of stakeholders simply lacks an understanding of the value the pending dialogue will have for them so that they can reconcile the "other" day-and-a-half event they will have to forgo when they sign up to the current event.

The dialogue management team has shared the names of the organizations that will be invited to join the event to help participants feel connected through recognizable names and feel engaged through opportunities to learn more about the challenges they share. However, there is still reluctance to commit. It is a fragile time. Even the sponsor's resolve can be shaken if the "community" hesitates. To address this challenge, the dialogue management team is considering ways to provide a prelude of the learning that will occur in the dialogue to the participants as a means of coaxing them up the ramp. The tactic involves launching preparatory research that will help link the core missions of each organization with the shared issues of the community. The rationale for this tactic is that the learning environment of the colaboratory (the forum within which the dialogue will be held) begins to emerge as soon as members of the community start to reflect and contribute from their individual perspectives.

THE TACTICAL PLAN

Team Leader: "Okay, we're having a familiar problem at this stage. How strong is the hesitation? How much coaxing can we reasonably provide?"

Team Member 2: "The community brokers for the event are well trusted by the invited participants, so we are not dealing with a question of questioned motives. The familiar problem we are seeing once again is that we are asking for a large block of time. Most of the deeply informed participants will be working on very tight daily work cycles with constant demands for their operational input. We need to build the participants' sense of value for the outcome of the dialogue. The sponsor and the community brokers are collectively suggesting that we might do this by 'hooking' the dialogue to some larger regional or national initiative."

Team Leader: "What are the prospects for doing this?"

Team Member 2: "We have included invitations to individuals who operate on the regional and national stage, but we don't yet know if there are any oars in the water from other initiatives at the moment. We are positioning our situation as being special—being a model. The brokers want to see some evidence that the model will be picked up by a 'key audience' beyond the dialogue itself so that they can cajole the full-time commitment from the invited participants. Without the evidence of a significant and imminent follow-up of some sort, the brokers don't see much leverage to get the time commitments."

Team Leader: "What do we think?"

Team Member 1: "I agree with everything that Jack has just told us. We are not yet positioned to make the appeal that the bulk of the value will have a local impact by enhancing the connectivity and coordination within the community. As we can appreciate, this value is easy to understand after the event but difficult to promise in advance."

Team Member 2: "Yes, Chris, and I would add that most of the participants routinely have been invited into 'meetings' where new information that is touted as the reason for the gathering has far less value than the freeform networking that gets done in the half-hour of open time before or after the main event. The community doesn't have a good mental model for dialogue in a large forum as a means of providing genuinely valuable outcomes. They expect the experience to be as dull as watching C-SPAN or position statements read by national legislators. Who wants a day and a half of that?"

Team Leader: "Okay, so we give them real value up front. What approach would you like to try? Tim, what's your take on this?"

Team Member 3: "In light of the scope of the dialogue, I suspect that interviewing representative stakeholders to collect a range of issues might be a bit overwhelming. It seems like the invited participants are focused on putting out fires in their own organizations and may not be particularly receptive to exploring fires that are raging nearby—even if the wind is blowing in their direction. Gathering a preliminary view of the scope of issues and sharing this with invited participants can help them understand the need to come together to construct a central view of their situation—if the group actually will read through a brief white paper. I do agree that we need something, but I'm not sure that this is information that this particular audience is craving just now."

Team Leader: "Yes, but we do need to serve the community by ensuring that it gets what it needs, not only what it initially thinks it wants. What do the brokers think about a survey? Do we have any ideas for modifying our survey for this specific community?"

Team Member 2: "The brokers are in unfamiliar territory with this approach to planning. They can't strongly sell the methodology, because they haven't yet experienced it themselves. The sponsor doesn't have much leverage with the community. Everything must be done by coaxing. Still, I do think that the brokers might underappreciate the opportunity of selling the value of looking internally within the community more than looking externally for outside followers. Part of this thinking may very well have been driven by the initial positioning of the event as a response to a national call for community input. My view is that the local participants will respond primarily because they have come to see a locally valuable payoff."

Team Member 1: "If we want to take a page from community organization approaches, we could work with Jim Capraro's model at the Greater

Southwest Development Corporation in Chicago. Jim engages the community by providing SWOT (strength–weakness–opportunity–threat) analyses as a means of demonstrating that his initiatives are all about creating value for participants. Commercial organizations call this "touching the customer" and count the touches needed to convert to a sale. We would be counting the contacts until we get a commitment to participate."

Team Leader: "Sure, but we can't control our costs if we take on the role that brokers typically play in community dialogue. When brokers are struggling to recruit the participants, we are actually able to be only a backup resource for them. If we provide SWOT analysis for all invited participants— and do this well, of course—we will be contributing a lot of value, but we will lose our shirts. Isn't there something else that we can provide this community of stakeholders that will light the fuse on the learning that we will be building when we have the dialogue?"

Team Member 3: "Well, actually, let's ask them if they already know each other."

Team Member 2: "Okay, Tim, this time you're really going to have to explain what you have in mind. It seems odd that they would not know each other."

Team Member 3: "Yes, but I mean *really* know each other, not just know *of* each other. Look, we all fully appreciate that dialogue can lead to social capital creation, right? We know that we're pulling folks together from across a very broad range of perspectives. We know that the health sector and the wellness sectors are almost independent—though complementary—ways of approaching the world. I think that we will find that many folks do *not* have a personal contact in many of the organizations we are inviting to the dialogue. One immediate outcome is that everyone will have at least one personal contact in each of the organizations that participates. We can predict that we will have a huge impact on social capital formation. Getting the contact data up front is a fundamental part of a research study, but in this case it is also a means to help each individual participant recognize how disconnected he or she currently may be. If they recognize the extent to which they are disconnected, they may have a clearer way to value what becoming connected may mean to their own operations. I suspect that they will come to view the dialogue as a team-building investment on an expansive scale."

Team Leader: "Interesting. The action research approach does have its appeal. It isn't without its costs, though. You'd have to think through the logistics to control time and effort for our team as well as for each of the invitees that you interview. Also, when you're talking to the invitees, you're going to get asked to explain the community dialogue. Let's grab a cup of coffee. We have some work to do on the evolution of our triggering questions. We may be here for a while yet."

WHAT HAS JUST HAPPENED

The first lesson that a community needs to learn is why it needs to learn together. In organizations where a CEO or a charismatic leader can "compel" a community to gather for an extended dialogue, brokers can extend "invitations" (which may have the power of a summons) and forgo the effort of building the participants' will to invest their own time in a community learning dialogue. In the situation described above, invited participants are asked to make a *significant* investment of time in a process that is difficult for them to value at the onset. If a design management team makes the claim that it is providing a powerful learning and problem solving capacity, that team may need to provide a sample of the quality of learning that it will cultivate. A generic approach is to gather up diverse ideas from a community and then present those ideas back to the community to highlight the scope of the learning opportunity. This is by no means a simple task. Some members of a community will want to see the "data" summarized. While one could identify the central ideas and, conversely, the fringe ideas, this risks prejudicing the community against the fringe ideas and biasing them toward the central ideas. Individuals who hold marginal viewpoints may feel that the community has already decided what it wants and may not feel that it is worth spending time and effort to argue for the marginal perspective. For this reason, two strong rules should apply for all preliminary surveys in advance of a community dialogue: (1) do not do statistical analysis of dominant perspectives; establish a level playing field for introducing a diverse array of ideas; and (2) do not attribute; the identity (and political power that is potentially associated with that identity) of any invitee should not add to nor detract from the merits of his or her expression itself.

In this particular situation, the dialogue management team has linked a means of creating a reflective awareness of interinstitutional connections as one significant anticipated outcome of the community dialogue. The dialogue management team will ask brokers to contact invited participants so that the participants will not be surprised when they get a call requesting a half-hour for an interview. The participants will be promised a summary of the interview in exchange for the time needed to participate in the survey. During the survey, the researchers on the dialogue management team will also answer questions about the forthcoming community dialogue. The invitation itself will remain as a contact from the broker. The design management team will step forward into the community to assist the broker by engaging community interests in an innovative learning opportunity. Most leaders will not want to be among the last to learn a lesson that is coming into the community, so the prospects for successful engagement through this mechanism are strong in this instance.

REVISITING THE TRIGGERING QUESTION

The Design Management Team began discussion of the triggering question with sponsors. The process is iterative, because the triggering question will focus the dialogue on the goals of the community and within the time-frame that the community needs in order to act upon the deliberations that are shared. It is not uncommon for sponsors to have multiple goals, nor for goals to shift in priority. The design management team challenges the thinking of the sponsors by reminding them of opportunities to extend the dialogue to be more inclusive of diverse perspectives.

Team Leader: "Let's review briefly. Six weeks ago, we received a phone call [see *Chapter 6*] and were asked to become involved in a design project. Peter Roberts, our friend from the World Health Organization project, told us that his friend George Bennet was, as Peter put it, 'heading into deep water.' Peter has been hoping that we might offer a 'simulation' for his partner and a group of associates, and we explained the shortfalls in attempts to convey an understanding how the technology works through a simulation. I mean, it's like trying to demonstrate a parachute by pulling the cord when we jump off a chair. When you don't need to manage a lot of complexity, it is a waste of everyone's energies to make a show of using the heavy artillery. In the end, Peter arranged for us to talk through the situation with his partner, George, over lunch. George was initially refer-ring to his stakeholders as the 'partners' forum,' and the problem was that the group wasn't able to come to a strongly shared understanding of what they were dealing with—and they didn't have the time to continue cycles of unproductive talk. We agreed to do some background work and launch with a white paper, so our discussion of a survey of the social network con-nections in the sector is consistent with the prep work we have agreed to take on. We explored the goals that the sponsor wanted to achieve [see *Chapter 7*], and last month [see *Chapter 8*], as we began the stakeholder assessment for the sector, we recognized that the sponsor had under-estimated some of the stakeholders who can help his group more fully understand the challenge. If you recall, Jack and Peter had felt that the group would be responding to something like, 'What barriers will we need to address in the next five years to open up a market for a global health curriculum?' And, Tim, you may recall that we brought you in because we were thinking that we might need some telephone interviews with some partners in the pharmacy or the pharmaceutical sector. Now, up to this point, we haven't tested the proposed triggering question with any of the stakeholders, and it may be that we now have a different goal to address given that the dialogue will be bringing in patients as well as community service groups. What had looked like an issue of cost and health care now involves a larger picture of health and wellness assurance. Does this bring us all up to date?"

Team Member 1: "In a nutshell, yes. The sponsor was trying to simplify the situation to talk about it in a simple way, but he kept running into a wall, because the situation simply wasn't as simple as he was hoping it would be."

Team Leader: "Yes, but remember that no one still fully knows just how complex the situation is. The stakeholders will determine this. What we know with certainty is that significant gaps exist in understanding the problem and finding a solution, which requires adding some missing voices, and, as is typical, once we named missing voices, the sponsor has had no problem agreeing with our findings. The goal of seeking to be inclusive is to break the habit of looking at the world only through familiar boundaries that could limit everyone's vision."

Team Member 3: "What is the most current iteration of the probable triggering question just now?"

Team Leader: "The sponsor is now less certain than he was three weeks ago, but we feel it will be related to identifying barriers to ensuring health and wellness in the immediate region as we increasingly rely on a uniform state health insurance plan. Peter has engaged Carolyn Smith as a cosponsor with the expanded set of stakeholders, and Carolyn has agreed to be the individual who will actually present the triggering question to the group, so we have settled some parts of the task. The intended action that will result for the dialogue seems to be solidifying, and the wording of the question still needs work."

Team Member 3: "This task is still new to me. What should we be keeping in mind as we frame a triggering question?"

Team Leader: "Well, to answer your question, Tim, let me tell you a bit about a recent engagement in the education sector. This is an interesting story, if you will indulge me, because we were preparing a triggering question for high school dropout students in the state of Wisconsin. We needed to concurrently consider conceptual complexity, linguistic clarity, and cultural acceptability. We need to address all three of these dimensions of the triggering question in the current project so that story is relevant."

Team Leader: "Let's begin.

"A major Community College was sponsoring a project designed to get an understanding of a student perspective on the drivers of high school dropout in a region encompassing a three-county area. Naturally, we needed to frame a triggering question. The project included the dialogue management team and a steering committee that was organized by the sponsor. The steering committee provided a sounding board for refining the triggering question much as any sponsor discussion will. The goals of this particular project unfolded as the triggering question took shape through some e-mail exchanges and postings on a wiki that we had put in place to support the dialogue management team. I recall one interesting e-mail 'thought sharing' exchange that I had with a teacher on the dialogue management team named Maria. Maria said: 'I am "thinking out loud" as I read the attachments you sent, and hope you will be open to my thought sharing! In all of our communications regarding the high school dropout rate reduction project in the steering team, the use of FaceBook and My Space with students, and the structured dialogic design process, the theme of "dropping out" permeates our language. Based on my past experiences, I have noticed that when we think about a problem in "the negative," the solution becomes more puzzling and evasive. This contrasts with the smooth results I have experienced when thinking about a problem within a "positive" framework. Even though the problem remains the same, using language that anticipates a positive outcome improves the process! This brings me to consider the opportunity to get our collective consciousness looking beyond the dropout rate problem. Rather than asking about ways to the "reduce the drop out rate," we might be better off asking for ways to "increase the high school graduation rate."'

"As you might appreciate, Maria was looking back at the framing of the triggering question from the preconceived 'solution' space. This is not unusual in itself. Good intentions lead us to anticipate what a solution might look like and to then coax the dialogue toward that end. Unfortunately, good intentions can preempt alternative solutions. What if students are really saying that the graduating itself is not enough to represent a real solution for them? This is not an easy situation to discuss, and it can be even more complex when we are using e-mail or wiki technology. I recall that I replied to Maria along the lines of, 'Maria, the way we define a problem is by focusing on the gap (or dissonance) between what "ought to be" and "what currently is." We begin with recognizing that the "ought" is graduation from school and the "is" is dropping out of school. The triggering question will need to make a clear distinction between the definition of the problem and the design of a solution. We believe that the stakeholders, in this case the students at "risk of dropping out," are the best people to define the problem. They might need help from other stakeholders to design the solution. We might therefore expand the community of stakeholders when we transition from the problem space to the solution space. At this point, we need to immerse ourselves in the challenge to fully discover from the students why they are at risk of dropping out of school. Please, let's plan to discuss this question at the training session next week. Let's also post it in the LCC community of learning wiki, and I will respond to the question once you post it so we can bring the rest of our colleagues into this very important, but also very subtle, discussion.'

"If you're following this, Tim, I moved the discussion onto the wiki so that we could share an understanding in some of the considerations as well as any prototype for the triggering question. We are dealing with issues of scope, vocabulary, and tone as well as general strategic intention. On the wiki, I summarized my initial response to Maria and then proposed that the triggering question for the students might be, 'What factors cause you to think about dropping out of school?' I then asked all of the dialogue management team on the wiki what they thought about the question. Penny, another member of the team, provided an answer along the lines of, 'I think that triggering question is wonderful, especially considering who our target audience is. Do we know if the target audience is going to be only students who are "at risk" for dropping out? If not, we may wish to further define the question just a bit, for example: "What factors or situations cause you to consider dropping out of school?" Looking forward to working with you next week! – Penny'

"I liked Penny's suggestion, and I replied to the group, saying that I liked it and proposed that we plan to discuss this variant of the triggering question when we meet along with the members of the steering committee. As planned at the time, students were the only participants. Observers would include members of our design management team and maybe some members of the steering committee, and observers would not be responding to or shaping any responses to the triggering question. I advised the dialogue management team to check in again with our team member who was playing the broker role (with the task of recruiting all participants into the dialogue forum) to provide the team with more details about the composition of the stakeholders participating in the dialogue. Even a subtle change in stakeholder composition, of course, can necessitate revising the structure of the triggering question. I was concerned that our broker may not have the names of all the participants so that they could join the MySpace site for some preparatory conversations. Our broker responded, 'Everest High School is still in the process of obtaining signed parental authorizations. We will be able to work with the students after this has been completed. It is anticipated that the needed legal paperwork will be in order so that we may proceed as planned on Friday!'

"And at this point Maria raised a critical point: 'These are not students who have dropped out of school! They are students who are struggling with their classes and have been identified by their teachers as being "at risk" for dropping out. They also may be defensive because of being viewed as "at risk" for dropping out. We need to find out more about them once the group has been identified. For the triggering question, maybe we should consider asking, "What stands between yourself and doing well in your studies?" or "What do you think are the obstacles to success in school?" The triggering question is very important. Input from the steering committee and discussions within our group will both be helpful in determining a strategic question!'

"Through the wiki, I thanked the group, and reminded them that Maria was absolutely correct. The framing of the right triggering question is the most challenging task of the structured dialogic design approach—and the discussion that we were having was proving that very point. Even though this point is raised in all training sessions with new dialogue management teams, the point is difficult to internalize without an experience of the challenge."

Team Member 3: "I can see that! So were there additional problems when you brought the triggering question to the steering committee?"

Team Leader: "Yes, there were. Within the dialogue management team, we came to favor the question, 'What do you think are the obstacles to success in Everest High School?' With the steering committee, we considered five triggering question variants, substituting "not doing well" for "dropping out," or "thinking of dropping out," as well as "obstacles for success." Actually, I was surprised when we ended up spending most of our meeting concerned about geography. We considered whether we wanted to gather school-specific data or whether we were critically interested in regional solutions, rather than in approaching each high school separately. After considering this goal, we realized that the phrasing of triggering question would not impact the outcome, because the students themselves would have experience that was limited to a specific school. The discussion did span all of the goals behind the reduction of the dropout rate initiative, including stakeholder profiles for both problem identification and solution design, resources available for replicating the student engagement in other schools, possibilities that some of these students may have had experiences in multiple schools, and plans for measuring the difference in the dropout rate for a cohort of students in four or five years. In effect, all of the goals of a project need to be looked at through the lens of the triggering question. If the triggering question impacts a goal, this has to be taken into consideration. The challenge is that sometimes there are latent goals that the sponsor may not have fully articulated earlier in the process. This can get tricky. In the end, we converged on, 'What do you think are the reasons for seriously thinking about dropping out of high school?' I think you get the picture, don't you?"

Team Member 3: "Got it. So how are we doing in our project?"

Team Leader: "It takes collective agreement to be certain. Jack and Peter have suggested, 'What barriers will we need to address in the next five years to open up a market for a global health curriculum?' I have an uneasy feeling that one of the goals that will crystallize on the design table is a goal to specifically link health and wellness in the effort. My intuition tells me that we need to name these two different aspects of the stakeholder group so that we honor them and legitimize their differences. In preparation, the survey that we discussed can help us all out. Based on my understanding of the sponsor's intentions, as the stakeholders identify links and gaps in their interconnections, they will develop a sharper perception of the artificial boundary that separates health and wellness. Addressing the boundary may surface as a major goal leading up to the overarching project goal. So we still have a ways to go, and I suggest that you keep an open mind.

We have—on several occasions—revised a triggering question even as we presented it to a group. When we are working with complex stakeholder assemblies, sometimes we cannot fully anticipate the source of potential dissonance with the question. We want to be confident that we are at least 95% certain of the wording. What we do *not* want to happen is to put the sponsor in a group authorship situation that involves more than a tiny tweak to the final phrasing."

WHAT HAS JUST HAPPENED

The dialogue management team is working to anticipate issues of scope, vocabulary, and tone as well as general strategic intention in a triggering question. The triggering question will both open a subject area for collective input and also focus the group on a specific output. The question needs to align with all of the project goals, engage and honor the participants, and remain clear and concise enough to easily guide the dialogue.

THE FINAL WORD

A learning environment needs both background context and a specific learning mission. Ultimately, the participants will bring together all the essential background information based on their diverse professional and life experiences. In some instances, the scope of the dialogue needs to be illustrated in advance of the gathering to build political will for attending the dialogue. This is true even if an authority may "compel" attendance, because dialogue will move most freely when all participants anticipate genuine value through a group learning opportunity. There are a variety of ways to capture a flavor for the subject matter that a group will engage. Traditions of providing documents to read in advance of a meeting are beginning to yield to newer traditions of providing a dialogue brief or "white paper"—or perhaps a converging perspective through some complementary group process or an audiovisual experience. The point is that sometimes groups will need support in making a commitment to willingly give a large block of time to be part of an unfamiliar dialogue process. In practice, individuals who have attended one structured dialogue design event are receptive to a future event. This receptive perspective is driven by the value that is created through collaborative learning. When invited to discuss a specific topic, the most typical first response is, "Who else will be participating?"

Once a dialogue management team has secured a commitment to participate, the opportunity then critically depends upon maintaining the flow and the focus of the dialogue. The triggering question plays a critical role in this task. The use of a triggering question is not unique to structured dialogic design. What is different about structured dialogic design is that one single triggering question is used uniformly throughout the dialogue. This places a burden on the design team to "get it right." Skill for doing this is honed through years of experience in the use of the process. Dialogue managers adopting the methodology will find strong support for hints at guiding the evolution of the triggering questions through the professional support group for structured dialogic design of the Institute for 21st Century Agoras.

CHAPTER 10

THE WORK: AGENDA AND ACTIVITIES

"When we try to pick out anything by itself, we find it hitched to everything else in the Universe."

John Muir
Founder of the Sierra Club

Most informed participants in a large-scale group design process approach the event with the giddiness of a school field trip or the dread of facing a protracted tax audit. Experience leaves little middle ground. Participants expect a lot of social interaction, a lot of information overload, or both. As individuals converge for a structured dialogic design session, they are certain to find some things that will look familiar to them. As the session gets under way, the participants are certain to recognize that they are going to be part of a new approach to building understandings of their problem situation and agreeing upon solutions. The dialogue management team works closely to manage the check-in process.

ENTERING THE ROOM

Team Leader (who also will be the dialogue manager in this particular structured dialogic design session): "The participants will be arriving very

The Talking Point: Creating an Environment for Exploring Complex Meaning, pages 133–176
133

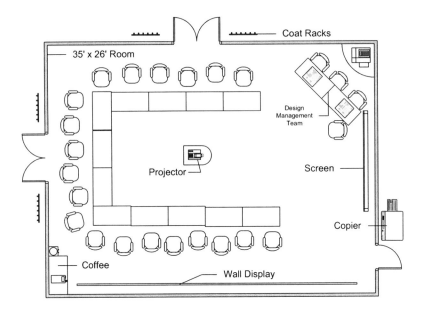

soon now. We need another three chairs at the rear of the table. The flip chart is fine. Our projector is running now, right?"

Team Member 1: "Yes, the systems are up and the participant name cards are in place. The hotel staff has given us the green light to use the walls for posting the ideas of the group and to access the copy machine for the work products we will be printing out. I'm confident they understand how critical this is for us. We are still setting up the workbooks. The room's floor plan needed to be updated to reflect what we have here today. We put an "observers' table" in the rear of the room in the event that any of the participants happen to bring along someone else from their organization today.

Team Leader: "Fine—the layout is for sixteen small groups of three participants each (triads), which isn't exactly what we are doing here, but the location on the design management team in the front of the room is accurate. Please make sure that this updated map gets into the participants' workbooks right away. Is the coffee here yet?"

Team Member 2: "Yes, the hotel guest coordinator will be coming in shortly, and she will welcome the group and remind folks about parking validation, and restrooms, and a few other features of the lobby. We had the typical give-and-take with the hotel folks about our need for these specific comfortable and rotating chairs at the table. They always want to put a dinner chair at the table, because they don't know how forty-eight participants sitting together for six hours creates a physical drain on folks."

Team Leader: "I know. Most hotel folks, and even many sponsors, think that we are going over the top when we worry about the physical comfort of the participants. They simply have no idea how hard it is to make contributions and draw distinctions, as well as to make decisions about relationships for extended spans of time. They think that a design session is a passive sport. Okay, I see we now have some folks arriving. Make sure that they find their way to their triads. There is a tendency for folks to rearrange things when they first arrive. I'll bring them up to speed when we introduce the agenda. Just help them settle in and get comfortable."

What Has Happened

The design management team has been working with the hotel staff for the past twenty-four hours to make sure that participants will have a room with enough wall space to display work products, enough table space so that no one will feel crowded, enough temperature control and lighting control and sound control so that participants will not be distracted, and enough physical comfort in the form of the chairs at the table and water glasses and hard candy on the table. Each participant has a nametag at the place he or she will be sitting. The design management team has meticulously considered seating to maximize the spatial distribution of different perspectives—so that the dialogue would be unlikely to represent folks on two sides of the room aggregated in differing points of view. The spatial dispersion is also a means of limiting distracting side conversations that are difficult to control when individuals who work together are seated next to each other. The setup also makes it explicitly clear that "observers" have roles that are distinct from the specifically invited design participants. While "observers" can be accommodated in a structured dialogic design session, it is generally desirable to make explicit their role, only because it can be distracting to the participants. The participants will be interacting intensely with each other—not as a "team," because the structured dialogic design process does not require team construction—but rather as a cohesive group. It is for this reason that structured dialogic design can forgo team-building exercises. Traditional team dynamics are not required for the purposes of collaborative design.

The dynamics of sustaining high performance in a cohesive group are slightly different from the dynamics that underlie interactions in established or newly formed teams. In structured dialogic design, group members will remain functional as individuals. Their bond to other individuals within the group will emerge around common commitment to an emerging understanding or to a collaboratively developed action plan. Teams build up their commitments to shared membership in an organization or to personal commitment to each other as part of a collective enterprise. Structured dialogic design is able to build strong social contracts in the absence of a strong overarching institution, organization, or enterprise because of the commitment that each individual participant adds to the shared understanding that cements them into a social contract that spans institutional boundaries.

The design management team's attention to providing workbooks that included information about the design methodology, the design event, the participants, the design management team, and even the layout of the room was just another part of ensuring participants that everyone has access to the same information. As the work session progresses, all participants will receive real-time copies of their work product that they will compile into their notebooks, so that at the end of the session everyone will be able to leave with "the complete story" in his or her hands in its authentic form. In this project, the real-time delivery of work products is relying on copy services of the hotel, so the design management team has concluded the last minute check-in with their hotel's office service unit to be sure that all systems are ready.

COMMITTING TO THE AGENDA

Dialogue Manager: "Ladies and gentlemen, welcome: my name is Alexander Christakis, and you will hear more about me and from me in just a moment, but I want to get us started by introducing you to your host and sponsor, Mrs. Smith. She will remind us why we have gathered here today, and then we will begin."

Mrs. Smith: "Thank you, Aleco. Greetings, everyone. Thank you all for coming. As you know, we have struggled with a huge challenge for several years now—and for some of us, this struggle reaches back even further. We have been working on various aspects of a problem that we all know is a shared problem. Our individual efforts have sometimes brought about a measure of success, but we all sense that we are not going to make real progress without understanding how to solve this thing together. For this reason, we have decided that we need to take a fresh approach, and in doing this, we are also using a design method that few of us have even heard of before. We will hear about the 'how' of everything from Aleco. I am here to tell you that your work for the nine hours that we will spend together in this room is of critical importance to all. This is why we have asked that you plan to commit to spending this full span of time here together. I am supposed to remind you, too, that this means no cell phones today. I am very excited about this project and I will be eagerly awaiting to see your work and to listen to your reflections. I will turn this back to Aleco now, and once again say that this is the way that we can begin to change the world."

Dialogue Manager: "Thank you, Mrs. Smith. Let me take just one short moment to allow Ms. Corey of the hotel staff comment on the facilities, and then we will begin."

	Day 1
9:00–9:15	Welcome
	Overview of the agenda
9:15–9:30	Introduce and explain the triggering question for our design work
	Individually generate lists of **key** ideas that we must address in responding to our triggering question
9:30–10:30	Post **labels** for our individual ideas
10:30–12:30	Clarify the **meaning** behind the labels of our ideas
12:30–1:30	Lunch
1:30–2:30	Continue to clarify the **meaning** behind the labels of our ideas
2:30–2:45	Break
2:45–4:30	Cluster our ideas into groups of related ideas
4:30–4:45	Break
4:45–5:00	Individually vote for our most preferred ideas in response to our triggering question
5:00	Adjourn
	Day 2
8:30–10:30	Structure the influence among our preferred ideas
10:30–11:00	Review the structure of influence among our preferred ideas
11:00–11:30	Augment/amend the structure of influence among preferred ideas
11:30–12:00	Report narrative summaries of our shared understanding
12:00	Close

[The hotel guest coordinator highlights the amenities of the building and offers recommendations for making dinner arrangements after the close of the first day's work.]

Dialogue Manager: "Thank you, Ms. Corey. Now, if I may have your attention, we will review our working agenda for the next day-and-a-half. On this flip chart, you will see an agenda for our group work. We will work through each of these steps of the agenda, and we will allow frequent breaks as we move through these tasks."

Dialogue Manager: "We are going to begin with an introduction of our triggering question by Mrs. Smith, and we will use this question to help us remain focused on our design objective. This triggering question has been framed with input from sponsors in all three of the sectors who have come here together to help us develop a shared understanding. We have input from government offices, nonprofit service and education organizations, and corporate partners. Mrs. Smith will explain the question, and we will have the opportunity to ask for clarifications so that we are all sure we understand what we need to do together in this design project. Is this clear?"

[The participants signal that they understand. The team leader puts a check on the task on the agenda.]

Dialogue Manager: "Next we will provide you with cards for gathering your thoughts on key issues that we need to keep in mind. Last week we had circulated copies of a white paper to you that provides an overview of the range of questions that members of the community have felt are relevant to consider. You will find a copy of that document in your notebook for future reference, but we are asking you to speak from your own perspective when you list your key issues. We will provide you with details about this task as we go forward. Is the nature of the task clear?"

[The participants signal that they understand. The team leader puts a check on the task on the agenda.]

Dialogue Manager: "Once you have your list, we are going to ask you to come up with a brief label for each idea, and we will then collect the labels using computer software. We will print and post the labels on the wall here at my left. This will give us a continuous view of what we are going to be dealing with. We will not clarify the meaning of the ideas at this point. We will go around the room taking one idea at a time until we have all the ideas up on the wall. I will be repeating your words as we enter your labels into a record that we will be giving to you. Do we understand what will be happening as we collect up your labels?"

A Participant: "What if we happen to name the same ideas?"

Dialogue Manager: "Yes—that is a good question. If you feel confident that the label that you hear is certain to express the same idea you have, then choose a different idea from your list when it is your turn to give your label. If you have any doubt, then keep your idea and give us its label. We can confirm distinctions among labels when we clarify meaning in the next step in the agenda. We will go around the table again and again until we have all of the ideas, and as we collect the ideas some ideas may cause you to think of other ideas. You may update your list, but please do write down the idea and provide a concise label for that idea. This can help us get a rich set of important ideas with reduced probability of overlap from the outset. Are we clear on this step?"

[The participants agree. The team leader puts a check on the task on the agenda.]

Dialogue Manager: "We will spend a considerable amount of time clarifying meaning, because if we do not clearly understand each other, we cannot get anywhere. We will clarify meaning for each label and will capture that clarification into notes that we will provide for you at the end of this task. During this step of the process, it is important that we *understand* each other even if we do not *agree* with each other. Agreeing and disagreeing are managed through a voting process that comes later in the design program. We are going to have lunch midway through the clarifications, so we will return to this activity after lunch. Is this clear?"

[All agree. The team leader puts a check on the task on the agenda.]

Dialogue Manager: "Once we have clarified the meaning behind the ideas, we will then sort the ideas into groups based on the similarity between ideas. This task is frequently more difficult than it sounds, because some ideas may belong in multiple groups, and some additional meaning behind ideas may also surface at this stage. We will get a stronger understanding of our ideas once we have completed this task, and our team will work to make this process as smooth and as pleasant as possible for you. Do you understand that we will be sorting the ideas into clusters?"

[No questions. The team leader puts a check on the task on the agenda.]

Dialogue Manager: "Once we have put ideas into groups, we are going to vote for the ideas that we feel are of the very most importance for all to keep in mind as we work together to resolve the challenge ahead. Voting will be done by adhesive dots: we will pass out the dots and have you attach your votes to the labels that we will have posted to the walls. Is this clear?"

A Participant: "How many votes to do we get?"

Dialogue Manager: "We will get into the mechanics of the voting process when we get to this task. Before we begin our work today, what we need to understand is the sequence of activities that we will be doing and the time when we will be doing them. There are questions about process that will certainly arise during this design program, but we ask you all to please hold process questions for individual discussion during breaks or at the close of the program. We are happy to address all of your questions, but we don't want to take up time right now with process questions. Right now, we're simply agreeing that we understand the nature of the tasks that we will be doing at this time. Do we understand that we will be voting on our most preferred ideas after we have sorted ideas into groups?"

[The group agrees. The team leader puts a check on the task on the agenda.]

Dialogue Manager: "After we have a collective list of our most preferred ideas, we will break for the evening. You will probably be exhausted. Take the rest of the evening off. You'll deserve it. When we return tomorrow morning, we will begin to explore and map the connections among the ideas. You have heard the expression 'connecting the dots.' It is a very popular expression these days, because people are beginning to realize that we are dealing with systems of ideas. Although it is a popular thing to do, it is not easy to do without some help, especially if we are going to do it as a group. I am not going to describe how this is done now. It is important that you understand that we will specifically examine how our important ideas connect to each other so that we have a 'systems view' of our challenge. You will create this view through your pairwise decisions by focusing on two ideas at a time, and we will track your decisions and illustrate your decisions in the form of an influence map. Do you understand that you will be asked to make decisions together about influences among ideas that you agree are of central importance to keep in mind as we address our challenge?"

[The group murmurs its agreement. The team leader puts a check on the task on the agenda.]

Dialogue Manager: "All right. I recognize that this task is much less familiar than the other tasks that we will be doing. Let me add that we will be using software to present you with a series of questions and that each question will ask you to make a decision between two—and only two ideas—at a time. After you have made that decision, we will track your response, and you will make another decision for another pair of ideas. Some of the decisions will seem strange to you, and—because a computer is prompting you with decisions that you have not yet made—some of the decisions that you are asked to make may seem a bit silly. The point of this task is that you will be 'connecting the dots' by explicitly agreeing upon the influence relationship where you see strong influence. Does this help? Do you understand this task?"

[The participants agree. The team leader puts a check on the task on the agenda.]

Dialogue Manager: "Once we have gathered your decisions, we will provide you with a structure that will show you how you collectively understand the ideas to be connected. We will explore this structure together and determine whether it is a good representation of your collective view. We will follow this task with an opportunity to amend or enhance the structure with additional ideas from your collection of preferred ideas. And we will follow this task with some work translating the structure into narrative form. You will have opportunities to use the map to explain where the strong influence acts upon the most central ideas related to our shared challenge. Do we understand this set of three tasks?"

A Participant: "What if we get a new idea that we think is really powerful at this stage?"

Dialogue Manager: "Sometimes participants do identify some profound new ideas as a result of examining a systems view of their situation. If this is the case, we can introduce a new idea, clarify that idea, and map that idea into the structure. This is a very powerful and flexible process. Because the world changes around us, the process that we are using is ideally suited to easy revision through deletion or inclusion of new ideas. We can discuss this in terms of how the process works at the close of the session. At this point, it is helpful to recognize that our work will not prevent us from working with what we discover along the way. Do we all understand that we will be making a structure, reviewing that structure, and converting the structure into narrative accounts of our challenge? Do you also understand that we are espousing and promoting learning and flexibility of thought and of structure?"

[The participants agree. The dialogue manager puts a check on the task on the agenda.]

Dialogue Manager: "Excellent. We have just completed our first task."

[The dialogue manager puts a huge blue check mark on the agenda next to the line

item that reads "Welcome/Overview of the agenda" and moves the flip chart with the agenda about four feet toward the wall, where it still remains in prominent sight.]

What Has Happened

The dialogue manager has just taken the group through a critical passage. A contract has been sealed. The group has collectively agreed that they understand what they will be doing. The contract will remain visible in the room throughout the design session. This is important because as a design process gets under way, some participants may want to take some "shortcuts" and may push for a change in the agenda. This is particularly true with groups that are confronted with an unfamiliar and exacting design process. The contract is the dialogue manager's tool to remind the group that for this project, we will stick to the existing approach and that in future work, there may be opportunities to work with teams that use different approaches. The agenda gives the group a general idea of what is going to be done and how long tasks are going to take—and the group implicitly understands that if members choose to step out of the process, they risk missing the progress that the group will make. The importance that is attached by the dialogue manager to the review of the agenda also signals the need to start on time so that the group will use the full power of the group work to its best advantage.

Presenting an agenda is not intended to be without fun. Humor is important, and icebreaking activities can be added to help groups get comfortable with each other. Typically each participant will introduce themselves to the group so that the group hears each person's voice. Introductions can also be combined with the first time that a participant is called upon to speak. For example, when idea labels are being collected, a participant may be asked to first give his or her name and add a comment about his or her connection to the subject. There are many ways to introduce an agenda—and there are just as many ways to be playful and rigorous at the same time. The agenda remains highly visible in the room, both to help the group chart its progress through its work and also to remind the group that that group is committed to work within the process of the structured dialogic design approach.

EXPLAINING THE TRIGGERING QUESTION

Dialogue Manager: "Mrs. Smith, will you please present and explain the triggering question to the group at this time?"

Mrs. Smith: "Gladly. Our triggering question is, 'What issues must we anticipate in our hopes to ensure health and wellness in our region in the next five years under the newly approved universal health coverage plan?'"

[As Mrs. Smith reads the triggering question, it is concurrently displayed on the projection screen in the room, and paper printouts of the question are attached high on the walls on both the left and the right side of the room by the members of the design management team.]

Mrs. Smith: "Jack Roberts, Eva Jones, Elly Sousa, and I spent about a week with the design management team framing this question. We were really challenged to focus our question in a way that would be most certain to get us the type of information that we can put to effective use."

Dialogue Manager: "Thank you, Mrs. Smith. Are there any questions for Mrs. Smith about the meaning of this triggering question?"

A Participant: "Why five years? We need to take some actions right away."

Mrs. Smith: "We discussed the idea of timeframe and agreed that there were certainly some ideas that we could put to use directly; at the same time, we felt that if we were planning ten years down the road, we might have too many unknowns emerging in that timeframe, based upon our experience. So when we say the next five years, this means that we want to act on this with things that can have some effect in the next five years, including things that we could do immediately. What are the barriers or the opportunities that we will need to consider to make real progress in the next five years?"

Dialogue Manager: "Any more questions?" *[The dialogue manager takes a long, slow look around the room.]* "Okay—if there are no mo questions about the triggering question, let's begin." *[The dialogue manager walks over the flip chart and puts another huge blue check mark next to the item that reads "Introduce and explain the triggering question for our design work."]* There! We're making great progress already!"

What Has Happened

The design management team has explicitly stepped out of the "content" area of the design program. The "context" for generating "content" was introduced in the form of a triggering question, which was brought to the group from Mrs. Smith—the group's host and sponsor. Mrs. Smith spoke on behalf of a team of individuals recognizable by name to the participants and clarified the meaning behind the triggering question. The group raised questions about the meaning of the context to Mrs. Smith, not to the design management dialogue manager. Because the sponsor of the design event has introduced the context and provided the clarifications, the design management team has confirmed its intention to remain fully neutral about any contribution or decision that the group of participants might choose to make with respect to the content of the design. At the same time, the design management team has affirmed its role as the custodian of the structured dialogue process for supporting the participants in generating content in response to the triggering question,

The dialogue manager adds a flourish as he returns to this designated task of managing the agenda in support of the design project.

GENERATING LABELS OF IDEAS

Dialogue Manager: "All right: let's begin. On the table before you, our design management team is placing large yellow index cards and some pencils. During the next five minutes, we are asking you to silently list five ideas or issues that you feel are highly important to consider in response to the triggering question. You should jot down each item using your own shorthand to capture the idea. Each idea should be a single idea, so if you catch yourself using the word "and" or "with" make sure that you don't have two ideas wrapped into one. When we have completed this task, we will move on to the next step."

A Participant: "What if I have more than five important ideas? This is a complex process, and I'm sure we could all come up with dozens of important ideas."

Dialogue Manager: "Yes, collectively and individually we will come up with between 50 and 100 ideas—at least, that is what we have observed in over 300 design projects such as this project. We ask you for five for two reasons: first, it eases the burden on you as individuals, and second, we need to be sure that we tap into all of the "most important" ideas, and empirical studies have shown that "five" is an optimal number for establishing "saliency"—which is to say, establishing a focus on what is agreed to be of most importance. Now, with this as a background, if you have six, seven, eight ideas—then yes, let's begin with those. Okay?"

[The participant agrees, and there is a clatter of pencils and scratching on paper as the participants begin to comply.]

Dialogue Manager *[ten minutes later]*: "All right; now we must choose labels for our ideas. As we do this we may discover that some of our ideas are actually more than a single idea. For your label, begin with a verb—like 'fixing' or 'avoiding' or 'capturing' or 'understanding/' This will help us when we compare ideas. We will project a slide on the screen with a range of verb forms that might work with your ideas. *[The systems operator projects a slide showing a list of verbs in gerund form.]* Try to keep the idea labels to fewer than ten words. If the labels are too long, they will be difficult to read and to track as a group. Don't rush on the labeling of your ideas. And be extra careful if you feel you must use the word 'and' in a label. Remember, we are coming up with labels at this point, and we will work on the clarification of meaning in the next step."

Dialogue Manager *[a few minutes later]*: "Okay. Let's begin gathering up the labels." *[The dialogue manager moves toward the end seat on the left of the horseshoe-shaped table, and approaches the participant seated there.]* "Please state your name and your affiliation or your connection to our project, and then provide us with a label for one of your ideas." *[Then the dialogue manager gently turns to face the audience as the participant is speaking.]*

[As the participant states his or her label, the label appears on the project screen, allowing the participant the opportunity to ensure that it has been accurately captured.]

Dialogue Manager: "Have we captured your label accurately?" *[Saying this, the dialogue manager then reads back the recorded label that has been displayed on the screen.]*

Participant: "Yes, that is what I said."

[With the soft whirl of machinery, a printer spits out a single sheet of letter-sized pink paper with the label printed on it in the largest possible font. The numeral 1 precedes the first label that is printed. A member of the design management team immediately takes the printed label to the far wall and tapes it in a highly visible location.]

[The dialogue manager moves on to the next person seated at the table. This time, no prompting is needed. The participant states his name and affiliation and provides the label, it appears first on the screen, and then is printed and taped to the wall, prefaced with the numeral 2. With a nod, the dialogue manager turns and moves to the next participant. With an economy of discussion, the labels are all collected, projected, printed, and displayed. During the fifth cycle, some of the participants say that all of their ideas have already been voiced, and several participants go on to add a sixth and possibly a seventh or eighth idea.]

Dialogue Manager: "Splendid—we are doing very, very well." *[He places another huge blue check mark on the agenda on the item "Post **labels** for our individual ideas."]* "It is 10:30, and we are right on schedule. We have generated fifty-three ideas that we will discuss and clarify. Let's celebrate with a ten-minute coffee break. You may bring your coffee to the table, and don't feel like you have to rush drinking it. Just rush to get back to the table."

What Has Happened

When participants initially responded to the triggering question with brief written statements, they edited their complex thoughts down into more concise statements. As participants crafted labels for their ideas, they again edited their expression to capture the essence of single thoughts. The group is moving toward concise expressions for sharing ideas originating by looking at the wicked situation from different portals. Their progress is visible both on the walls and also on the agenda. The transparency with which ideas are collected and the authenticity with which they are recorded are clear to all. Some learning is occurring as some members of the group recognize that some of their ideas have also been voiced by others. Flexibility of the process is demonstrated by accommodation of additional ideas from some individuals. The roles of the design management team are beginning to become apparent as the participants recognize the recorder capturing input and the production manager generating work product that an additional team member then brings to the wall displays. There is progressively less said by the dialogue manager, and only rarely is the flow of ideas to work product punctuated with any obvious communication among the design team itself. It seems to participants that the design management team has faded a bit into the background. Participants are progressively focused on the content itself. The prevailing atmosphere in the facility is one of humility, equity, and empathy.

During the coffee break, some of the participants are already chatting to each other about the labels on the walls. Some individuals are engaged in a focused exploration of the wall displays. A few seem to give a nod to one or more ideas from within their conversations, referring to them by their numbers. In other words, the problem situation has now been digitized completely, since the linear prose for discussing the wicked complexity has been substituted with the more efficient labels of the ideas represented by their numbers. Some participants are already connecting the ideas displayed on the wall by saying, "I see how number 15 is strongly linked to number 42." Of course, the labels by themselves are not sufficient to capture the depth of meaning of the ideas, or the various nuances covered by the labels. The labels will have to be elaborated by the authors to make the meanings of each label transparent to every member of the group.

There is an energy and excitement in the room about the next step of the process.

What is likely to be less obvious to the participants is the fact that by collecting and displaying labels for a large set of ideas first, the group has not only painted a broad brushstroke for what lies ahead, but also relieved some tension within the group. Tension comes from several sources. One source of tension comes from a sense of urgency in getting an idea onto the table for the group to consider. It is not uncommon for participants to seek to launch into an explanation as soon as they voice an idea. The dialogue manager can coax an eager participant to relax by reminding them that the group is collecting all the labels first—the next cycle will include capturing meaning. In short, an urgent desire to speak and be heard is provided as a cathartic release through the reassurance that their statements have been recognized and that their explanations will not be overlooked. By delaying the explanations, we enable all participant voices to be heard at the level of specificity of the label before we indulge in explanations and clarifications of the meanings underlying the labels.

A second source of tension comes from the labels themselves, or, rather, the interpretations that participants may attach to labels as they are being voiced. The dialogue manager needs to model and impose an environment of tolerance to labels, something that might be displeasing to some members of a community under pressure. While personal attacks cannot be accepted at any time during a structured dialogic design process, the process does allow participants to voice statements that will not win universal agreement. All members of the design group will be coached specifically about how "understanding" is distinct from "agreeing" with the ideas that are coming to the table. Even at the early stage of putting idea labels on the walls, some participants may become stressed with the notion that certain subject matter is going to be part of the group deliberation. Participants can become irritated with each other for any number of reasons—they can consider some ideas to be silly, foolish, or frivolous and other ideas to be insulting, threatening, or risky. They are invited to propose an antithetical idea to the one that has been voiced by another member of the group. They can also feel intensely attached to an idea and stressed to hear it voiced by someone who they may feel is a poor spokesperson for the idea. At no point does a dialogue-based design process assume that human emotions do not need accommodation. Structured dialogic design makes accommodations by equitable, transparent respect for each and every participant's ideas. A dialogue manager leader may at times need to diffuse tensions by stepping in the line of sight and conversation between two individuals at the table—and it is for this reason that the table is an open horseshoe with access to central space for dialogue management.

CLARIFYING MEANING

Dialogue Manager: "Let's start once again. At every break, there always are one or two individuals who fail to make it back in time, but we can't spend time waiting—your time is too valuable." *[The dialogue manager walks to the flip chart.]* "We have almost an hour-and-a-half before lunch arrives, and we will have a full hour for lunch. We have a lot to do in the next ninety minutes. We will explore the meaning behind each label by asking the author to explain their idea. As you listen to the author's explanation, you need to be sure that you understand. You do *not* need to agree. If you attack each other because you do not happen to like ideas that are very important to others, the group cannot go forward together, so for this reason we do not allow ideas to be criticized as they are being introduced—and if you do come to understand ideas, you may find them to be less difficult for you than you might originally think. So, we will ask each author to clarify his or her meaning, and while the author is clarifying the meaning, our team will work to capture the essence of that idea for your records. Our design management team has an individual who will be serving as a recorder. It is important that only one person speak at a time, because our recorder needs to hear clearly, and the recorder is sitting up in the far corner of the room. Let's begin. The author of idea number 1 is sitting here in the first seat at the table." *[The dialogue manager turns to the participant in seat number 1.]* "Will you please explain the meaning of your idea for the benefit of the other members of the group." *[The dialogue manager reads the idea labeled "1" from the wall display—"Standardizing our information systems." The Dialogue Manager nods to Participant 1 and then turns slowly toward the rest of the group.]*

Participant 1: "This means that we need to use the same information system so that we can share data."

Dialogue Manager: "Okay. Do you understand what this means? Are there any questions or comments?"

Participant 16 *[looking at the dialogue manager]*: "Is she saying we need to use her information system?"

Dialogue Manager: "How would I know what she is talking about? I don't know anything about any of this. All of you are the expert stakeholders. You must ask each other."

Participant 16 *[looking at Participant 1]*: "Do you have a specific information system in mind?"

Participant 1: "Well, we have a pretty good system, but I wasn't specifically expecting everyone to jump onto ours. It is just that we do need to have a better way to share information."

Dialogue Manager: "Does this answer clarify for you?"

Participant 16: "Yes. I am clear now."

Participant 12 *[looking at Participant 1]*: "We could use our system. It is probably the best value for the cost that we would be facing."

Dialogue Manager: "Excuse me, excuse me—excuse me. Please. I know that you are trying to be helpful, but our point here is to understand the idea. This is our only goal at this time. If you would like to make a comment, that is all right, but questions must be limited to understanding what our author has in mind. Your statement clearly changes the meaning and intent of the author at this stage. You are free to propose a similar statement with your own intent and interpretation."

Participant 12: "Okay, I would like to comment that we probably have a variety of systems that we could choose from."

Dialogue Manager *[to Participant 1]*: "Would you like to respond to that comment, or not?"

Participant 1: "That's fine. I am really only concerned that we choose one."

Participant 23 *[to Participant 1]*: "I think we could have more than one. We don't need to pick just one."

Dialogue Manager: "Excuse me, once again. Please. This is a good example of a temptation we all need to resist. You do not have to agree with an idea. You need only to understand it. If you feel strongly that an additional idea should be added to our list after we have gone through clarification of our current list, then we can accommodate such an addition. For now, we need to focus on understanding each other."

Dialogue Manager *[to Participant 23]*: "Do you have a question about idea 1?"

Participant 23: "No, I understand the idea quite well, thank you."

Dialogue Manager: "Are there any other questions or comments about idea 1?"

Dialogue Manager *[turning to Participant 1]*: "Thank you." *[He then slowly moves toward Participant 2, reads from the screen the label of idea 2 and asks Participant 2 to explain what he means. Participant 2 picks up the cue, reads from idea 2 on the wall display, and then offers a clarification.]*

Participant 2: "What I am thinking is that as we reimburse the caregivers for services aimed as preventing lifestyle illnesses, we need to have a way to stay in touch with the patients over time so that we can determine how much service has been delivered. This is not so much an issue of capitation in health care as it is a value-based fee-for-service pricing scheme. I once read about how this worked for a group in . . ."

Dialogue Manager: "Please, let me be sure that we are keeping up with your pace of explanation. I noticed that our recorder hasn't been able to capture much so far, and it seems like you are giving us a great deal of information. Let me ask our recorder to tell us what he has." *[to Team Member 2]* "What do we have in the record?"

Team Member 2 (Recorder) *[immediately]*: "We must reimburse caregivers for lifestyle illness services. Not like capitation. Value-based service."

Dialogue Manager *[to Participant 2]*: "Have we got the essence right?"

Participant 2: "Sort of. I was trying to make it clearer with a story."

Dialogue Manager: "Okay, let's see if we can get some help. Is the meaning of idea 2 clear to everyone?"

Participant 15: "Are you thinking along the lines of teenage pregnancy prevention counseling?"

Participant 2: "Yes, that's it. It's a good example. The story that I wanted to share involved my work with tribal elders in a United Nations program several years ago. I was fresh out of med school at the time and I had been selected from a national program for . . ."

Dialogue Manager *[to Participant 2]*: "I am sorry once again. Because this has been a complex thought, let's be certain that we are capturing the essence of what you are saying." *[quickly nods to the dialogue management recorder]*

Dialogue Management Recorder (played by Team Member 2 in this session) *[immediately]*: "We must reimburse caregivers for lifestyle illness services. Not like capitation. Value-based service. Question: Like counseling for teenage pregnancy prevention? Answer: Yes."

Dialogue Manager *[to Participant 2]*: "If we have captured the essence of this idea, we should move on now. We will have opportunities to share many stories over lunch, and also at the reception that that will be held in the hotel this evening. Have we captured the essence of idea 2?"

Participant Member 2: "Well, yes, I guess you've got the gist of it."

Dialogue Manager: "Participant 3, can you help us understand your idea?"

Participant 3: "Idea 3 is 'Helping community health workers build up translation skills.' I am not really sure how to say this. Community health workers are bilingual or multilingual in almost all cases anyway."

Participant 7: "You probably mean community nurses. They need the translation skills."

Participant 3: "Well, I guess that I could mean them, too."

Dialogue Manager *[to the group]*: "We have to slow down for a moment. What is happening is that we are being too helpful at this moment. We are not looking for collective authorship here. We need to let Angela first explain her original meaning. I am concerned that we may be changing or adding onto the intent of Angela's idea by expanding it." *[to Participant 3]* "Angela, could you first tell us what you originally had in mind."

Participant 3: "I don't know much about the community nurses, but the community health workers need to translate medical situations that are sometimes complex into a way that makes sense culturally with families in the community. I don't really know what to call it. Maybe it's cultural translation of medical practices."

[The dialogue manager turns back to the group; without verbal command, he nods to a participant who is starting to raise her hand.]

Participant 9 *[to Participant 3]*: "Is this a bit like the need to explain why birth control pills don't protect from sexually transmitted diseases?"

Participant 3: "That's a good example. Yes, the community health worker needs to know that that is a common misunderstanding in some parts of our community so that they will know that they should discuss it."

Dialogue Manager: "Are there any other questions? If not, let's hear the record from our recorder, because this has been a particularly complex clarification."

Team Member 2: "Clarification record for idea 3: 'Community health workers are bilingual or multilingual already but need support in understanding where confusion exists in some health practices, such as why birth control pills do not protect against sexually transmitted diseases.'"

Dialogue Manager to Participant 3: "Have we got it?"

Participant 3: "Yes, that is what I was trying to say."

Dialogue Manager: "All right. Participant 4."

Participant 4: "My idea is actually the same idea that Angela has, but I am saying it in a different way."

Dialogue Manager *[to Participant 4]*: "Well, let's first explain it and then see if your idea is identical to or different from Angela's idea. What is your idea?"

Participant 4: "Idea 4 is 'Making things more clear to families in poor parts of town.' I know that the information that comes to many folks isn't very helpful. You would need a PhD to understand what type of a health plan to choose. You cannot get the information that others get if you don't have a computer with Internet access."

Dialogue Manager: "Let's ask Angela first, now, because she is the author of idea 3, which John has just told us is identical to his own idea."

Participant 3 (Angela): "Well, I wasn't thinking about things that get mailed to families. That is an important thing, but community health workers are not necessarily going to make that a lot easier on their own. I think that it could be a larger problem."

Dialogue Manager *[in a joking tone, to Participant 4]*: "Well, John—it looks like Angela says you don't know her quite that well yet. John, what do you think?"

Participant 4: "Okay. I guess I'm found out. It *is* different."

Dialogue Manager: "This is fine. We want things to be different. It is more fun for everyone this way, isn't it? Incidentally, we can expect to find ideas that actually *are* the same. When that happens, we will ask the author who first expressed the idea to continue to own that idea, and we will ask the author of the second expression of that idea for permission to delete it from the list. The idea will not vanish, but we will mark it as "merged with idea *x*" so that you will always know where it went. Now, do we have any further questions for John on idea 4, 'Making things more clear to families in poor parts of town'?"

What Has Happened

First of all, the dialogue manager does *not* address participants by number. The name of each participant is located on a folding card in front of him or her at the table. In advance of the session, each participant was asked how he or she preferred to be addressed. Frequently, a participant with high credentials may want to use a title in their name card—but such participants frequently ask to discontinue using the title when they realize that the event is most clearly egalitarian.

Second, the participants learn how to learn with each other. When a group begins to explore meaning behind statements, the group needs to develop some norms for managing the give-and-take. The ground rules are clear: questions for clarification only—no premature value judgments. Still, the dialogue manager may need to intervene to remind the group that the rules need to be enforced. Ideas have labels, and they also have numbers, and the dialogue manager uses both the label and the number in order to reinforce their interchangeability.

Groups tend to rapidly learn to track ideas by both label and their number. They understand that each numbered idea has a specific owner, and that the owner's rights to the full authorship of the idea are protected. This gives ideas authenticity and integrity. Joint authorship of ideas is actively discouraged, but other participants are welcome to gently offer help to any one participant in externalizing the meaning behind their idea, as long as they do not violate the original intent of the author. We see this in the example above when Angela (Participant 3) was put under pressure to expand her statement to include not only community health workers but also community nurses. The dialogue manager stepped in to limit the imposed expansion of the concept. If this step had not been taken, then Angela would, at some point, have had to turn to someone else to explain what her statement related to community nurses meant. Angela needs to be in complete control of the meaning behind the idea that she is presenting for group consideration. This can only be ensured by protecting the authenticity of individual authorship for each idea.

The reason for protecting authorship and ownership of ideas is because as a dialogue progresses, meaning unfolds and evolves; if one idea has more than one author, there can be serious confusion over what a specific idea actually means. A second dimension of the individual ownership of ideas is the group's need to retain the original author as the design session moves through its stages. In cases in which an author happens to permanently leave a dialogic design session, another participant can agree to "adopt" an orphaned idea. At that point the idea becomes the exclusive new property of the adopting participant, and the same rights, rules, and obligation of ownership apply.

Sometimes a group will have participants who will want to tell long, tangential stories. Early in the process, the dialogue manager can lean on the team recorder to help the group recognize that a living record is being constructed and that lengthy excursions into side conversations are indeed difficult to support. This gentle illustration is often all that is needed to cultivate the norm of communicating the essence of ideas and remaining responsive to questions as a prompt for providing more detail. This is, however, a thin line and one cannot constrain a group with a recorder who is unable to keep pace with the flow of dialogue.

In this stage of the process, we can see emotions running through the participants. Some will seem to be thinking, 'I cannot believe we are spending time talking about something as basic and clear as this,' and others will be thinking, 'that idea is so esoteric that it probably belongs only in someone's thesis'—and still others will be thinking, 'yes, I understand, but that type of backward thinking is the reason we are in trouble in the first place.' All of these feelings are fully legitimate at this stage of the design program. Some tensions can be defused using humor, but some individuals' body language will betray their growing frustration as they cross their arms and button their lips. As ideas that don't fit neatly into each individual's existing framework for viewing the wicked situation, they can become excited about a possible learning opportunity, or they can become hardened about the threat that seriously considering all of the ideas will have upon their worldview. As a result, *this stage of the design process cannot be rushed.* The exploration of meaning has both the obvious components of getting the words right, and also the subtle internal issue of getting the required variety fit right. In a sufficiently complex situation, all participants are likely to experience at least a partial collapse of their original view of how the world works. When this worldview collapse happens, individuals can face a personal crisis. Design management teams need to recognize the magnitude of personal investment that participants can have in a social systems design, and for this reason they need to be sensitive to subtle signs of struggle shown by participants.

CLUSTERING SIMILAR IDEAS

Dialogue Manager: "Congratulations—we have just checked off another milestone on our agenda. We are now ready to cluster similar ideas in categories of similar meaning. Our design management team has printed out a table of the clarifications of the labels that we have generated, so this work product can help us as we now assign ideas into affinity clusters. I will start this task with you, and then I will step back and have you all come up to the wall display, pick an idea off the wall for which you are the author, and assign it into an existing cluster or create a new cluster for it.

"Now, to start: on the screen before you, you will see ideas presented and you will be asked if the ideas 'belong together in the context of the triggering question.' If you think that they are similar in meaning, explain why they are similar. Okay. Are the two ideas shown on the screen related?"

[A few hands go up]

Dialogue Manager: "Why?"

Participant: "Well, they both involved hospitals."

Dialogue Manager: "Okay, then why not?" *[A few different hands go up; the dialogue manager nods to them.]*

Participant: "One is related to billing, and another is related to clinical care."

Dialogue Manager: "All right, we have to dig deeper. What else can we say?"

Participant: "Yes, they differ with what they affect, but they are in the same organization, they serve the same medical population, and they both require links to translators. I would say that they have a fair bit in common."

[A few more heads seem to nod in agreement]

Dialogue Manager: "Okay, do these two ideas belong in an 'affinity cluster' together?"

[The group agrees they are similar, the software operator on the design management team records the decision, and a new idea appears beneath the first two.]

Dialogue Manager: "What about this third idea? Does it belong in the same cluster?"

Participant: "No, the new idea relates to "marketing" and doesn't have much to do with 'operations.'"

[The group agrees that the idea does not belong with the others, the software operator on the design management team records the decision, and the third idea is removed from the screen; a fourth idea then immediately appears beneath the first two in cluster 1.]

Dialogue Manager: "Now take the fourth idea. Does in go into the cluster with the first two ideas?" *[pause]* "You say, 'no,' so now does the idea go into the second cluster along with the third idea?" *[Idea 4 now appears below idea 3 in cluster 2]* "You say 'no' again, so this fourth idea goes into a third cluster. Do you see what we are doing here? You have just identified three clusters. We may decide to rearrange where we have parked ideas as we go forward, but for now, we're building up clusters."

[The group catches on and works through about twenty ideas, building up about seven clusters.]

Dialogue Manager: "Let's pause for a second. What you have constructed so far is a 'skeleton structure' of clusters. We haven't used many of our ideas, and we have already found seven clusters. As we go forward, it will help for you to see all of the clusters up on the wall as you continue to expand and extend the clusters. At this point, we are transposing the work you have done using the projection screen onto a wall display on the side of the room. We will carry the same task forward that we have started using the projection screen. We will test to see whether a new idea 'fits' with other ideas in a cluster, and if it doesn't fit, we will 'walk it down the wall,' testing other clusters until we find a fit or end up defining a new cluster. Let's do a few with this manual process now."

[The group structures another ten ideas and in doing so identifies another two clusters, but some of the ideas evoke detailed discussion.]

Participant: "I see things in common with the idea about the 'insurance issue,' but the 'peer pressure' part of idea 21 doesn't seem to fit too well. Maybe if we think of peer pressure as some form of social capital, it might fit. I am not sure that that is what the author of idea 21 had in mind though."

Participant 21: "I am the author of idea 21, and I was thinking along those lines. I guess I would have to say that I do see a fit. I didn't realize it at first, but it does match what I had in mind."

Dialogue Manager: "Great, we're using our experience well here. Let's put them together for now and see where a fifth idea goes."

[After another ten minutes, the group has nine clusters and has a good idea of how to put ideas into clusters together.]

Dialogue Manager: "We are ready to change gears. I want you all to individually pick up an idea from the wall display that we used when we were doing clarifications. If you can pick up an idea that you authored, this will be helpful. Take that idea and then walk along the wall from left to right. If you get to a cluster where you feel an idea fits, stick it there and then go and pick up another idea you authored. After we have done this for a while, we will then see whether we should revise the location of any of the ideas that we currently have put into our clusters. In this way, we will refine the clusters through iteration—picking up items that seem to fit very poorly and then walking those items through all of the other clusters once again. Then we will discuss our results."

Participant: "We haven't named the clusters. If the clusters had names, it would sure make this a lot easier."

Dialogue Manager: "You are exactly correct. The problem is that we haven't yet discovered the clusters, so we don't know what to call them. If we started out with names for clusters, this would prevent us from discovering them, so although this is a lot of work, it is really unavoidable right now."

[Participants pick up ideas and march along the wall with the growing clusters. After about ten minutes, the position-swapping seems to slow down. The dialogue manager moves back to the wall.]

Dialogue Manager: "We are probably just about finished. We can now assign names to the clusters. Consider all of the clusters without considering any one idea too deeply. What do the clusters suggest to you? Let's have some one- or two-word labels."

Participant 4: "The first one says 'lifestyle illnesses' to me." *[Others in the group signal that they agree. No other suggestion is offered, so the dialogue manager writes "lifestyle illnesses" on top of the cluster.]*

Participant 17: "The next cluster says 'education' to me."

Participant 5: "I was thinking that it said 'training'—how about 'education and training'?" *[The group agrees, and the dialogue manager writes "education & training" above the second cluster.]*

Dialogue Manager: "This is good progress. Once we've finished naming the clusters, we will make sure that we have not made any bad assignments of ideas into the wrong cluster. Then we will take a break, and when we come back we'll vote for ideas that we feel are relatively more important to keep in mind as we continue our work." *[As he speaks, he makes a sweeping gesture at the triggering question that is posted on the wall above the clusters: "What issues must we anticipate in our hopes to ensure health and wellness in our region in the next five years under the newly approved universal health coverage plan?"]*

What Has Happened

Clustering ideas serves as a catalyst for getting a deeper appreciation of the inner meaning of ideas. The struggle to make assignments of similarity are difficult, and the magnitude of the task is beyond what one might reasonably expect of the participants working as individuals. As we struggle to make relational judgment among the ideas two at a time, we recognize that suddenly what seemed to be crystal clear when the author clarified her idea is not clear enough to be able to make a judgment about the similarity of two ideas. The authors are asked to offer additional clarification, and sometimes to vote about the positioning of their ideas so that others can hear the rationales of the authors before they vote.

The collective results generally have some features that do fit well with all individual participants. The fact that the ideas have been "organized" makes it much easier to deal with them in terms of judgments of relative importance. Also when grouped as similarly related ideas, similarities fade a bit and differences stand out. Selecting preferences will be based on making distinctions, and what the group has done is assembled ideas into affinity clusters that represent different "dimensions" of their thinking. Within each dimension, there will be ideas that will now "stand out." Organizing information in this way helps a group apply a gestalt impression of sameness that acts as pass-through filter for seeing distinctions among sets of ideas. Each individual will be processing this information using his or her individual frameworks, but collectively the group will select a set of preferred ideas assembled into a collective—or shared—framework. This process will begin with the next step of the design project: the expression of individual preferences.

EXPRESSING PREFERENCES

Dialogue Manager: "Welcome back. We gave you that extra unscheduled break because we know that you have all been working very, very hard. Now on the table in front of you, you will see a set of five blue dots and a summary of your work with the affinity clusters. First, write your name on each of your voting dots. Sitting at your table, you can then go through the cluster maps and refer to clarifications of meaning in your prior work product, and you can make choices in response to our triggering question, which you see on the wall and which we are again displaying on the screen in the front of the room. Take the time that you need to choose as wisely as possible. We want your top five choices in the context of the triggering question. You can choose only five, and you must choose five. Putting multiple votes on a single statement will distort the results. Are there any questions?"

Participant 4: "Why only five votes?"

Dialogue Manager: "The use of five votes has been found to be optimal through empirical studies in the field of collaborative design. Our goal here is to identify high-priority preferences that will be used to construct a strong backbone for the group's understanding and planning purposes."

[The group studies their work products and makes selections, and blue dots begin appearing on the ideas that are sorted and displayed in clusters on the wall.]

Dialogue Manager: "We are almost finished for today. As you can see, we have seven—or eight—ideas that have clearly been named as highly preferred by the group, and another half-dozen ideas that also have captured at least 50% of our total set of votes. We are in the process of printing up a summary of this voting results for you to have as you leave for the evening, so we will now check off 'Individually vote for our most preferred ideas in response to our triggering question'." *[He puts a check mark on the agenda.]*

Dialogue Manager: "Let me say the following things about our voting results. Some of you might feel satisfied to see an idea that you have authored get a lot of votes. It is like having your horse win at the races. Let me say that the race is far from over. This means that for those of you who do not see your idea as among the most popular at this point are all still very much in the game. In fact, as you will see, none of the ideas we have gathered have been left behind. They are all in the record, and they are all valid expressions from the individual authors' perspectives. They are all also understood by all participants in this design project. The voting results are important to use because they give us a place to start when we build a structure that will reveal other relationships among highly preferred ideas that we need to consider as we build our understanding and our plans. Furthermore, by taking the time to vote, you have internalized the ideas more and are more prepared to explore other relationships and build a system of ideas.

"Once we have handed out the voting results to you, you are free to go, or you may join the design team for some refreshments and share thoughts on the processes you have experienced so far."

[The dialogue manager walks to the agenda on the flip chart and places a huge blue check mark next to the item that reads "Adjourn."]

What Has Happened

Without putting too fine an edge on it, the dialogue manager has just told the participants that their votes don't matter much. This message will seem irrelevant to those who may be feeling as if they have "won" a contest of sorts, and it may be somewhat consoling to those who may feel as if they have lost. Once the first wave of celebration or despair passes through the now exhausted participants, they will begin to reflect on the extent to which the full list of highly preferred ideas compares and differs with their own list of preferred ideas. It is most likely that they will sense the discrepancy between their view and the group's collective view, and this can trigger a crisis of worldviews. The emotional fabric is ripped. Participants invest their time in the project because of the importance that they attach to it, and all of that importance is tethered to emotional anchors. Participants will feel the anchors giving way. They may feel the collapse of the inner cognitive frameworks that helped them in earlier understanding and ascribing meaning to the situation that they face. Much as a person who is facing a terminal illness must pass through phases of psychological adjustment for his or her mortal life, the design participants must face what our colleague Kevin Dye has called "grieving for the loss of a worldview." This takes time, and for this reason schedules should allow ample time for participants to go through the grieving process.

As participants pass into the new territory that exists beyond protecting their old worldview, the participants can be expected to engage each other at deeper (though perhaps not desperate) levels. The quality of dialogue can shift for different individuals at different times in the design process, but we usually see it establish itself as the norm by early in day 2. For individuals who may have been "holding back," the qualitative change in their participation impresses members of the design team as a "transformation." For some, the transformation may already have happened, for others the transformation may happen overnight, and for some the transformation will surprise them as they find themselves confronting their sincere desire to be understood when the group explores other relationships among strongly preferred ideas.

EXPLORING RELATIONSHIPS OF INFLUENCE

Dialogue Manager: "Welcome back. I hope you've had a good evening. It's good to see that everyone has returned here on time to start our new task. This task begins with a review of what we have accomplished so far in six hours of work." *[He walks to the flip chart and points to the agenda.]* "We have identified and understood our triggering question. We have silently generated our individual list of what we feel is most important to keep in mind. We have collectively generated a set of fifty-three key ideas to keep in mind. We have clustered our ideas into seven categories of related thought. And we have collectively identified a set of fourteen ideas that all have captured at least 50% of our total set of votes. All of these work products are in your notebooks. We are going to start today with this set of fourteen ideas, because at least four of you have voted for each of these items. We will use all of the ideas that have received four or more votes to create a structure that will tell us how we—as a group—understand our situation and our options for action. We then will come back to this list with a deeper understanding of our situation and select additional ideas that we might want to add to our structure. Are we ready to begin?"

[The design management team hums into action, and the projection screen, which was displaying the "triggering question," switches to a display that the group has not seen before.]

Dialogue Manager: "What you now see on the screen before you is a display from a 'tracking program' that will help us work with our set of ideas. The software will prompt us for connections and will record our answers. It then will convert the pattern of our answers into a 'tree.' This is all that the software does. It also has an algorithm that selects which ideas to ask about so that it will extract the maximum information from the participants and minimize the number of questions before the construction of the tree is complete. This gain in efficiency helps groups converge in the construction of a tree with fifteen ideas in, say two hours, instead of eight hours, of group work. However, it should be realized that the software does not think for us. We do all of the thinking, and the software is doing the bookkeeping. The software is prompting us with the following question: 'If we make significant progress on idea 1, "Standardizing our information systems," will this help us significantly in making progress on idea 14, "Teaching children about their responsibilities for staying healthy" in the context of ensuring health and wellness in our region under universal health care coverage within the next five years?' Now, before we answer this question, I must ask if we all understand the question."

Participant 7: "What happened to idea 2?"

Dialogue Manager: "The software selects the ideas to choose based upon the votes that we have gathered. Idea 2 is still in the software file, but we did not give idea 2 enough votes to have it included in the structuring process at this time. We are not saying that idea 2 is a bad idea, and we may come to love it very much as we go forward. What we are saying is that based on our voting results, we should start with the ideas that you see on the display at this moment. The display will change once we have made our choice, and we will consider the influence relationship between two different ideas. This is why we are making this particular relational judgment at this particular time. Are there other questions?"

Participant 19 [who has been sitting back with her arms folded across her chest for much of the activity over the past day and seems to be holding back]: "We probably have good reasons to come up with different answers for this question—in fact, for any connection we might make. How are we going to know whether we agree with this statement or not? After all, what does 'significant' mean? We each have our own ideas on what is significant."

Dialogue Manager: "You raise a very good point. In fact, this is central to our design approach. As a group, we will agree that the relationship exists if 75% of us or more agree. This is a supermajority vote for a *yes* answer. Some designer situations accept 66% as a supermajority, but in this project we are applying this threshold stringently because we need to see a structure that shows very strong connections between ideas as captured by the word 'significantly.' About the meaning of 'significant'—well, this is more subtle. If you vote *no*, then this means that either you don't see any influence or you feel that the influence is weak. The very strong *yes* votes will lead to a specific connection that we will see in our tree. We will have to explain to each other what we feel is significant in each connection, and we may or may not be able to convince each other of what we see as being significant. If a connection does not meet the 'significant' threshold, the idea will still appear in our map, just in a different location in the map. We are not going to leave any of these highly significant ideas out of the structure that we are creating. And we are relying on your discussions with each other to resolve borderline questions about what the group sees as a significant relationship. Anything else?"

Participant 4: "What actually do we mean by 'making progress on' in the question? There are probably a variety of ways that acting on one idea might help us to act on another idea."

Dialogue Manager: "Precisely! We are asking a "generic question" here. There are many ways that successful action on one idea could influence the outcome of action on another idea. We must expect to hear of different ways that acting on one idea may influence the outcome on another idea. For these reasons, some will see a significant impact that others may not yet have recognized. And some will see the same impact but not feel that the impact is 'significant.' Shall we start?"

[The group says yes.]

Dialogue Manager: "All right, now, reading from the screen: 'If we make significant progress on idea 1, "Standardizing our information systems," will this help us significantly in making progress on idea 14, "Teaching children about their responsibilities for staying healthy" in the context of ensuring health and wellness in our region under universal health care coverage within the next five years?' Point your thumb up if you say yes, and down if you say no. Let's see the votes."

[Eighteen of the group show thumbs down, two show thumbs up, and the remaining six seem unsure of themselves.]

Dialogue Manager: "Okay, we have some disagreement, but we also seem to already have a supermajority that does not see a significant influence in this relationship. Because we are just starting with this new task, we should talk about our decisions a bit. Whenever we have a split decision in a group, we always go first to the 'minority' opinion—the smaller side of the split— because a minority view can have the power to transform the opinion of the entire group, and this is powerful. So let me first ask Angela here: why do you vote *yes* and think that there is a significant impact?"

Participant 3 (Angela): "If we have the same information, we have a consistent message that we can give to our kids. We have the real data from the streets where we live. This will make what we say as relevant as possible to our kids."

Dialogue Manager: "Other minority opinions?"

Participant 23: "Yes, I agree—and we also can get access to sets of messages that we know work. We can use our information systems to discover and share best approaches for educating the kids."

Dialogue Manager: "Okay, let's hear now from the majority side. Who will speak?"

Participant 16: "Well, you've got me thinking now. I had felt that the link simply would not be significant. I guess that this will depend upon whether we are talking about an information system that is designed for sharing medical records or whether we are talking about something else."

Dialogue Manager: "Okay, let's go to the author of idea 1 for a clarification. Are we thinking of an information system that will carry more than medical data alone?"

Participant 1: "I didn't mean to exclude information that could be used for working with patients, and since wellness is the front end of health care, I would expect patient counseling information to be included in what the system can deliver. So, I guess that I am saying yes."

Dialogue Manager [to Team Member 2]: "Okay, please update the clarification statement for idea 1 to show this additional information. We will print out a revised clarification document for all participants at the close of this task."

Dialogue Manager: "Now let us vote again. I know that we have had some folks who have not felt like voting on this topic, and it is okay to be unsure. Sometimes the discussion helps us clarify our thinking. Votes, please."

[This time, all but two participants have shown a thumbs-up vote.]

Dialogue Manager: "Okay, now we have a new minority perspective to hear from, so I'll ask if you have a new or a different perspective to offer to the group."

Participant 11: "No, I don't have any new information. I just don't think that information alone is going to make the big difference in educating the kids to practice wellness behaviors. I think that more is needed."

Dialogue Manager: "Okay, we have a difference of perspective on 'significance.' I want to caution you to recognize a distinction between a significant influence and a 'necessary and sufficient influence.' If we were asking if one idea were sufficient—in itself—to influence another, we would be mapping sufficiency. We are not doing that here. We are mapping strong influence. When we individually consider the significance of an influence, we are making assumptions about the world within which that idea will be applied. It is certainly appropriate to see the world differently, and what we are doing as we make these relational judgments is bringing our different worldviews together to establish where we as a group agree upon strong influences."

Dialogue Manager to Team Member 3: "Enter a 'yes' for this question, and let's move on."

[The yes vote is entered and the software program flashes up a second question, which happens to be the inverse of what was just asked.]

Dialogue Manager: "If we make significant progress on idea 14, 'Teaching children about their responsibilities for staying healthy,' will this help us significantly in making progress on idea 1, 'Standardizing our information systems' in the context of ensuring health and wellness in our region under universal health care coverage within the next five years?"

[All thumbs immediately point down.]

Dialogue Manager: "Okay, that was easy. Because your response was so rapid and strong, we won't belabor this connection, but if the group is struggling to make a choice, we should consider discussing that choice even if we do seem to all agree. Let us enter a 'no' vote and move on. We will pick up speed as we continue."

[The screen prompts with a new question, but the question has reused one of the previous ideas.]

Dialogue Manager: "If we make significant progress on idea 1, 'Standardizing our information systems,' will this help us significantly in making progress on idea 19, 'Providing incentives for individual wellness efforts' in the context of ensuring health and wellness in our region under universal health care coverage within the next five years? Point your thumb up if you say yes, and down if you say no."

[The group seems to be about evenly split.]

Dialogue Manager: "Okay, we certainly have to talk about this one. Where do we start? We are about evenly split. First let's hear from the author of idea 19, and then let's hear from a 'no' vote. Will the author of idea 19 explain the idea and then tell us how she voted?"

Participant 19 *[who has been sitting with arms across her chest for most of the group work so far]*: "The incentives really are needed, but they have to be the right ones. Like I said originally, incentives can be free memberships to health clubs or to weight loss clinics, but there has to be feedback. I felt that having a strong information system in place is going to be critically important for implementing an effective incentives program, so I voted yes." *[leaning forward now and speaking in an earnest tone that others have already begun using]* "Look, I know that incentives are going to be costly. This is really the reason why we do too little and then convince ourselves that we cannot succeed. If we use incentives, we have to do this right. This means that we will have to have some accountability at the health clubs and at the diet centers. It does cost to build accountability into programs, but this is really what the entire mission needs. We need to ensure everyone that we are going to be accountable for wellness if we want them to be active partners in protecting health."

Dialogue Manager: "Thank you." *[The dialogue manager smiles inwardly and notices a similar knowing smile on other members of the team. A reticent participant has just converted and jumped earnestly into the talking point.]* "And now for a 'no' vote."

Participant 5: "I have to agree that I see Victoria's point. I can agree that if we first succeed in providing effective incentives, this would help a great deal in getting others on board with a standard information system."

Dialogue Manager: "We have to be careful here. The question asks if the information systems will impact the incentives, and not the reverse. We may see the reverse question on the screen in a bit, but for now we need to be focused on the direction of the relationship. Let's read the question once again and take another vote."

[This time a supermajority rapidly votes in favor, and three participants seem unsure.]

Dialogue Manager: "It is not uncommon to be unsure. If we strongly agree or strongly disagree, we are probably working at a 'significant influence' threshold. If we feel unsure, we are probably sensing a connection, but not feeling the 'significant' of that connection. It is the strong 'yes' votes that signal where our understandings converge. Let us continue."

[The software prompts the group as they work through pairwise connections for the next hour-and-a-half. The tone of the group is one of deeply inquiring and earnestly explaining differing perceptions. Many of the connections open new windows of understanding, and the expression "I guess I never thought of it quite that way" is frequently heard. Finally, the last prompted pair of ideas has been evaluated, and the software program signals "session complete" and begins producing the tree structure.]

Dialogue Manager: "All right, in just a moment the screen will display a view of our tree." *[The dialogue manager puts another huge blue check mark on the agenda—right next to "Structure the influence among our preferred ideas."]* "Let's stand up and stretch for a moment as we print out maps and then take a close look at the tree structure you've generated."

What Has Happened

A great deal is going on as groups work through a set of relationships among fourteen ideas of higher relative importance. Indeed, this process is complex enough that it deserves a book of its own to fully explain (see Christakis & Bausch, 2006, *How People Harness Their Collective Wisdom and Power to Construct the Future*, Information Age Publishing).

The task discussed in the illustration in this chapter would certainly trigger information overload if the group were not supported with a tracking system. The number of possible pairwise relationships to consider can be calculated by multiplying the total number of ideas by the total number of ideas minus one. In this case, 14 times 13 gives 172 pairs to assess, and at a rate of two minutes per assessment, the group would spend almost six exhausting hours completing this task. If an idea is discovered to be in error and must be removed from the structure, or if a new idea needs to be added, the group has a tremendous problem in trying to rethink its decisions. As important as we will show this process to be for the group, few groups would even consider the task. It is simply too much. However, work that began in a think tank at Battelle Memorial Laboratories in a field of study called uniform program planning nearly a half-century ago engaged the problem of cascading matrices of complexity.

In the late 1960s, Doug Hill and John Warfield were seeking a means to ease the burden that engineers were facing in calculating cascading matrices in program planning. The complexity they were engaging was selected specifically because it represented the most challenging problems in the world. Several years later, at a UN-sponsored conference in Budapest, physicist Alexander Christakis (one of the authors of this volume) was presenting a paper on his work on the use of field anomaly relaxation matrices to explain trends in growth in agricultural demand. Dr. Warfield was in the audience and was amazed to see the tremendous amount of effort this physicist had done in producing all of the matrix calculations in the rather esoteric demonstration project and approached him after the talk. When asked, Dr. Christakis admitted that his adopted Chinese son Quan Yang Duh had performed the calculations because the sheer volume of the work was too arduous for him to do himself. Dr. Warfield laughed and said, "Come over to the labs at Battelle, we'll show you the easy way to do it." Christakis knew immediately what this breakthrough meant. The ability to translate the geometry of the resolution of the matrix calculations into an easily interpreted tree structure could be placed within the reach of the average citizen of the world. Christakis and his colleague Hasan Özbekhan teamed up with John Warfield on what would be a twenty-year campaign to refine a methodology for empowering groups with a world-class situation analysis tool. For the group using this tool in the example in this chapter, a team of over twenty individuals working comfortably together achieved in an hour-and-a-half what previously could not have been achieved by a team of expert engineers skilled in cross-impact analysis given four times as long. In many cases, the time savings is even more dramatic, and this means that, *through a combination of deeply reasoned scientific and engineering tools, problem solving capacities are able to reach into complex situations today where they could never have gone before.*

There are a few additional points that are illustrated in the example presented above. First, the participants need to come to agree that assessing what may be "significant" is a matter of perspective. The task explicitly surfaces differing perspectives. Participants are not expected to change their perspectives, although they are indeed invited to consider adopting a new perspective. Because individuals retain their individuality, they may agree to disagree about the significance of specific pairs of relationships. As they present their perspectives, participants frequently express themselves in the form of an appeal for understanding by the group. This is very, very different from an authoritative "telling" to a group, and leveled power of the voting leads some leaders to present themselves in ways that their colleagues may not have experienced before. In some cases, such as the case of Participant 19—Victoria—in the example above, a transformation in an individual's posture to the group can be strikingly obvious. Victoria abandoned her crossed arms and beseeched the group to look at a situation in a new way—and in this case, it worked.

Groups may need a bit of coaching to remain consistent in the direction of the relationship that they are assessing, and they may need to be reminded to go to the minority side of a split vote first to share perspectives. If the group goes to the majority side first, then the volume of argument in majority direction can repress one or two individuals who happen to think differently. Pressure of this sort creates lost opportunities to learn from each other. The example presented is fairly typical of the swing in perceptions that arise as a result of the discussions fostered by this task. Participants realize that they are learning as they change their minds, and they realize that others are learning as they change their votes. Some decisions are really difficult, and the group struggles together as it learns. The shared pain of the struggles and the pleasant feeling of learning something new helps build a social connection among the participants.

The confidence that the group has developed in the meticulous information tracking practices of the design management team relieves stress and anxiety that would come from trying to track decisions individually. The group has all of the up-side of a powerful learning experience with few of the stressful downsides. This is not to say that some individuals will not feel "defeated" when the group does not share their view. On balance, though, group participants consistently report that the discussions were rich and rewarding.

REVIEW THE INFLUENCE STRUCTURE

Influence diagrams or influence maps (such as shown in Chapter 4) are generically the same. At one edge (frequently the bottom of the page), ideas are described as "deep" within the structure, and at the opposite side of the page (again, typically the top of the page), ideas are "strongly influenced" by the system of ideas that lie beneath them. Influence is thus propagated through the "tree." When groups first see the tree that they have created, there is usually a silent "aha" moment, and then a growing curiosity about the "other" implications of the structure.

Dialogue Manager: "So here it is: this is the result of the many decisions that you have made. Idea 7 was judged to be the deepest idea in the structure. It influences ideas 4 and 22, and then also influences a "cycle" of ideas consisting of ideas 11, 18, and 37. This cycle means that this set of three ideas are influenced by the same idea or ideas, and also that they exert influence on the same other ideas. A cycle suggests that a set of ideas might benefit from being investigated more closely as a single unit. As you look at this structure, pay particular attention to ideas that seem to be uninfluenced by other ideas in the set. Idea 7, because it is the deepest idea in the structure, is an example of an uninfluenced idea. Also look over at idea 44. It sits in the middle of the structure, and none of the other ideas in the system seem to influence idea 44. Examine the structure and ask yourself whether the influences that are represented in the tree make sense to you in light of the discussions that the group has shared."

Participant 8: "This is very cool. The structure captures a great deal of talking and thinking in a nice snapshot. I guess that it wasn't really what I had in mind, but it seems to make sense. Is this what we can call a consensus statement?"

Dialogue Manager: "Yes, the influence map does result from consensus. By this we mean that it represents an understanding that the supermajority supports, and it does not portray a relationship that any individual feels is strongly objectionable."

Participant 4: "A lot of the work we have been doing really comes flooding back as I climb through this tree. Just how elaborate can these trees get?"

Dialogue Manager: "There are some practical limitations due to the resolution of font size on the labels. The rule of thumb is that a model of a situation should be as complete as possible, but no more so. For our purposes, we have created a model of our situation that tells us where our

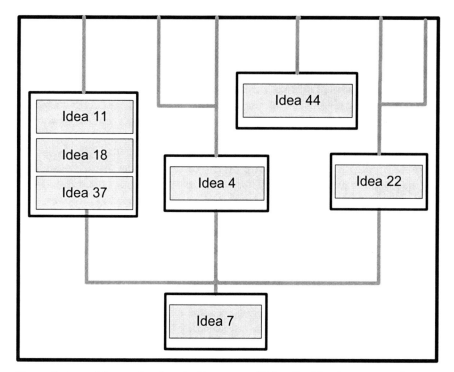

Figure 2. A partial map showing the "root cause" identified by the group and revealing the propagation of its influence onto other ideas mapped by the group.

strong agreements lie, and because we know where we hold strong agreement, we can understand how action on these points of shared agreement can improve the depth and quality of our collaborations in the future. In a few moments, I am going to introduce a task that will show you how to extend this model. For the present moment, please do 'climb through the tree,' as you say, Jack, and let us know how you find the view.

"I want to point out one thing for you. On your map, your most preferred idea did not end up being the most influential idea. In fact as our design management team now rearranges the ideas on the wall into the structure that you have created, you will recognize that few of your most preferred ideas actually had influence on the system of ideas that you need to resolve. The implication of this is important. What it means is that when you are in a situation in which a whole set of ideas need to be attacked as a system, the key leverage points for action cannot be anticipated without mapping influence. With a show of hands now, how many of you will agree that idea 7—which you had ranked ninth based on your preference voting—now is our most preferred idea for designing an approach to resolve our situation?"

[All hands are raised.]

What Has Happened

The group members have been presented with an artifact that they have collectively created. The structure does not fully represent any single individual's preconceived view of the situation. Instead, it precisely captures the strong agreement of the group. The group recognizes that based on the discussions that have been held so far, the structure rings "true." This creates a sense of shared ownership and a sense of closure with respect to addressing the triggering question. At the same time, the group senses that an opportunity exists now to use this new information to create new possibilities. And there are also a few backward glances to see what has been "left behind." In truth, the group does not leave ideas out. Rather the group has captured the strongly held center of the understanding that the group shares. Because an influence structure—whether it is called a map or a tree—is new to most group members, it takes a while to explore.

The dialogue manager drew specific attention to the lack of correlations between a highly preferred idea based on accumulated individual votes and a most preferred idea based upon accumulated consensus votes on pairs of relationships of influence among ideas. Individual voting on subjective preferences, even though it may be shaped by the opinions of others in the room, fundamentally differs from aggregated consensus voting on influences between a pair of ideas at a time. The transparency of the methodology creates conviction in the legitimacy of the results.

AMEND OR AUGMENT THE INFLUENCE STRUCTURE

Dialogue Manager: "All right, I now want you to realize that it is possible that we did not select the 'real' deep driver as a result of our current work. We have created a structure that shows idea 7 as the deepest, and thus most influential, of all of the ideas in the system. I want you now to search very carefully for any idea that we have discussed that you feel may significantly influence idea 7. Use your 'clarification tables' to check on meanings, and let's see what we find."

[A few moments later . . .]

Participant 14: "Idea 2 looks like it might significantly influence successful response to idea 7."

[The group murmurs in fragmented discussions.]

Participant 23 *[jokingly]*: "You're going to have to put it to the thumb vote, Tony!"

Participant 14: "All right, thumbs, do your stuff."

[About a third of the group gives a weak "thumbs up," and the majority signals a more convincing "thumbs down."]

Participant 14: "Okay, I recant. It doesn't fit that well."

Dialogue Manager: "That was good. You may have given in a bit too easily, but you all clearly understand what you are doing. Sometimes we do find a deeper driver through this 'final pass,' but usually the group does pull the deep drivers into the top 20% of its ideas. The rank order, however, is always different. This is the erroneous priorities effect. We cannot trust ourselves as individuals or as groups to sense the influence that is propagated across a set of strongly preferred ideas that are part of a complex social system."

Participant 21: "Wait a minute, though—we haven't used all of the ideas yet. I feel that we have left important things behind. How do we handle this?"

Dialogue Manager: "There are several options. First, the group can decide that it needs to add one or two more items—the software could be used to continue to build the structure. The second approach is that you—collectively or as individuals—can use this core structure as a means of explaining where you would insert an additional idea. This second approach would involve the use of a 'manual' construction that does not require a computer. Here—I'll show you so that you'll have the power to use the structure to explain relationships we haven't yet mapped."

[The dialogue manager goes to the wall and picks up an idea that captured only three individual votes during the voting phase. He holds the idea up in his left hand and points with a laser pointer to a position on the influence structure that is being displayed on the screen.]

Dialogue Manager: "I am trying to find a place on the map for idea 41. What do you say? Does idea 41 influence idea 7 here at the bottom of the tree? Yes, or no?" *[Thumbs point down.]* "How about over here on idea 4?" *[Suddenly all thumps point up.]* "There—that was easy, wasn't it? But first, does idea 41 significantly influence idea 22 also?" *[Thumbs slowly agree that there isn't a significant influence on idea 22.]* "Now we have to also ask about each of the three ideas in the cycle too, and also idea 44, which we recognized had not yet been influenced by any other idea. You can see that this process is very easy with the software tool, but difficult on its own."

What Has Happened

The group has been given a specific search image that was informed from the position of ideas within the influence structure. At this point, the approach to improving the group understanding has been strongly aligned. Participants communicate to each other using idea labels and code phrases that have emerged during the design process. The group shares some of the "in-house" culture and norms of a team. While this team environment is not expected to persist beyond this assembly of individuals, it may be reassembled when the individuals reconvene at some future time and reconnect through the shared understanding that they have cocreated in their influence structure.

The group also understands that the influence structure is a living artifact. They can use it to explain other ideas, or they can augment it to enrich its explanatory power. The most important aspect about the influence structure is the fact that it is a secondary product. The primary product is the bond that exists through the shared—or distributed—ownership of an understanding or an action plan by the participants. Coownership is a powerful basis a social contract, and this is essentially what has been created. The artifact represented by the influence diagram serves as a collective reminder of the social contract that has been constructed. In the next (and final task) for this session, the group will "customize" the meaning represented within the influence structure through the use of narrative so that members can carry that meaning into diverse audiences.

CREATING A NARRATIVE FROM AN INFLUENCE STRUCTURE

Dialogue Manager: "We're almost finished here today. To close out on our response to the triggering questions, we now need to use our influence structure to respond with the strongly held preferences of the group. We can append this statement with a comment on other actions that will impact the system of ideas that represents our understanding of our situation, but our most strongly unified response is found in the influence map itself:

'To ensure health and wellness in our region in the next five years under universal health coverage, we will begin by addressing idea 7, because addressing this idea will help us to address all the other ideas related to our success in this effort.' This answer begins at the bottom. 'To ensure health and wellness in our region in the next five years under universal health coverage, we must address ideas 13, 12, and 23, but to succeed in addressing these ideas, we need to address idea 4 first, because the success of idea 4 will improve prospects of succeeding with the top three ideas—and to improve chances of succeeding with idea 4, we will need to do ideas 7 and 14 first.' This answer begins at the bottom. You could even start in the middle, or you could start by saying that to succeed we need to address fourteen core ideas, and then work in any way that you choose. You will be guided by your grasp of what your audience will understand, and your own ability to manage expectations through narrative means. I want you to form small teams of three people and quickly craft a narrative using the influence diagram. We will then share our stories with each other, and the three members of the winning team will win a copy of a book from me as a gift. Okay? Let's go."

[Teams of three rapidly self-assemble, and the participants begin crafting their summaries. Ten minutes later, all teams seem ready to report. In sequence, they present stories that weave the ideas captured in the influence structure into their response. The presentations are all different, yet they are also all remarkably similar—and certainly internally consistent.]

Dialogue Manager: "Bravo! By your applause, team 5 has won the books. Before we turn the meeting back to Mrs. Smith for a final word or two, let me say that you have done a strong job in developing a backbone for collaboration. You also have a strong story to tell. As stories are told in the community, they can take on a life of their own—and this is not always a bad thing. You, however, will have a script to which you can return if you find that you need to refresh a narrative that is causing tensions in the community. The influence structure is that script. It does not have the syntax of the English language or of any other spoken language, but it is an authentic expression—it is the cognitive product of more than a single human mind, it is the product of the collective mind of the group. You can speak on behalf of the group at any time, but only the influence diagram authentically represents what the group itself has expressed here today." *[check the time]* "We have finished precisely on time." *[A huge blue check goes on the agenda next to "Report narrative summaries of our shared understanding."]* "Mrs. Smith, the group is in your hands, and I and my team will head out to the lobby. As you leave this conference room, please do complete and leave us a subjective assessment of the design project based upon your individual expectations and perspective. Thank you—most sincerely. Goodbye, and good luck." *[SDD session assessment sheets are placed on the table near the exit as the dialogue management team leaves the room.]*

What Has Happened

The group has applied the graphic summary of the decisions that they have made together to produce small group narrative summaries. In this task, the decision map (or the tree structure) is introduced as a catalyst for carrying the learning of the group forward in what can become a transformative wave of agreement for the community. The participants recognize that they have been provided with a vehicle for taking the work of the group back into their personal worlds through narratives that will be tuned for their communities. The impact of narrative on organization alignment and management is reemerging in the forefront of management thinking. As practical scholars such as Stephen Denning have been telling us, storytelling is becoming rediscovered as a powerful and artful means of managing changes. Entrenched myths in organizations can only be displaced with new stories that uproot old beliefs and tumble them from sight.

The narratives crafted through influence structures are all about the power of strong agreement—not disagreement—in lifting people up to an inspired course of action. The telegraphic outline structure of the influence diagram supports impromptu composition of narrative, and the participants experienced this through observation when the dialogue manager illustrated one way to tell a story using the influence tree. The participants experienced the power of using the influence tree as a script for creating narratives when they rapidly crafted stories in small groups. Notice that as narratives are constructed, the structured dialogic design method does *not* seek to collaboratively produce a single grand narrative for the group. While the group might choose to agree upon a consensus statement, the business of creating a group statement involves joint authorship, and our experience is tuned to the tradition of preserving individual authorship and hearing every voice. In our experience, multiple narratives can peacefully exist and can support each other when they are crafted from the same authentic script. Allowing flexibility of expression of an underlying shared understanding helps move that understanding into diverse audiences. For this reason, we promote the idea of using the tree structure of the decision map in concert with narrative when a group wishes to present a consensus statement.

In certain instances—such as when groups cannot meet frequently yet will need to remain connected so that they can pick up phases of collaborative work that spans long periods of time—narrative has a sustaining effect. The stories we tell are who we are and who we wish to become. The stories will rekindle the memory of the moment when they are retold in each others company. While this power is rarely fully appreciated in top-down technical management, it is the very fabric of truth in missions that sustain themselves on social capital.

FUTURE PHASES

Team Leader *[talking once again to his design management team]*: "That session worked well. I know we expect it, but we never take success for granted. I can feel their strength. What do you think?"

Team Member 2: "I would guess they're ready to start planning options for action at this point. Have the sponsors discussed this with us yet?"

Team Leader: "No. We did not want to make our offering too complex for our new sponsors. They are very smart, but we are still a new experience for them. We did back them up to get them to focus on a definition of the problem first, so they realize that there is more that we can do here. Sponsors will want to move into action planning when they feel that they will have the resources to meet the expectation that always follows action planning. I mean, everyone wants to get to work. If the sponsor had to say, 'that's nice,' and then put a hold on the project for several months, this could cause some unnecessary pressures. Remember Tom's work in Ireland—he had all of those folks come together from the UK, the States, the North, and the Republic, and they got so excited about their new diabetes management approach. Tom's company appreciated the design work but realized that the capital risk was really too great. Tom says he got calls from folks for the next six months trying to coax him into changing his CEO's mind. Tom didn't mind the calls, of course, but you can imagine that if a group that lived in the same town or worked with a closely linked set of companies got as excited as Tom's group did and then they were put on hold, they could bubble over and perhaps burn out. We have to cook carefully, and we know that we always cook with gas. So, we should put a proposal on the sponsor's table when we get back and remain patient. Everyone is happy now. The success of the current work will linger for long time. We will tell the sponsor that if we wait too long, the situation may change, and this might require a reexamination of the situation. We really cannot be any more forward than that."

Team Member 1: "It is not only the situation, though. We also have a group that has gotten into the rhythm. They will be using pretty much the same skills to nominate options for action as they did to name ideas for consideration in the current work. It is such a nice group."

Team Leader: "Yes, I liked them very much too. Did you notice when Victoria left her shell and really joined the group? It was early in the pairwise relational analysis segment. The body language and the tone of voice—wow, she really did step into the group at that moment. Her comments were often aimed at the solution space, too. I think that she may have been holding back because she might have felt that discovering the situation was 'so yesterday' for her. I mean, she is sharp, but, heck—the whole group was smart. They are all stakeholder experts."

Team Member 3: "The sponsors are sure to grasp the fact that moving from the problem situation space—where we were today—into the solution space is very similar, mechanically, for us. What I think they will have difficulty with is recognizing that our approach also achieves convergence on an action plan after we have led a group through an exploration of the influences among action options. They may or may not anticipate the methodological consistency in which a problem is identified through a problematique and action options are structured during the design of solutions."

Team Leader: "This is probably not a big problem here. When we tell the sponsors that we will be using an extension of tools we have used to define the problem as we move into defining solutions, they will have confidence in us. After we have explored options for action, we then divide the group up into small teams and have them construct narrative scenarios. The sponsors will be recalling our closing task today. We will need only tell them that the action option scenarios are constructed from the preferred options that will be selected by the small teams from the action affinity clusters. We will be sure to tell them to pick action items from among all of the clusters to construct balanced scenarios. We may have to explain how ideas drawn from all dimensions of the solution space contribute to a balanced plan, but this is not generally a problem for us. We present the work that groups have constructed in the past, and we explain the tasks, but nothing really matters until each new group has experienced the methodology."

Team Member 2: "Ah, yes—but the evolution of the right language within the group to assist convergence is the magic. And this is more than just a bit subtle."

Team Leader: "Indeed. What can we do about this? When we start talking about shared meaning, we are on solid ground. When we talk about language and semiotics and symbolic statements such as the influence map, we get into that deep academic mire that we both love and hate. Language is profound. It is everything. It is the geometry that allows impossible solutions to be realized. Maybe we should specialize and work for CEOs who have had PhDs in physics?"

Team Member 3: "Only if they happen to still like physics, I would caution. I do think that as far as the language creation aspects of boundary-spanning design is concerned, we are better off presenting the jargon metaphor—you know, just as technology groups working together will invent shorthand for communicating complex ideas and thereby come up with some super-effective ways of communicating creative challenges, we are helping groups build a language for accelerating their rate of learning together."

Team Member 1: "Well, the proof is in the pudding, as they say. The rate with which the group processes information continually accelerates, even when we know that the group is growing progressively more fatigued."

Team Member 2: "I have to agree with you there, Chris. I mean, about the accelerated learning bit—even though we have got the data to show the rate of increase. About the 'proof is in the pudding'—I actually don't know who the 'they' is that is supposed to say that."

Team Leader: "Back to reality, folks. We should be able to explain how a language that is based on shared meaning and consensus-based assessment of relationships expressed in graphic form accelerates learning and establishes a firm foundation of planning action. And then we should be able to say that that same language enhances and accelerates developing deeply shared understandings around options for action, when it enables the group to construct a series of distinct yet internally related action plan scenarios. This lets us align the internal structure of the scenarios to get consensus on a core action plan, which the group then augments with additional action options that are assessed as tradeoff choices given the core structure of the plan. When the action plan is in place, we marry the plan with project management tools to establish critical paths, and this tells the managers the level of resources that they will need to allocate to keep the plan on schedule."

Team Member 3: "Beautiful! You should always explain the big picture that way—at least, when you sell it to me. Project managers do get this picture. The problem they have is that they cannot sell the picture to their higher-ups, and then there is the personal career risk for a project manager whenever they attempt to sell up into the chain of command. Project managers have the capacity to appreciate the integrated approach, but not the authority to embrace it. Top policy managers have the authority to embrace it, but rarely do they have the capacity to truly appreciate it. Top management plans, and project managers manage. And eventually, things break."

Team Manager: "Tim, is this your way of telling us that you are off to join McKinsey?"

What Has Happened

The design management team is debriefing after the close of a situational design session (formally called the "definition stage") and is contemplating a segue into the solution space (formally called the "design stage") of structured dialogic design. The stages of the situation analysis were presented in the story from the arena of practice.

The solution stage is frequently constructed on top of the situation stage, because options for solving complex problems should be linked to specific high-leverage elements in the problem situation that needs to be resolved. By convention, structured dialogic design uses red or pink to indicate that groups are working on the definition or anticipation of the situation (which could be either a problem definition or an anticipation of an opportunity). Structured dialogic design uses blue to indicate that groups are designing solutions for the situation. Blue solution options can be mapped directly on

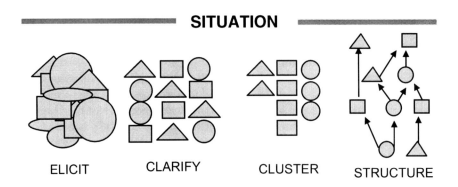

top of pink situation elements within an influence structure. By convention, this has been called a superposition (i.e., positioning the design option on top of the situation element).

As a group moves into the design of a solution, there are options for the design process. For example, structuring the solution options will reveal their influence upon each other, but this may be redundant if the solution options are mapped on top of the situation elements—because the influence structure generated in the situation definition already describes influence across the system. In the solution options stage, the more relevant work is the clustering of options for action. This is more relevant, because a "balanced" action plan will pull action from across all the dimensions of the solution space. Clustering will heighten the planners' awareness of the dimensions of their solution space.

When a group has used structured dialogic design to define a situation, the group can make reference to the influence structure from

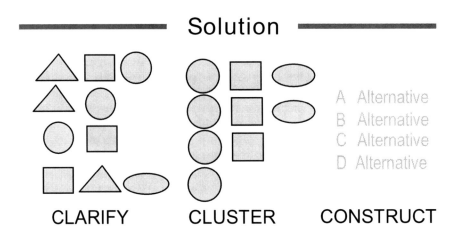

the definition to elicit options for action. In this fashion, one ensures a point-to-point correspondence of options for action in response to elements in the situation definition that must be addressed as priorities. The participants then construct alternative action plan scenarios by drawing from the clustered solution options. The same discipline of option labeling and numbering, meaning clarification, and cluster construction and naming apply to this stage of activity. When alternative action scenarios are constructed, they contain shared "language elements," which makes it far easier to move toward convergence. Without the work leading to this stage, alternative scenarios would be win–lose options. In this case, solution options that are used across multiple scenarios represent preferred or highly preferred solution options, and it becomes rational to begin a core structure with those design elements that are most universally used by the participants. The design management team struggles with this aspect of structured dialogic design, because the structured dialogic design approach does not have familiar precedents in the practice that many managers use.

Once a preferred action plan has been selected by a team, the issue of timing and resource loading is addressed. These tasks are significant, but they are also familiar tasks for professional project managers. A project manager can appreciate the savings that will result from having a group strongly buy into "what" must be done. The issue of "how" time and resources will be assigned to the essential tasks is the source of many sleepless nights for project managers. Where project managers are working with teams that have split accountabilities (i.e., to department leaders as well as to project managers), many hours can be spent continually negotiating with team members to get them to accept the priority of a task. It is for this reason that project managers can be quick to appreciate the value that can be produced using structured dialogic design. The design management team continually struggles to find ways to make this value increasingly visible to executive managers.

THE FINAL WORD

Structured dialogic design creates a powerful environment for collaborative learning that is mission- or task-focused. The methodology has been rigorously validated and has been designed to marry with traditional project management practices. It is an approach that is particularly well suited for working through "fuzzy front-end" problems with large, boundary-spanning groups who are dealing with truly complex challenges.

The design approach uses sequential refinement of expression to lead participants into telegraphic expression of their ideas. Through nominal group technique, participants first write down their ideas, and in doing this they edit their thoughts. They then create a shorthand label for their idea, which provides an even more concise expression. Idea labels are recorded and numbered, and participants come to refer to complex ideas not only by their label, but also—eventually, exclusively—by their number. Complex ideas are clarified through open and focused dialogue, and records of this clarification are provided in real time. These refinements preserve meaning while increasingly speeding the efficiency of sharing and working with complex ideas.

Structured dialogic design provides a rich environment for learning. The first major evidence for learning occurs when participants create clusters and discover the dimensions of the complexity in their situation. The second measurable learning exists when individual voting converges on preferred ideas. If no learning had occurred, all participants would have voted only for their own initially preferred ideas. The third major evidence of learning occurs when participants change their votes during pairwise relationship assessments. Without learning, individual voting changes would not occur. The fourth evidence of learning occurs when participants observe the influence structure that they have created and agree to accept a "deep driver" as a highly preferred idea. Participants also learn to respond to the triggering question using the group's collective set of preferred ideas, and in doing this they learn to speak for the consensus that they have established.

Structured dialogic design is rich with emotional experiences. Participants move through individual cycles of inquiry, barrier, appeal, and resolution. Feelings of cohesion and joint ownership are constructed through a highly transparent consensus approach to identifying priorities. Collective satisfaction with the group dynamics, the information content of the work product, and the depth of learning leads participants to form a social contract for supporting the authenticity of the work that they have done together. This contract can be leveraged into collaborative action through extension of the definition of the situation that the group shares.

CHAPTER 11

THE RESULTS: SUBJECTIVE AND OBJECTIVE ASSESSMENTS

"As the circle of light expands, so does the circumference of darkness."

Albert Einstein
Theoretical physicist and philosopher

The dialogue management team is "debriefing" after their structured dialogic design session. The team is seated comfortably around a huge stone fireplace in the early evening at Skamania Lodge in Stevenson, Washington. Beverages are refreshing, and the tone is rich with relaxed tension now that everyone has gathered off-stage. It is a moment for celebration and reflection.

THE IMMEDIATE IMPACT

Team Leader: "Well, what do you think? Where did you see the breakthroughs? Where do you see the action?"

Team Member 1: "When Victoria transformed from the uncertain watcher to the active participant, I could feel the ice thawing. She so clearly

The Talking Point: Creating an Environment for Exploring Complex Meaning, pages 177–186
Copyright © 2010 by Information Age Publishing

connected with the spirit of the process. And she was quite effective in putting her perspective into the mix. Several of the reversals during the pair-wise relationship connections were strongly impacted by her input. She moved from being a quiet student to being a compelling peer educator."

Team Member 3: "I was struck by that, too. I am certain that Victoria has made some enduring friends here over the past two days. They are going to make her stronger and more effective in her day job too—and vice versa, of course."

Team Member 2: "At the end of the day, I was most impressed with Tony. As Tony was commenting on the 'influence structure' that the group constructed, he was consistently saying 'we,' and he connected the dots powerfully. I do feel that we had several fine narrative summaries of the structure of the problem, but Tony got my vote for the very strongest expression—of course, different narratives are going to work effectively with different audiences, so I am not counting any of the stories out. They are all leading toward the action phase. Did you catch Joan inserting her 'for instance' examples into her narrative? She is already moving forward."

Team Leader: "Yes, Joan really did take her full measure of ownership of the structure of the challenge. She is working it even now, I suspect. Everyone was impatient to get into the action phase, but now they have a language and a structure to do it together. I have to confess that I am really looking forward to getting together with this group for the next phase—of course I say this all the time, but I do always mean it."

[general laughter]

Team Member 2: "Have we got any feedback from the sponsors yet? George Bennet was present for the narrative summaries. What did he have to say?"

Team Leader: "What do you think? He loved it. He has a tight team to work with now. They don't need any coaxing. They are ready for action. Yes, there are real challenges ahead, but no one feels that he or she is facing them alone. George summed up his satisfaction with one word: 'Amazing.' Regardless of the fact that we do promise compelling results, our sponsors are all sincerely amazed when the result is delivered. George is going to check in with the stakeholders individually in about a week or two and confirm that their commitment is durable. We are not too worried about this. Conditions might change in the arena a bit, and there may be some sense that shifting conditions could impact the group's priorities, but unless we have another global meltdown like the collapse of the financial sector, we are on firm ground to proceed with action planning."

Team Member 3: "The dialogue flowed smoothly. We can count the pace when we have time back home, but my guess is that we were running par with the recent project on the creative economy task force in New Bedford. Both groups identified, clarified, clustered, and voted on approximately fifty complex ideas within about five hours, which means that we were resolving ideas at an average rate of one idea roughly every five-and-a-half minutes. The pairwise relationships were being assessed at a rate of about two minutes each. I am estimating that the group worked through about ninety decisions and will be taking home a lot of learning. The disconnect between the initially preferred ideas and the ideas that were subsequently identified as highly influential also signaled the group's learning. While we will tally these metrics into the final report, the key deliverable is the contract to move into action. That seemed evident today."

Team Member 1: "I have to agree. We delivered, even with a bit of technical difficulty with the copy machine. We need to be watching this going forward. We also were getting a bit close to the bottom of the barrel with some of the printer supplies. We didn't anticipate the three revisions that we would need for the clarification document. We did specify that we would need backup supplies on site, and we trusted the logistics manager without confirming. We were lucky this time, but next time . . ."

Team Leader: "Yes, we'll need to bring everything that we do think we might need. That reminds me, do we have the replacement bulb for the LCD projector with our kit now? We have to guarantee to our sponsors that we will be fully functional in rain, sleet, and snow."

Team Member 1: "Hmm . . . maybe a backup generator or two as well?"

TEN-YEAR IMPACT ON THE LAUNCH OF
A GLOBAL PARTNERSHIP

Team Member 3: "Taking this back in a serious direction, do we think that this group will choose to internalize the structured dialogic design process?"

Team Leader: "Now that is an interesting question. It's a bit early to say. Generally, it takes about a dozen uses of the process before an organization will agree that it makes sense to internalize the process. Some organizations capture a breakthrough, and then that specific project takes on a life of its own."

Team Member 2: "You mean a one-shot experience leads to a sustainable launch?"

Team Leader: "Yes, sometimes it is like that. Here is a case in point. About a decade ago, in 1997, the World Health Organization needed to engage the global philanthropic community in support of a very large, very long, and very costly plan to break a self-sustaining cycle of disease affecting the futures of 20% of the world's population. The idea was to globally eliminate *lymphatic filariasis*, which you may recognize as elephantiasis. The experts felt that it would take just over twenty years to reduce the incidence of infection sufficiently to break the cycle. At that time, 120 million people were already infected, and 40 million of those people had been incapacitated or disfigured by the disease. In seventy-three countries throughout the world, 1.2 billion people were at risk of becoming infected. Attempts to control the insect that transmits the pathogen from person to person had failed. The new approach involved using medicines that halt the development of the pathogen, but treatments would have to include all people at risk and would have to be continued for twenty years.

"We were called in because the sponsors recognized the complexity related to uncertainties about commitments and capacities of local authorities to manage the program. Philanthropic sponsors would need to understand the program's goals, risks, costs, and capacities before they would sign the checks. Philanthropic advisors to the sponsors for the program recommended the application of structured dialogic design to build a strong partnership. They convened over seventy world experts from fourteen distinct types of organizations that would be working together, and we helped the group develop an explicitly shared understanding of the nature of the challenge and preliminary actions that they would need to take together. For example, we worked with international agencies, philanthropic organizations, nongovernmental organizations, national government agencies, academic research communities, professional health care associations, health service oversight bodies, pharmaceutical suppliers, monitoring and testing equipment systems suppliers, primary health care providers, public health field workers, health training and education programs, patients, and even the media.

"During this design project the voices of the participants needed to be balanced so that all relevant perspectives were presented and understood. We met in Geneva in October, and our triggering question was something like "What barriers/inhibitors do we anticipate in the quest to eliminate lymphatic filariasis by the year 2020?" Differences in familiarity and ease in the use of the English language were supported with concurrent audio and visual display of each individual's observations. Understandings were clarified, mapped, and structured using tasks within the structured dialogic design process.

"The participants identified and discussed over fifty unique challenges related to this mission and sorted them into seven clusters that represented distinct dimensions of concerns. After deliberation, the partners agreed that the essence of the challenge that they were facing was represented by about a dozen key challenges, and we helped them structure these challenges into a system. The 'deep' challenges included the need for a clear statement of the public heath situation and the need for a clear action plan, but in this instance it was important that the group agreed that 80% of their concerns could be dealt with once they got under way. In essence, the group agreed that most of their collective concerns were readily manageable.

"We helped the partners focus on the 20% of the challenges that were collectively identified as high-priority challenges. The group came up with about seventy specific actions that they could take to begin to address these challenges. So in this sense the group felt it was well armed to begin to attack the core challenges. Some of these actions included clarifying some mutually agreeable goals, organizing a steering committee, and defining sources of support for capacity building. Folks were getting comfortable with the prospects of attacking the challenge.

"Now here is where you might ask if the group chose to continue to use the structured dialogic design process to construct sets of specific action plans. They certainly could have done so. We would have been more than happy to have worked with them. The choice was taken, however, to move from this high-level strategic partnership building phase directly into a more traditional tactical project design and management phase. The transition was exceptionally smooth and rapid. We declared victory for our work because today the Global Alliance, which was established immediately after our work with the Partner's Forum, includes the ministries of health of the endemic countries as well as more than forty organizations from the public and private sectors, academia, international development organizations, and nongovernmental organizations. They have succeeded."

Team Member 2: "Yes, they have succeeded, and they have been thriving ever since. An impressive ten-year track record. So how do we report the magnitude of the contribution that we made using structured dialogic design?"

Team Leader: "Actually, we claimed victory for the smooth transition. The Global Alliance itself proclaims the fact that some magic was present when the program was launched. On their Web site, they say, 'No public health program has ever expanded as quickly as the Global Program to Eliminate Lymphatic Filariasis.' You see, our work forged the political will that was needed to move forward and begin constructing a detailed work plan. We did create an authentic spirit of collaboration among the partners.

"Now, I must add that many tactical leaders with strong project management skills sometimes feel that 'nothing' real has been done until the tactical action plan emerges. This is because human beings are often unable to individually see the full extent of the complexity that surrounds them. Attempting to plunge directly into crafting a complex plan with a large and diverse set of stakeholders frequently results in failure, a delayed start, or a slow expansion of collaboration. None of these negative impacts plagued the advance of the Global Alliance. The wisdom of the sponsors of the launch of the partnership invested in getting the partnership bonded in trust before it became entangled in details. This story is fresh in my mind because last year we conducted our own ten-year retrospective on the project through a small e-mail survey involving thirty-five of the original participants. Some respondents remembered a positive feeling about the design event but did not specifically recall why they had come away from the event with such hopefulness. Others remembered the complexity of the times. And some retained a strong impression of the structured dialogic design process itself. One individual acknowledged that he actually tried to replicate the success himself with another project."

TEN-YEAR IMPACT ON INDIGENOUS CULTURE

Team Member 3: "And there are examples in which a group has internalized the process as a part of their organization's core skills too, right?"

Team Leader: "Of course, and you'll know several of these cases. My favorite example involves our work with indigenous peoples. In 1987, Reuben Snake, chairman of the Winnebago tribe, had a problem. His people had been spinning from conflict to conflict, with no remedy greater than the next conflict resolution initiative. He wanted a new approach to collaborative planning. LaDonna Harris, a Comanche born on an allotment in southern Oklahoma in the 1930s, is a close friend of mine now. She knew of Reuben Snake's needs through her work as a presidential appointee on the National Indian Opportunities Council. LaDonna and her husband, Senator Fred R. Harris, actively sought transformative solutions for all Native Americans. While attending a seminar that I presented in Washington, D.C., LaDonna sensed that she might have found the solution that Reuben Snake was seeking. Six months later, seventeen Native American leaders gathered to put structured dialogic design to work understanding what factors were giving rise to disputes within and among tribes.

"The tribal leaders who engaged in these deliberations were acutely aware of their sense of presence as they participated in the collaborative planning project. They seized upon how the method matched traditional Native American approaches to deliberation and consensus building: it honored everyone by listening to their voice, it treated the spoken words as sacred and captured them in print, and it uncovered collective wisdom. The tribal leaders discovered that their conflict related to the ways that they 'filtered' the information that they shared. This shared wisdom crystallized their understanding of the seriousness of their predicament and committed them to resolve this situation.

"The appreciation for structured dialogic design for boundary-spanning problem solving led the Americans for Indian Opportunity to use the method extensively, and then in 1996 to adopt it for all of their complex problem solving needs. They have rechristened the process the Indigenous Leaders Interactive System (ILIS) and share the process with indigenous people globally. In 2002, the AIO forged a relationship with a group of Maori leaders in New Zealand to diffuse the use of the planning method, and in 2008 they brought the methodology to their Ambassadors International Gathering in Bolivia.

"In retrospect, having an overarching organization such as AIO support the diffusion of structured dialogic design into indigenous communities has been critically important. Working from a foundation of cultural acceptance with a critical mass of tribal communities, AIO has moved beyond the frustration of seeking 'grant funding' for special collaborative problem solving projects to a wholesale adoption of the methodology as a core capacity. Internalizing the methodology was important because granting institutions often did not understand the language of structured dialogic design, and as a result it was difficult securing grants rapidly enough to bring the methodology into the places at the time when it was most needed. This is precisely the model that the Institute for 21st Agoras is seeking to cultivate globally."

TEN-YEAR IMPACT ON NATION-BUILDING

Team Member 1: "My favorite example involves the adoption of structured dialogic design into the peace-building initiative in Cyprus. Turning conflict to peace is real magic."

Team Leader: "Yes, this is another great story, but you must be a bit careful here. Structured dialogic design can help design strategies for conflict resolution, but it is not a conflict resolution tool itself. There are actually two stories to tell about the use of structured dialogic design in Cyprus. One begins almost fifteen years ago, in 1994, when Ben Broom—a student of mine—started using structured dialogic design in an experimental support of conflict resolution in Cyprus. The second story begins a decade later.

"Ben Broom responded to growing political will to move beyond conflict through a more collaborative approach with the goal of addressing one conflict at a time. As a result, over a three-year period, he exposed two to three thousand Cypriots to the structured dialogic design process, and he nurtured a regional capacity for grassroots problem solving. In 2004, a wave of hopefulness led to negotiations between the political leaders of the Greek and Turkish communities in Cyprus under the auspices of the United Nations. This culminated in drafting a plan for resolving differences known as the Annan plan—named after the then UN Secretary General Kofi Annan.

"The plan was put on separate referenda on the two sides of the island on April 24, 2004, and was subsequently rejected by the Greek Cypriots—though accepted by the Turkish Cypriots. This failed UN-sponsored effort at reunification of island left behind it a climate of disappointment, and disempowerment.

"In the shadow of this disappointment, a second initiative was launched that was made possible in large part due to the many Cypriots who had experienced the structured dialogic design process in the prior decade. The renewed effort was inspired by a team of six veteran peace pioneers, who met in September 2006 to discuss the post-referendum political situation. Two years earlier, as the Annan Plan was coming to a vote, the Cypriot government had begun using structured dialogic design internally. Government offices were developing familiarity and confidence with the process, and skill in understanding its authenticity as a means of extracting and sharing deep understandings.

"In 2006, the peace pioneers pulled together influential citizens from both sides of the island and launched a session using the triggering question, 'What obstacles must we deal with as we engage in our peace-building efforts in Cyprus?' Working together in response to this triggering question, fourteen Greek Cypriots contributed sixty-seven obstacles, and the ten Turkish Cypriots contributed eighty-seven responses—showing significant bilateral contributions to a shared understanding of the problem. The group "clustered" the factors into twenty categories, voted for factors that they had come to consider most important, and structured the factors into a systems view. This experience is now being replicated and extended under the leadership of our colleague Yiannis Laouris, and a bottom-up culture of collaboration is emerging on a national scale.

"In 2008, the reconstruction efforts of the civic sector in Cyprus were acknowledged to have reached a milestone by the UN with a visit from 'the elders.' And the Cypriot experience is beginning to spread through Europe. Between 2005 and 2008, structured dialogic design has been used to support more than ten large-scale (eighteen-nation) pan-European groups struggling with complex societal problems. Today, five EU countries have come together to begin plans to establish a training school for structured dialogic design in Cyprus.

"Reflecting on the experiences of structured dialogic design in Cyprus, sustained local activity is an important part of building a capacity to both believe in and apply collaborative approaches. Structured dialogic design was the means of creating the shared understandings that have liberated the people from their quagmire of conflict. Without the benefit of early "experiences" with the power of structured dialogic design, the people of Cyprus may have become trapped within the myth that there was no way that they could develop a shared understanding."

Team Member 1: "Compelling stories of enduring impact. The short-term recruitment and alignment of resources speaks for itself. Before we head back and pack up our equipment for the trip home, maybe you could share the story of the origins of the practice with Tim."

Team Leader: "Sorry—we really don't have time for the full story. Tim, you should read *How People Harness Their Collective Wisdom and Power* to fill in the story. But what I will do is tell you how I have come full circle from the Club of Rome to the Institute for 21st Century Agoras. We may not have all the time in the world, but we do have time for this short story.

"The Club of Rome itself can be traced to an executive committee meeting in a New York City restaurant in 1969. Over food and drinks during a conference, Aurelio Peccei, Hasan Ozbekhan, and I discussed ways to start an international initiative to address the global problematique, namely the technology chasm as initially conceptualized in Aurelio's book *The Chasm Ahead*. This book described the escalating technological chasm between the advanced industrialized countries and the third-world countries.

I had systematically collected and assembled a set of validated methodologies in parallel with the emergence of systems dynamics as a planning approach. My method, however, embraced a social system to enable groups to directly and collaboratively construct systems views of their shared situations. The result of the use of structured dialogic design is not only a systems view that parallels the power of systems dynamics, but it is also a social contract for action based upon a transformed future that cannot be captured through the purely descriptive power of system dynamics.

Today, structured dialogic design is perpetuated through the Institute for 21st Century Agoras, a 501(c)3 membership organization incorporated in the State of California with 300 members distributed in over thirty nations. It was established "to build the capacity of civic groups so that they can engage in complex boundary-spanning initiatives." Even though the Institute for 21st Century Agoras is a young organization, many of its members have been interacting professionally for decades. The principals associated with the institute are versed in multiple approaches to dialogue and collaborative design, and we share a conviction for the power of structured dialogic design as a breakthrough methodology.

End of stories. Back to work.

THE FINAL WORD

The design management team is considering the short-term impact of structured dialogic design on a problem solving project. The metrics include participant satisfaction and motivation to move forward. Satisfaction alone is insufficient. The ethos behind structured dialogic design states that it is not ethical to consume costly community time in a dialogue that is not designed in a specific way to improve the situation of the participant community. The momentum toward collaborative action is an essential dimension of any measured impact. In this reflection, the team also considers examples in which structured dialogic design has made enduring and transformative impacts on large-scale social systems.

CHAPTER 12

EPILOGUE: WHY DO PEOPLE HAPPILY AND HOPEFULLY STRUGGLE TO COLLABORATE?

"Someday, after mastering winds, waves, tides and gravity, we shall harness the energy of love; and for the second time in the history of the world, man will have discovered fire"

Pierre Teilhard de Chardin
French Jesuit priest, 1881–1955

Anyone who has ever managed a group of any size at all recognizes that it is generally faster, easier, and less stressful to do a complex task individually than as a group, when it is possible for an individual to act alone. Collaborating differs from other forms of recreational socialization in the way that it involves pulling together multiple ideas and converging upon a single, specific action plan. Some ideas get left behind, and if the group moves too rapidly, there can be hurt feelings and anger among its members. On the other hand, once a powerful plan is accepted by a group, the social aspects of implementing that plan can combine work and play. Barn-raising, for example, requires a complex plan to secure and manage resources: once the plan is in place, individuals can join into a celebration of collaborative

The Talking Point: Creating an Environment for Exploring Complex Meaning, pages 187–198
Copyright © 2010 by Information Age Publishing
187

action. The trick is to present a group with an acceptable plan or a more acceptable means of creating their own plan. When people share a sense of purpose and achievable goals, and demonstrate their willingness to contribute, the social cohesion can be both energizing and comforting.

MANAGING COLLABORATIVE GROUPS (PROJECT MANAGERS)

This particular book is intended for individuals who plan, who sponsor plans, or who in some way help planners deal with complexity. Individuals who have been managing groups understand in the face of genuinely complex problems that authentic collaboration is driven by necessity because of the steep cost of time, energy, and morale that is consumed in putting together a complex collaborative plan. For this reason, collaborative planning is most frequently done in small groups (less than ten individuals). In these small groups, facilitators seek to manage participation so that everyone contributes to the plan. With this mental model in mind, project managers might hope that with a sufficiently talented facilitator, the size of the group could be significantly raised so that more experts could contribute to building a better plan. The universal truth in the trenches is that as the group gets larger, as the planning horizon gets more remote, as the subject matter takes on more hidden meaning—problems surface. The problem is not a function of the skill of the facilitator—the problem is a result of the mismatch of design processes with the cognitive burdens that are imposed upon the group. To effectively manage genuinely complex problems (what some are calling wicked problems)—where many components interact in unexpected ways—groups need to be supported with advanced information management and decision support capacities. Cognitive limitation of individuals and of groups set thresholds for moving into different approaches for handling complexity. Because this is a problem that is so exquisitely felt by project and program managers, professionals in this field are among the very strongest advocates for the use of structured dialogic design. Formal training that predisposes individuals to adopt the practice of structured dialogic design includes experience in managing details such as in mathematics, accounting, science, engineering, and computer systems. This does not limit the capacity of program and project managers in human resource fields to appreciate this methodology. Managers can draw the false conclusion that structured dialogic design presents itself as a preferred alternative for managing all complex projects. In humble truth, structured dialogic design is costly to implement and is thus best used in those situations that genuinely require a powerful methodology. An agile manager will draw upon a range of tools to deal with any specific situation.

Managers who have struggled with only marginal success in their best efforts to align groups in collaborative resolution of complex problems can perceive structured dialogic design as a silver bullet. While we are happy that structured dialogic design has been strongly embraced, we do want to caution managers that the process is a strong spice that can be used to transform an organization's culture or to enable a specific breakthrough on a critical path project. The lead time required to prepare for the use of the method does not lend itself to ad hoc applications, so we recommend that managers continue to hold their traditional facilitators closely. An experienced facilitator is an excellent resource to play a role as a broker in engaging an SDD dialogue management team.

EXPERIENCING AND PROMOTING DEMOCRACY (CIVIC ACTIVISTS)

As we are writing this book, it is the first decade of the twenty-first century, and almost 250 years after the launch of the experiment in democracy named the United States of America. In twenty- to thirty-year cycles since the launch of the nation, the people of the United States have experienced fiscal crises that culminated in the Great Depression of the 1930s. Safeguards which were put in place at that time were sequentially rolled back in the beginning of the "end of big government" movement of the 1980s—and the consequences of the repeal of these safeguards corresponds with the Savings and Loans Crisis, the Enron/Arthur Anderson frauds, and the ultimate collapse of the global financial sector. American democracy is not an ideal form of democracy, because—guided by the early wisdom of our founders—we embraced a representative form of governance in our efforts to hold the generally independent colonies into a federated union.

In the wake of the global financial collapse of 2009, President Obama issued a memorandum for the heads of the executive departments and agencies calling for "transparency and open government." Does this signal a rebirth of American democracy? Traditionally, when representatives meet and take action "for the good of the people," their actions are guided either by well-positioned special interests or very well expressed general interests—and at times, these interests force representatives to make uncomfortable compromises. In rare moments, the general public comes together to directly vote on a referendum—such as a motion to change the provisions of some rules by which government functions. When this happens, the referendum itself is fashioned by agreements among representatives, and not by the people themselves directly. Thus, even when given an opportunity to vote, American democracy provides little assurance of its citizens' opportunity to provide input that will shape the issue that is put to the public vote. These are imperfections that clearly relate to that scale with which democracy is practiced.

If a representative isn't strongly pressed one way or the other by the visible and vocal needs of his or her own constituents, then that representative is accessible to the influence of his or her peers with respect to the way that they will vote. Special roles exist in the legislature for political parties to round up flexible votes and mold them into a political block. American democracy uses advocacy as part of this political process. Advocacy purchases votes with promises of paying back the favor for those who agree to support a specific bit of legislation. In this way, party leadership (and even lobbyists) can "buy" representatives' votes with a currency that is independent of purely logical argument on specific issues. Representatives may vote for things that they do not believe in as a means of securing promissory notes for votes on issues that they feel a strong need to put into law.

American democracy is further complicated with legislative processes that allows "unrelated" line items to be added into a legislative bill which, if passed, will drag or piggyback those unrelated actions into law. This is worse than an imperfection. This process evades the necessity of putting a logical argument on the table to secure the wise support from a majority of representatives. Not only does this process cloud the view of what is happening from the eyes that see the process only at street level, but even among the voting representatives the implications of many of the unrelated add-ons may go unnoticed. Authentic democracy will not slip unrelated ideas into a decision making process. A democratic decision is a decision about a specific issue or set of clearly interrelated issues. American democracy at the national level (as well as at other levels) is a market where political favors are swapped in exchange for political power. If one trusts in the honor, wisdom, integrity, and global fairness of a complete body of representatives, perhaps the fact that votes are purchased through advocacy and through political alliance might not offend us greatly. However if one looks at the state of the national and global economy—and accepts it as even the poorest index of national and global inequity—then one is likely to conclude that change is long overdue. Legislature should be collaboratively "constructed" by a body of legislators rather than crafted by a small set of individuals and then either whittled away or burdened with unrelated add-ins as a means of pulling sufficient advocacy to the bill to affect its passage.

Individuals who have experienced structured dialogic design find themselves immersed in a powerfully democratic process. They find that the process is under control, and that the group work is clear, strong, and durable. They also find that they have the means of explaining to others what was decided and why the decision was taken. For many participants, structured dialogic design will have been their first exposure to authentic democratic practice in a large group setting. No, we don't mean voting.

We mean democratic design of the issues that are put to the vote by the group. Elsewhere we have described structured dialogic design as being based on "peoples' science." This is not a folksy marketing ploy. The codesigner of the method (Alexander Christakis) was rigorously trained as a theoretical physicist at Princeton University and Yale University and has served in the capacity of the president of the International Society for Systems Science. The reason that such a highly technocratic innovator elected to describe structured dialogic design as a peoples' science is because the approach uses only methods that have been individually validated in fields of sociology, psychology, philosophy, logic, and engineering and then further validated their combined use in the structured dialogic design methodology through forty years of "testing in practice" with peoples across the world. It is enticing to experience authentic democracy, and it is intoxicating to actually bring authentic democracy to the mission of solving complex problems for other people. This is one reason why practitioners are often drawn to support to groups through structured dialogic design.

When one brings authentic democracy as a tool for solving complex problems, individuals who participate in the democratic definition and resolution of their shared problems are appreciative and directly express that appreciation in ways that transcend financial gains that practitioners might otherwise expect as the primary reward for their labors. In some cases, a participant group may come to see the leader of the dialogue management team as an extraordinary presence; in others, groups appreciate that the leader of the process is every bit as constrained by the rules of structured dialogic design as are the participants themselves. It is natural to personify the power of the methodology, yet it is also powerful to appreciate the methodology itself.

Among practitioners of structured dialogic design, a "game" has emerged that is jokingly called "the humility game." The objective of the game is to shed all possible personal credit for the success of the use of the methodology. One must remain humble yet also recognize that he or she wields considerable power through the privilege of guiding the group with the methodology. The demeanor is that of a warrior priest or priestess. The paradox, of course, is that no one can brag upon winning the humility game. The rules, of course, insist that the trophy must always remain invisible.

TRANSFORMATIONAL SOCIETIES (ORGANIZATION CHANGE AGENTS)

Transformation occurs as a result of catastrophe or as a result of directed learning. Individuals who desire to foster a transformation in decision making and governance systems have a real problem. Without the benefit of having had an experience with a powerful and efficient process to enable authentic, participatory democracy, citizens are trapped between their hopes and their doubts. One might hope for a better process, but they might also doubt that it exists. Sadly, inspired yet underinformed champions will insist that they have a magic bullet and cajole, badger, or otherwise coerce groups to drink their own particular flavor of Kool-Aid. In part, we are guilty of the same charge. We have presented a story that illustrates an approach that has been profoundly successful in a great range of complex decision making processes. We haven't tried to present the case histories or to argue for the philosophical and logical legitimacy of the science behind the approach. That story is presented in another volume (*Co-Laboratories of Democracy: How People Harness Their Collective Wisdom and Power to Create the Future*, Christakis & Bausch, Information Age Publishing, 2006). The process that is presented here competes with processes that offer either a race to closure (which typically results in a poor social contract among participants for genuine collaboration) or a festival of ideas (which typically results in no consensus on a strongly held common path for action). Structured dialogic design is, in real ways, a painstaking process. The process is not painful for participants, although there is a psychological adjustment that all individuals do make as they come to terms with a new set of norms applied in an unfamiliar process. The difficult and uncertain part of structured dialogic design is in the work that needs to be done to raise a community's political will to be part of an extended (some would fear "protracted") dialogue—and specifically in an era in which so many large group planning approaches make the increasingly hackneyed claim of ensuring a breakthrough. This book is intended to present a picture where aspects of structured dialogic design that exist in some form in other practices can be recognized by the reader. At the same time, aspects of structured dialogic design that are unique to this approach are also presented.

A genuine difference exists between structured dialogic design and all of its contemporary large group design approaches. Structured dialogic design ensures greater clarity in distinction making than other processes. This is essential because structured dialogic design employs a continuous process of decision making that leads a group to discover the way that it thinks. To sustain the integrity of this decision making process, structured dialogic design needs to implement a consistent yet flexible quality control on the information that is gathered and on the decisions that are recorded. Structured dialogic design additionally applies a reflective phase of analysis based upon systems thinking and then uses narrative management to further internalize and solidify the group learning. These features of structured dialogic design specifically lend the approach for transformational campaigns. This is true because the learning that is achieved in one design session is strong, clear, and captured in narrative. Proponents of this approach to transformational missions recognize that structured dialogic design provides a firm foundation for group learning and a culturally acceptable environment for future learning sessions. It is possible for groups to collectively envision a desired or a dreaded outcome with vivid clarity and shared certainty that collaborative response becomes the only practical option for the group. This is to say that structured dialogic design may uniquely preempt catastrophe when truly complex problems rise up to confront communities. Structured dialogic design cannot ensure that responses will be easy or painless, but the collaborative design approach can be applied to chart a new course before a community must confront the reality that it has hit bottom.

One of the goals of this book has been to illustrate how uncertainty can be voiced and discussed in the context of a complex system. Structured dialogic design helps groups because it brings a group into a unified systems view of their situation through a common path of issues and understandings. When critical uncertainties are introduced into the discussion, the group shares a language and a set of understandings for efficiently communicating perspectives on this uncertainty. Multiple perspectives on an uncertainty can either help to mitigate the concern for the impact or can focus the community's resolve to investigate the uncertainty more deeply. Either way, community concerns during cycles of transformation become either milestones for measuring security or goals for measuring future collaboration. Individuals who feel the need to guide the transformation of communities recognize the power of structured dialogic design as a tool for aligning understandings and coordinating responses.

FOSTERING COLLABORATIVE LEARNING (EDUCATORS)

Like dialogue, design is a ubiquitous human activity. Great design is emotive, meaning that an individual who observes the product of the design activity experiences a powerful feeling that may prompt specific action. This emotive aspect of design exists in performing, visual, and cognitive arts. The greatest of designs may be attributed to a design genius. In all fields of human activity, there have been geniuses. Much has been written and said about the magic of the genius mind. One view is that a genius can tap into a collective conscious or subconscious wisdom through synchronicity—that process whereby great minds are the product of their times. At the close of the twentieth century, a second world war had scarred the face of three continents, a military–industrial sector had emerged, large-scale engineering had become constrained by limitations in information processing and decision making capacities, and trajectories had been set for the emergence of environmental protection agencies, world governance bodies, revolutions in scientific understanding of living systems, and a transformation brought on through the information age. Futurists emerged to forecast how technologies would transform individual lives and public systems. From health care to education to global financial markets, the many spinning gears of huge machines changed shape before the very eyes of the world. Municipalities—many of which still have water lines constructed of wooden pipes—now contemplate uncertain futures with hugely risky infrastructure costs. And global warming casts a shadow over not only the evolution of the uses of all coastal lands and resources, but the survival of systems as extensive as agriculture itself. In efforts to deal with complexities of this order, technical experts frequently lead toward the mapping formalism of system dynamics. This tool integrates materials and flows with regulatory processes and describes an overall dynamic picture as various patterns of change in regulatory processes act on the system.

The most elusive—and perhaps also intrusive—regulatory process in our complex sociotechnical systems is the impact of human will. Given a specific understanding of a complex system, what will people choose to do? The question is complex for two primary reasons: (1) it is difficult to give a group a specific understanding of a complex system, and (2) it is difficult to extract a statement of what a group will collectively decide to do. Decentralized decision making in complex situations makes outcome unpredictable—the decision will be a function of the specific understanding of a situation and options for action at the moment, the influence of the impressions that are shared through advocacy along communication nets, and the emotional frame with which individual decision makers individually act. Consider the challenge faced by a coastal municipality faced with a multibillion-dollar investment in wastewater management and an opportunity to make a transition from an antiquated tradition of highly centralized treatment plants toward emerging distributed, modular treatment networks. The burden of learning is huge, and it is impractical for only a few individuals in the decision network to take on the socio-technical-economic learning challenge as individuals. How do we learn to think our way out of our increasingly complex problems?

Individuals who are group learning consultants will recognize the power of structured dialogic design to break the learning task into manageable assignments, while focusing on the salient points for decision making. Municipal leaders rarely come into their offices profoundly well equipped for complex group decision making challenges. Most municipalities will defer to a consultant to provide an answer. Consultants may need to gather a lot of research before they can offer a credible recommendation. When in doubt, consultants will advise municipalities to do what they know has worked in the past. Municipalities who default to traditions of yesterday's thinking will be trapped. Even the municipal bidding process traps the city into asking for a recommendation when the city leaders may know that they need an innovation. Structured dialogic design was developed originally to help engineering teams manage just these types of decisions, but the wisdom behind the method embraced the view that the important social decision would not be made exclusively with engineering experts, but also with mixtures of individuals with very different backgrounds and decision making approaches.

Learning consultants (an emerging consulting profession) who must guide a group through complex considerations will appreciate the power of structured dialogic design as a means for ensuring comprehensive coverage of the issues. The challenge in applying structured dialogic design as a learning tool rests in the need to prepare communities of learners to embrace an unfamiliar way of collaborative learning. To build this capacity, one of the authors of this book (Thomas Flanagan) has established a capacity-building learning project through a community foundation that serves cultural and civic service missions in an aging gateway city in New England. As with all group processes, new users require an experiential learning opportunity before they can get excited about investing their individual time in a new approach.

The application of structured dialogic design certainly can be introduced at early stages in education systems. In applications for reforming education systems, the methodology has been used to engage high school dropout students in redesign efforts for their schools. In college classrooms, structured dialogic design can be introduced as a means of promoting a diversified class of learners in a capstone summary of the "significance" of key aspects of a course.

FOLLOWING SPIRITUAL AWAKENINGS (VISIONARIES)

There is something special about dialogue. Dialogue opens up a space for sharing ideas by creating a space where individuals can exercise their trust, compassion, or power through their speech acts and utterances. This space has been recognized as being special—even sacred. The poet Lowry Pei tells us that "[l]ove is a property of the space between two people." Austrian–Israeli–Jewish philosopher, translator, and educator Martin Buber (1878–1965), said that "God exists in the space between human beings. God isn't found in people, but rather in that space between, where two people are present for one another, in relationship." And Japanese philosophy has defined a concept called "ma" to characterize the boundary zone between self and other: "the distance between the talking self and the talked about self in one's internal world—the space created in inner conversation between the internal author and the internal addressee—the space between two people when they are joined in conversation," and that is lost when the mutual engagement is lost.[1] Sacred spaces call for devoted protection.

---

[1] Eells, T. D. & Stiles, W. B. (2008). Utushi and Ma: Infusing two Japanese concepts into Western psychotherapy. *International Journal for Dialogical Science, 2*(1), 115–122.

We want to walk very, very lightly with respect to spirituality as it relates to group support practices. Let us first agree that spirituality relates to the way that individuals feel when they perceive themselves to be doing something that is so very, very important and so very, very right. This is neither a comment on religion nor on a human tendency towards being self-righteous. There are moments in all of our lives when something—no matter how small it may be at that moment—just fits perfectly to fill a need or solve a problem. Finding your aging grandmother's long-lost favorite earring, perhaps. Or helping a lost kitten find its way home. These are small acts of humanity that make huge differences in the experience of life in others, and they reward us, too. We are not talking about the recent quest for altruism genes or altruism centers in the brain. There is something deeper than altruism where without sacrificing or disadvantaging ourselves, we genuinely feel rewarded when we ease the pain in others. Empathy is our capacity to feel a shadow of the pain that others feel. Spirituality is the privilege to be able to have eased that pain, a bit.

In general, individuals who take up a professional practice in the field of structured dialogic design appreciate the sense of spiritual connection that emerges during the actual group process phase of the practice. Spirituality is certainly not unique to structured dialogic design and related group support practices, but because practitioners bring an awakening of the possibilities of authentic collaboration and genuine democracy to the many different and diverse groups that they serve, there is a certain evangelical tendency that comes from proselytizing the deep philosophy and science upon which structured dialogic design is based. Where democracy, and collaboration, and structured dialogic design differ from a "religion" is in the fact that the public does not need to hold specific beliefs—and certainly not a single set of core beliefs—to make these systems work effectively. A harmony and feeling of community emerges when individuals of different backgrounds and distinct perceptions come to walk together in the same direction. Through the shared voyage, we share our humanity. For some of us who practice structured dialogic design, this call has been irresistible. It has pulled us from secure careers and put us on uncharted paths.

Reynaldo Trevino, our colleague and fellow practitioner in Mexico, provided us with this relevant insight:

> The great philosopher Dilthey said in *Introduction to the Sciences of the Spirit* (1883) that the method required for the sciences of the spirit should not be sought in the "causal explanations" of the science of physics, but rather must be found in what he named the "comprehension" (*Verstehen*) of the "nexus of meaning" within shared linguistic domains. Dilthey thought all of the familiar sciences were derived from a more fundamental science that should be recognized as their common basis. Specifically he stated that a "comprehensive science" of the human being should inquire about human life in its totality of thinking, wanting and feeling, going against the traditional epistemology

of Kant which reduced science to a mere intellectual dimensions. Dilthey named this progenitor science *selbstbesinnung,* and Ortega y Gasset translated it into "autognosis" or "becoming aware of our own self" (see Garrido Manuel, *The Philosophical and Scientific Legacy of the XX Century,* Catedra editions, 2nd edition, Spain, 2007, pp. 25 and 26).

THE FINAL WORD

In tragic ways, as a culture we have poisoned the well just when we need it most. We have touted design charettes and stakeholder processes as engagement vehicles and then ignored, marginalized, or corrupted the very input that we swore to hold as sacred. This has created a myth that large-scale collaboration is not possible—and this myth has led to considerable disillusionment among would-be participants and could-be sponsors. Structured dialogic design seeks to bust the myth about our limited capabilities to sustain boundary-spanning collaboration. To bust this myth, structured dialogic design needs to usher in a new wave of collaborative planning. Scholars have identified the SDD methodology as the cutting edge of "third phase" science—where the reality of a situation embraces interactions between objective findings and subjective intentions. Managing structured dialogic design is not an easy art to practice. It cannot be done with less than a fully focused effort. While software for tracking group decision making and generating the tree structure of the strongly held common understanding enable the practice, certification to practice SDD additionally requires training in social systems and an apprenticeship with a practitioner. The authors have contributed to installations in multiple organizations, and an international nonprofit affiliation of practitioners (the Institute for 21st Century Agoras) exists to provide peer support and to foster adoption of the practice.

C. Thomas Michell reminded us that the evolution of a methodology must parallel the evolution of the will to reach out for that new methodology when he wrote in *Redefining Designing: From Form to Experience* (1992) that

> [t]he new methods, properly used, release everyone from the tyranny of imposed ideas and enable each to contribute to, and to act upon, the best that everyone is capable of imagining and doing. It is not easy. It requires not only new methods but a new conception of self.

The only way that the power of structured dialogic design will be realized is through experiential learning with the types of real-world problems that have not yielded to existing alternative approaches. Individuals who take up the call to practice structured dialogic design management are cultural change agents who share a sense of purpose. Without casting these individuals as starry-eyed zealots, it is fair to say that every practitioner had suffered through the trials of struggling with social complexity before he or she was introduced to structured dialogic design. In effect, then, structured dialogic design changed the course of their lives. And now their altered paths seek to change the course of human history through a revival of authentic participatory democracy in application to real world problems.

APPENDIX I

THE STRUCTURED DIALOGIC DESIGN PROCESS

Structured dialogic design (SDD) is a rigorously validated collaborative design methodology that effectively and efficiently integrates input in the form of tacit knowledge from diversified design perspectives into a unified systems construct that represents the group's shared understanding of its problem situation or its plan for action. The process supports groups in a dynamic systems analysis, linking situation description with a prescriptive model for transforming the situation. Moreover, participating stakeholders from all walks of life need no special training to fully participate in collaborative planning that is managed with structured dialogic design. This is in part because, like all good social system design methods, SDD is free of overarching metanarrative and therefore does not presuppose consensus among stakeholders on questions of values, or even on the meaning of words and phrases. SDD sessions first create a consensual linguistic domain in the boundary-spanning subject area under design. People listen to each other and clarify each other's meanings, and only then proceed with designing alternative solutions. This creates a common spoken and symbolic vocabulary, as well as an environment of mutual respect.

Validations studies of the components and principles of the SDD approach—as well as of the integrated process itself—have appeared in over 400 professional journals of systems science over the past four decades, including journals such as *Cybernetics and Systems, Design Management Review,*

Human Systems Management, International Journal of Applied Systemic Studies, International Society for General Systems Research, Journal of Product Innovation Management, Journal of the International Society for the Systems Sciences, Journal of the Operations Research Society, Journal of Transdisciplinary Systems Sciences, Management Accounting Research, Psychology Review, Systems Research and Behavioral Science, Technological Forecasting and Social Change, and *World Futures.*

The forty-year track record of the use of process in communities across the globe by the co-developer of the process (A. N. Christakis) has recently been summarized in book form (Christakis & Bausch, 2006). In this appendix, we offer a high-level overview of the process and encourage the technical reader to explore additional resources by contacting the Institute for 21st Century Agoras (http://www.globalagoras.org; see Appendix II).

FACE-TO-FACE SESSIONS WITH STRUCTURED DIALOGIC DESIGN

In severely simplified form, the SDD process consists of a three overlapping stages: problem definition or anticipation, designing alternative solutions, and implementing action planning. The narrative account of the SDD process provided in this volume is focused on the definition stage of the process, but the principles of SDD remain the same throughout all three stages, with the inclusion of some specialized tasks appropriate for the distinct requirements of each stage. The generic steps for each stage of the process are shown below:

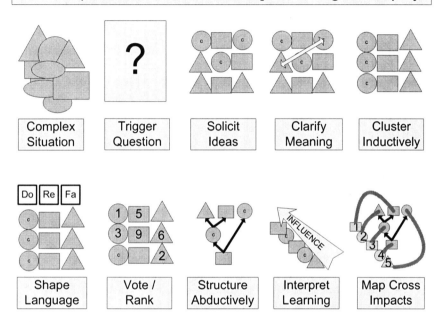

The Steps in the Definition/Anticipation Stage of Inquiry

Complex Situation	Trigger Question	Solicit Ideas	Clarify Meaning	Cluster Inductively

Shape Language	Vote / Rank	Structure Abductively	Interpret Learning	Map Cross Impacts

Problem Definition Stage (1½ days)

1. Community leaders identify a complex social systems situation that needs a collaborative response and that has been unsuccessfully served by alternative approaches, and they agree upon a coordinating platform for design work.
2. Design management team conducts a stakeholder analysis and identifies a community of representative collaborative designers.
3. Community leaders and design management team jointly frame and refine a triggering question to focus the dialogue.
4. Community leaders launch an SDD problem definition session by engaging a collaborative design group.
   - Participants acknowledge their status as stakeholders to discover a shared understanding of the community problem.
   - Participants individually generate and collectively clarify ideas/ issues/elements of the problem situation.

- Relationships among problem statements are examined and decisions are recorded.
- Connections among pairs of problem statements are evaluated and decisions are recorded.
- A systems view of the connections among key problem statements is reported based on the group's supermajority decisions.
- Narrative summaries of the shared view of the community problem are crafted.
- Participants commit to reflect on the problem and to reconvene to design solutions.

5. Design management team delivers a complete document of all of the group's ideas and decisions—along with a graphic summary of the systems view—to each participant at the close of the session

Designing Alternative Solutions Stage (1½ days)

1. Community leaders confirm the strategic target(s) from the community problem definition for high-leverage impact.
2. Augmentation of the collaborative design group is considered (possibly including invited technical experts).
3. Collaborative designers (stakeholders) reconvene, and community leaders launch an SDD solution design session.
   - Participants individually generate and collectively clarify action options that address elements in the problem situation.
   - Relationships among action options are examined and decisions are recorded.
   - Connections among pairs of action options are evaluated and decisions are recorded.
   - A systems view of the connections among key action options reveals high-leverage actions.
   - Action options are "superimposed" on top of the systems view structure of elements of the problem situation.
   - Narrative summaries of the superposition of action options on the community problem structure are crafted.
   - Collective estimates of time/cost for action options may be displayed as individual estimates mapped on grids.
   - Participants commit to reflect on the options for action, and to reconvene to construct an integrated action plan.
4. Design management team delivers a complete document of all of the group's ideas and decisions—along with a graphic summary of the superposition map—to each participant at the close of the session

Action Planning Stage (1½ days)

1. Community leaders confirm that the group's definition of the problem and options for action appear comprehensive.
2. Augmentation of the action planning is considered (possibly including technical experts).
3. Collaborative designers (stakeholders) reconvene, and community leaders launch an SDD action planning session.
   - Participants assemble into three or more "small teams" to construct action scenarios.
   - Teams each identify highly preferred action options from the clusters that the group had previously constructed.
   - Teams consult the "influence map" (superposition systems view) that the group had previously constructed.
   - Teams build a sequential model (an action scenario) using their team's selected action options.
   - Teams compare action scenarios with other teams and identify action options that are shared across scenarios.
   - Participants work as a single group to assemble the shared structure of their action scenarios.
   - Participants discuss the "significant improvement" that comes from adding in individual nonshared action options.
   - Process continues until all "significant improvements" have been added into the shared plan.
4. Action plans are resource-loaded (options are identified for unavailable resources).
5. Time schedules are added into action plan (time and cost tradeoffs are balanced).
6. Design management team delivers a complete document of all of the group's ideas and decisions—along with a graphic summary of the fully integrated, resource-loaded, and-time sequenced action plan—to each participant at the close of the session.
7. Participants define options for updating the action plan during project implementation cycles.

Very few folks are currently even attempting to construct systems views with live audiences, and of those who are trying this, far fewer can actually achieve closure on a systems analysis and synthesis project within a tightly forecast timeframe. Our sweet spot is in guiding a discussion so that groups are prepared to cocreate a systems view, and then allowing them to consider this systems view *before* they set priorities. SDD saves time, resources, and group confidence by helping groups set their priorities with authentic systems thinking.

ONLINE SESSIONS WITH STRUCTURED DIALOGIC DESIGN

Experiments have just begun using online platforms to support aspects of SDD projects. The coordination platform of choice for preparation phases of sessions is a wiki (a multiauthor Web site that accommodates a range of access control). Each individual SDD session is now supported with a task-oriented wiki to (1) enhance coordination between the design management team and project sponsors, (2) provide a "sign in" point for project participants, (3) present warm-up or preparatory materials, (4) sustain cohesion among participants between project phases and stages and between projects. A more aggressive use of the wiki includes gathering up responses to triggering questions (idea generation) and preliminary clarification. Dialogic design does depend profoundly upon dialogue, so one can appreciate the limitation that a text-only environment imposes on this design process. Experiments are under way to evaluate "simulated" gathering through the Second Life platform (where individuals participate through avatars who mingle in shared spaces in an artificial environment). The online technology reduces costs (largely by saving participants travel time and substituting some synchronous exchanges with some asynchronous post-and-reply tasks. Through a combination of voice over IP (VoIP) and screen-sharing software, we have managed the pairwise relationship evaluation task of structured dialogic design with promising results (see http://obamavision.wikispaces .com). This prototype application involved fifteen active participants and several observers located in Canada, United States, Mexico, England, Germany, Cyprus, South Africa, Australia, and Japan. Our point is that this international collaborative design session would not have been possible at all without the use of Internet tools. Successes that we have experienced in applications of online SDD have involved experienced SDD participants, and for this reason, although we are optimistic about the potential for improved technology to extend the reach of online SDD into new audiences, we are cautions about predicting the general utility of this approach.

A BRIEF HISTORY OF STRUCTURED DIALOGIC DESIGN

Interactive Management (an ancestor of SDD) was employed early on as a descriptive methodology for technological problems. In contrast, SDD is social, participatory, and consensual. It was learned from practice that the methodology needs to be open to intentions, intuition, and individual expression. This shift was made clear by Christakis and Shearer (1997), who integrated Habermas's theory of communicative action within IM as a way to overcome the complexities inherent in participatory group planning.

Communicative action instilled a fundamental shift in emphasis, toward the "emancipatory intent" (Habermas, 1987), an orientation to bring about change in social power distribution through linguistic process. Thus SDD addresses both intention and objective fact. It is both powerful and liberating because it provides a prescriptive reflection of intentions that are informed largely, but not dogmatically, by fact.

The well-validated descriptive methodology inherent in SDD finds higher value as a powerful prescriptive tool. The key metric for assessing the power of a prescriptive tool is the extent to which its recommendations are implemented, and the extent to which those implemented recommendations do lead to the desired end result. The track record has been exceptionally good.

THE INSTITUTE FOR 21ST CENTURY AGORAS (THE AGORAS)

The Institute for 21st Century Agoras (AGORAS), an international nonprofit 501(c)(3) [EIN 03-0466448] education entity incorporated in the State of California in June 2002, is a membership organization composed of university-affiliated, independent, and corporate social system design managers who promote and enable the practice of authentic, large group, collaborative design. The AGORAS operates as a "virtual organization," conducting most of its business through conferences and convened regional and international meetings. Corporate headquarters are located at the executive director's preferred mailing address, which at this time is 8213 Hwy 85 #901, Riverdale, GA 30274, USA. The corporate Web site is www.globalagoras.org.

By corporate charter, the AGORAS will

- Promote the idea of human connectedness and interdependence (the "global village")
- Promote democratic processes for addressing the problems and opportunities associated with global economic and political integration ("globalization")
- Promote the establishment of colaboratories of democracy (also known as 21st Century Agoras)

The AGORAS is led by an executive director who reports to a board of directors, each of whom serves a four-year, renewable term of office. Board members are elected by a vote of the seated board of directors. The board is composed of no fewer than six and no more than twelve seated members who convene through voice over IP board meetings no less than quarterly. Board members are recruited globally.

TO PROMOTE THE IDEA OF HUMAN CONNECTEDNESS AND INTERDEPENDENCE

The AGORAS has an e-mail practitioner and interested party base of 300 professionals distributed worldwide as of December 2008. The AGORAS communicates to this practitioner base through an electronic newsletter called *The Agora eBuzz* and through a corporate Web site.

The AGORAS provides informational seminars, published reports, and training opportunities on structured dialogic design and provides resource identification assistance for individuals or organizations who are looking for certified SDD practitioners in their geographic region or in their specific field of application. This social networking includes linking practitioners on the basis of SDD project histories.

The AGORAS identifies and engages sources of philanthropic and competitive grant support to convene practitioners into campaigns for social transformation through authentic democratic processes.

TO PROMOTE DEMOCRATIC PROCESS

The AGORAS maintains an archive of field applications of SDD under the oversight of a corporate research director. Archives will be accepted from any and all individuals who use structured dialogic design for democratic social system services, and collaborative research proposals will be seriously considered from all professional organizations addressing complex challenges that can advance resolution of global economic and political isolation.

The AGORAS maintains an active presence at societies and associations that promote applied democracy through citizen engagement and participation.

The AGORAS will seek to host no fewer than one international summit or retreat for the global practice of structured dialogic design on a five-year cycle, and will derive from these summits a consensus view of the barriers, opportunities, or essential action options required to advance the global democracy.

TO PROMOTE THE ESTABLISHMENT OF COLABORATORIES

The AGORAS maintains and distributes free Microsoft DOS software (with a user's guide) to introduce emerging practitioners to tools for constructing influence maps under the structured dialogic design protocol.

The AGORAS holds the service mark (trademark) from the U.S. Patent and Trademark Office for the commercial use of "structured dialogic design" (SDD) in the field of social system design, and the AGORAS certifies participation in official SDD informational events as well as achievement of levels of proficiency of practice through its certified SDD training and apprenticeship programs. SDD training is currently provided by individually recognized SDD experts in classrooms and communities in Cyprus, Mexico, the United States of America, the United Kingdom, India, Japan, and Australia. In all locations, SDD differentiates itself as a technical collaborative design practice distinct from traditional facilitation service. Making this distinction, however, can put SDD into a position that may seem to compete with local group facilitation practices. The AGORAS seeks to support local group facilitation practices when these practices find themselves dealing with a social system problem that is genuinely a wicked problem (e.g., when the important elements of the problem are misunderstood or poorly understood, rapidly evolving, and interacting with each other in unpredictable ways).

The AGORAS pioneers technological evolution of SDD, both through online implementation and through fusion with compatible social system design methodologies. The commitment to continually advance the science and the art of structured dialogic design draws the AGORAS into alliances with a range of dialogue management and design management communities.

The AGORAS coordinates practitioner teams for groundbreaking applications of structured dialogic design. Some of these innovative applications include

1. Curriculum design and education system reorganization
2. Online decision making platforms
3. Health care system evolution
4. Municipal decision making process enhancement

HISTORY

The AGORAS is a reincarnation of a lost tribe of the original Club of Rome. Some histories report that the Club of Rome was founded in April 1968 by Aurelio Peccei, an Italian scholar and industrialist, author of *The Chasm*

Ahead, and Alexander King, a Scottish scientist, and that it was operated with an informal "inner group" that included four others: Hugo Thiemann (director of the Battelle Institute in Geneva), Max Kohnstamm (former secretary general of the ECSC), Jean Saint-Geours (ministry of finance in Paris) and Erich Jantsch, author of *Technological Forecasting*. Aurelio Peccei brought Hasan Özbekhan and Alexander Christakis into the circle in 1970. Shortly thereafter, Alexander N. Christakis and Hasan Özbekhan discontinued their affiliation due to profound philosophical disagreements about the hierarchical nature of the global planning process that the Club of Rome chose to adopt. Forty years later, Alexander Christakis has returned to launch the AGORAS equipped with tools that enable the bottom-up planning capacities so critically missing from the Club of Rome (for an update on the Club of Rome, see www.clubofrome.org/eng/about/4/).

GENERAL REFERENCES

Many individuals have contributed to the evolution of the ideas and expressions in *The Talking Point*. Some contributions have been subtle—yet still powerful—while other contributions have influenced us in obvious and enduring ways that shape our reflections of the arena of practice. Authors whose works we recognize as direct contributions are listed below. Some authors may not recognize the nature of their contribution, for in some cases we used ideas as a springboard to move our discussion into new areas. It is certainly also always possible that authors whose ideas which have found expression in our narrative may have been unintentionally omitted in the brief list of published works cited below; if this is the case, we are fully responsible and truly sorry.

Argyris, C. (1990). *Overcoming organizational defenses: Facilitating organizational learning.* Boston: Allyn and Bacon.

Banathy, Bela H. (1996). *Designing social systems in a changing world.* New York: Plenum Press.

Bausch, Kenneth C. (2001). *The emerging consensus in social systems theory.* Norwell, MA: Kluwer Academic Plenum Publishers.

Bens, Ingrid. (2005). *Facilitating with ease: Core skills for facilitators, team leaders and members, managers, consultants, and trainers.* San Francisco, California: Jossey-Bass.

Bens, Ingrid. (2006). *Facilitating to lead: Leadership strategies for a networked world.* San Francisco: Jossey-Bass.

Block, Peter. (2008). *Community: The structure of belonging.* San Francisco: Berrett-Koehler Publishers, Inc.

Bohm, David. (1996). *On dialogue.* New York: Routledge Classics.

Christakis, Alexander N. (1973). A new policy science paradigm. *Futures, 5,* 543–558.

Christakis, Alexander N. (1988). The Club of Rome revisited. In William J. Reckmeyer (Ed.), *General systems,* Vol. 31, pp. 35–38. New York: International Society for the Systems Sciences.

Christakis, Alexander N., Warfield, John N. & Keever, D. (1989). Systems design: Generic design theory and methodology. In Michael Decleris (Ed.), *Systems governance* [Greek]. Athens-Komotini, Greece: Publisher Ant. N. Sakkoylas, pp. 143–210.

Christakis, Alexander N. (1996). *A people science: The CogniScope™ system approach. Systems, 1*(1), 16–19.

Christakis, Alexander N. & Bausch, Kenneth C. (2002). Technologue: Technology-supported disciplined dialogue. In Robert, N. (Ed.), *Transformative power of dialogue,* Atlanta, GA: Elsevier Publishing Co.

Christakis, Alexander N. & Bausch, Kenneth C. (2006). *How people harness their collective wisdom and power to construct the future.* Charlotte, NC: Information Age Publishing.

Christakis, Alexander N. & Kevin M. C. Dye. (2007). The Cogniscope™ lessons learned in the arena. In Patrick M. Jenlink & Bela H. Banathy (Eds.), *Dialogue as a collective means of design conversation,* pp. 187–203. New York: Springer.

Denning, Stephen. (2005). *The leader's guide to storytelling: Mastering the art and discipline of business narrative.* San Francisco: Jossey-Bass.

Eells, T. D. & Stiles, W. B. (2008). Utushi and Ma: Infusing two Japanese concepts into Western psychotherapy. *International Journal for Dialogical Science, 2*(1), 115–122.

Ellinor, Linda. (1998). *Dialogue: Rediscover the transforming power of conversation: Creating and sustaining collaborative partnerships at work.* New York: Wiley, John & Sons, Inc.

Flanagan, Thomas R. (2008). Scripting a collaborative narrative: An approach for spanning boundaries. *Design Management Review, 19*(3), 80–86.

Floor, Robert L. & Carson, Ewart R. (1998). *Dealing with complexity: An introduction to the theory and application of systems science.* New York: Plenum Press.

Gladwell, Malcolm. (2002). *The tipping point: How little things can make a big difference.* New York: Back Bay Books.

Goodman, Michael. (1991). Systems thinking as a language. *Systems Thinker, 2*(3).

Hallinan, Joseph T. (2009). *Why we make mistakes: How we look without seeing, forget things in seconds, and are all pretty sure we are way above average.* New York: Broadway Publishers.

Isaacs, William. (1999). *Dialogue: The art of thinking together.* New York: Currency.

Jackson, M. C. (2000). *Systems approaches to management.* New York: Springer.

Jenlink P. M. & Banathy, B. H. (2007). *Dialogue as a collective means of design conversation.* New York: Springer.

Jones, Peter H. (2002). *Team design: A practitioner's guide to collaborative innovation.* Bloomington, IN: Xlibris Corporation.

Kahane, Adam. (2004). *Solving tough problems: An open way of talking, listening, and creating new realities.* San Francisco: Berrett-Koehler Publishers, Inc.

Kuhn, Alfred. (1975). *Unified social science: A systems-based introduction.* Homewood, IL: The Dorsey Press.

Laouris, Yiannis & Christakis, Alexander N. (2007). Harnessing collective wisdom at a fraction of the time using Structural Design Dialogue Process in a virtual communications context. *International Journal of Applied Systemic Studies,* *1*(2), 131–153.

Laouris, Yiannis, Michaelides, Marios, Damdelen, Mustafa, Laouri, Romina, Beyatli, Derya & Christakis, Aleco. (2008). A systemic evaluation of the state of affairs following the negative outcome of the referendum in Cyprus using a structured dialogic design process. *Journal of Systemic Practice and Action Research,* *22*(1), 45–75.

Laszlo, Ervin. (1996). *The systems view of the world: A holistic vision for our time.* Cresskill, NJ: Hampton Press, Inc.

Lehrer, Jonah. (2009). *How we decide.* Boston: Houghton Mifflin Co.

Magliocca, Larry A. and Christakis, Alexander N. (2001). Creating transforming leadership for organizational change: The CogniScope system approach. *Systems Research and Behavioral Science, 18,* 259–277.

Matthews, D. (2008). Metadecision making: Rehabilitating interdisciplinarity in the decision sciences. *Systems Research and Behavioral Science, 25*(2), 157–179. Special Issue: Ethics, Democracy, Boundaries and a Sustainable Future.

McIntyre-Mills, J. (in press). *Systemic governance and accountability: Working and reworking the conceptual and spatial boundaries.* New York: Springer.

Meadows, Donella H. (2008). *Thinking in systems.* White River Junction, VT: Chelsea Green Publishing.

Medina, John. (2008). *Brain rules: 12 principles for surviving and thriving at work, home, and school.* Seattle: Pear Press.

Michell, C. Thomas. (1992). *Redefining designing: From form to experience.* Hoboken, NJ: John Wiley & Sons, Inc.

Norgaard, Richard B. (1994). *Development betrayed: The end of progress and a coevolutionary revisioning of the future.* New York: Routledge Press.

Ogle, Richard. (2007). *Smart world: Breakthrough creativity and the new science of ideas.* Watertown, MA: Harvard Business School Press.

Özbekhan, Hasan (1968). Toward a General Theory of Planning. In Erich Jantsch (Ed.), *Prospectives of Planning.* Washington, D.C.: OECD Publications Center, pp. 47–158.

Pei, Lowry. (1987). Love and space. *Missouri Review, 10*(2), http://www.lowrypei .com/memoirs/on-love-and-space.

Pierce, C. S. (1977). *Semiotics and significs: The correspondence of Charles S. Pierce and Victoria Lady Welby,* Ed. C. S. Hardwick. Bloomington: Indiana University Press.

Pink, Daniel H. (2005). *A whole new mind.* New York: Riverhead Books.

Pinker, Steven. (1994). *The language instinct: How the mind creates language.* New York: William Morrow and Company.

Pinker, Steven. (1999). *How the mind works.* New York: W.W. Norton & Co.

Putnam, Robert D. (1993). *Making democracy work: Civic traditions in modern Italy.* Princeton, NJ: Princeton University Press.

Putnam, Robert D. (2003). *Better together: Restoring the American community.* New York: Simon & Schuster.

Robert, Nancy. (2002). *Transformative power of dialogue: Research in public policy analysis and management.* Greenwich, CT: JAI Press.

Sandquist, Gary M. (1985). Introduction to system science. Englewood Cliffs, NJ: Prentice-Hall, Inc.

Schön, Donald. (1983). *The reflective practitioner: Toward a new design for teaching and learning in the professions.* San Francisco: Jossey-Bass.

Schreibman, Vigdor & Christakis, Alexander N. (2007). New agora: New geometry of languaging and new technology of democracy: The structured design dialogue process. *International Journal of Applied Systemic Studies, 1*(1), 15–31.

Schrage, Michael. (1990). *Shared minds: The new technologies of collaboration.* New York: Random House.

Senge, Peter M. (2006). *The fifth discipline: The art and practice of the learning organization.* New York: Broadway Business.

Shore, Zachary. (2008). *Blunder: Why smart people make bad decisions.* New York: Bloomsbury.

Snowden, David. (2002). Narrative patterns: Uses of story in the third age of knowledge management. *Journal of Information and Knowledge Management, 1*(1), 1–6.

Sparrow, Malcolm K. (1994). *Imposing duties: Government's changing approach to compliance.* New York: Praeger Paperback.

Thaler, Richard H. & Sunstein, Cass R. (2009). *Nudge: Improving decisions about health, wealth, and happiness.* New York: Penguin (Non-Classics).

Warfield, John N. & Cardenas, A. Roxana. (1994). *A handbook of interactive management.* Ames: Iowa State University Press.

Warfield, John N. (2006). *An introduction to systems science.* Danvers, MA: World Scientific Publishing Co.

Wellman, Bruce & Lipton, Laura. 2004. *Data-driven dialogue: A facilitator's guide to collaborative inquiry.* Sherman, CT: MiraVia, LLC.

Wittgenstein, Ludwig. (1953). *Philosophical investigations.* Oxford: Basil Blackwell.

Yankelovich, Daniel. (1991). *Coming to public judgment: Making democracy work in a complex world (The Frank W. Abrams Lectures).* Syracuse, NY: Syracuse University Press.

Yankelovich, Daniel. (1999). *The magic of dialogue: Transforming conflict into cooperation.* New York: Simon & Schuster.

LaVergne, TN USA
03 February 2011
215110LV00001B/54/P